The Complex Web of Inequality in North American Schools

The Complex Web of Inequality in North American Schools analyzes and challenges the critical gaps and inequalities that persist in the American school system. Showing how historical biases have been inherited in current policies relating to nondominant youth, the text calls for educational reforms that perform in the name of social justice.

This edited collection carefully interrogates how technocratic educational policies and reforms are often unequipped to address the interplay of political, social, economic, and ideological factors that are at the roots of educational injustice. Considering the most vulnerable student populations, original case studies explore how inadequate structures, practices, and beliefs have increased marginalization and highlight those instances in which policy has proved effective in reducing opportunity gaps between economically rich and poor students; between White, Asian, Black, and Latino youth; between native English speakers and second-language learners while highlighting racial integration and unequal American Indian education and for students with special educational needs. The insights into such policies shed light on the complex web of historically embedded inequities that continue to shape the construction, rollout, and consequences of education policy for the most marginalized youth populations today.

This volume will be of interest to graduate, and postgraduate students, researchers, and academics in the fields of education policy, sociology of education, economics of education, and history of education, as well as policy evaluation.

Gilberto Q. Conchas is Professor of Sociology of Education at the University of California, Irvine, USA.

Briana M. Hinga is Assistant Professor of Clinical Education at the University of Southern California, USA.

Miguel N. Abad is Doctoral Candidate in Educational Policy and Social Context at the University of California, Irvine, USA.

Kris D. Gutiérrez is Professor of Learning Sciences, Research Methodology, Policy, and Literacy at the University of California, Berkeley, USA.

Routledge Research in Education

This series aims to present the latest research from right across the field of education. It is not confined to any particular area or school of thought and seeks to provide coverage of a broad range of topics, theories and issues from around the world.

Recent titles in the series include:

Assessment in Mathematics Education Contexts
Theoretical Frameworks and New Directions
Edited by Jonathan Bostic, Erin Krupa, Jeffrey Shih

Examining the Use of Online Social Networks by Korean Graduate Students
Navigating Intercultural Academic Experiences
Joong-Hwan Oh

Stories from Inequity to Justice in Literacy Education
Confronting Digital Divides
Ernest Morrell, Jennifer Rowsell

Issues in Teaching and Learning of Education for Sustainability
Theory into Practice
Edited by Chew-Hung Chang, Gillian Kidman and Andy Wi

Young People's Transitions into Creative Work
Navigating Challenges and Opportunities
Julian Sefton-Green, S. Craig Watkins and Ben Kirschner

The Complex Web of Inequality in North American Schools
Investigating Educational Policies for Social Justice
Edited by Gilberto Q. Conchas, Briana M. Hinga, Miguel N. Abad, and Kris D. Gutiérrez

For a complete list of titles in this series, please visit: www.routledge.com/Routledge-Research-in-Education/book-series/SE0393

The Complex Web of Inequality in North American Schools
Investigating Educational Policies for Social Justice

Edited by Gilberto Q. Conchas, Briana M. Hinga, Miguel N. Abad, and Kris D. Gutiérrez

LONDON AND NEW YORK

First published 2020 by Routledge

2 Park Square, Milton Park, Abingdon, Oxon, OX14 4RN

605 Third Avenue, New York, NY 10017

Routledge is an imprint of the Taylor & Francis Group, an informa business

First issued in paperback 2020

Copyright © 2020 Taylor & Francis

The right of Gilberto Q. Conchas, Briana M. Hinga, Miguel N. Abad, and Kris D. Gutiérrez to be identified as the authors of the editorial material, and of the authors for their individual chapters, has been asserted in accordance with sections 77 and 78 of the Copyright, Designs and Patents Act 1988.

All rights reserved. No part of this book may be reprinted or reproduced or utilised in any form or by any electronic, mechanical, or other means, now known or hereafter invented, including photocopying and recording, or in any information storage or retrieval system, without permission in writing from the publishers.

Notice:
Product or corporate names may be trademarks or registered trademarks, and are used only for identification and explanation without intent to infringe.

Library of Congress Cataloging-in-Publication Data
Names: Conchas, Gilberto Q., editor.
Title: The complex web of inequality in North American schools : investigating educational policies for social justice / edited by Gilberto Q. Conchas, Briana M. Hinga, Miguel N. Abad, Kris D. Gutiérrez.
Description: New York, NY : Routledge, 2020. | Series: Routledge research in education | Includes index.
Identifiers: LCCN 2019026578 (print) | LCCN 2019026579 (ebook) | ISBN 9781138048539 (hardback) | ISBN 9781315170152 (ebook)
Subjects: LCSH: Educational equalization—United States. | Discrimination in education—United States.
Classification: LCC LC213.2 .C67 2020 (print) | LCC LC213.2 (ebook) | DDC 379.2/6—dc23
LC record available at https://lccn.loc.gov/2019026578
LC ebook record available at https://lccn.loc.gov/2019026579

ISBN: 978-1-138-04853-9 (hbk)
ISBN: 978-0-367-78417-1 (pbk)

Typeset in Sabon
by Apex CoVantage, LLC

Dedicated to our immigrant ancestors, our living communities, and our future who speak up for justice, even when it seems like no one is listening; resist oppression, when the tides seem impossible to swim against; and hold us in hope, with visions of collective liberation.

Contents

List of Contributors ix

1 Ambitious Imaginations and Education Policy: Swimming
  Upstream and Unsettling Neoliberal Enclosures 1
  MIGUEL N. ABAD, SOCORRO CAMBERO, BRIANA M. HINGA,
  GILBERTO Q. CONCHAS AND KRIS D. GUTIÉRREZ

PART I
"False Choices" 21

2 How Long Do We Have to Wait? Examining School Choice,
  Selective Enrollment Schools, and the Reproduction of
  Racial Inequality in a Southern Community 23
  SOPHIA RODRIGUEZ, DAVID BONEZZI, AND KYRA KOEHLER

3 Education for What and Whom? The Paradoxical Nature
  of an Upward Bound Program 46
  KEVIN CLAY

4 Turnaround, Mayoral Control, Minoritized Communities,
  and Dirty Water: School Reform in an Urban District in
  Connecticut 62
  JAMES S. WRIGHT

5 The Influence of School Turnaround Leadership: An American
  Indian School District Case Study 76
  JAMESON D. LOPEZ AND EVELYN C. BACA

PART II
Technical Solutions for Justice Issues 97

6 (Dis)Connected: Youth Peer Culture During a School Racial/Ethnic Integration Reform 99
ANA LILIA CAMPOS-MANZO, GRACE HALL, LUIS ENRIQUE RAMOS, AND CHRISTINA IGNATIADIS

7 Unfinished Bridges Over the Digital Divide: Engagement and Equity in 1:1 Technology 121
STACY GHERARDI

8 How the Free-Market Approach to Charter Schools Has Failed the Minoritized Students Who Were Intended to Benefit the Most 139
BRITTANY LARKIN AND CARLEE ESCUE SIMON

9 When Achievement Gaps Are Acceptable: School-Level Data Practices and Subgroup Accountability Pressure in Economically and Racially Segregated Schools 154
RACHEL GARVER

PART III
The Legacy and Futures of Special Education 171

10 The Individuals With Disabilities Education Act: The Further Marginalization of Racially and Ethnically Diverse Students for More Than 40 Years 173
JENNIFER M. MCKENZIE AND AMBRA L. GREEN

11 Civil Rights Remedies and Persistent Inequities: The Case of Racial Disproportionality in Special Education 189
CATHERINE KRAMARCZUK VOULGARIDES

12 "PAAP Season": A New Rationale for Segregating Students With Significant Cognitive Disabilities 202
MARIA TIMBERLAKE

13 Theories From Below: Imagining Policy Making and Policy Analysis Beyond "Achievement" Paradigms 218
SOCORRO CAMBERO, MIGUEL N. ABAD, BRIANA M. HINGA AND GILBERTO Q. CONCHAS

Index 227

Contributors

Evelyn C. Baca is Assistant Professor of Education at Bucknell University, USA.

David Bonezzi has a master's in teaching, learning, and advocacy from the College of Charleston and is an elementary public school teacher.

Socorro Cambero is a doctoral student studying education sciences, gender and sexuality studies at the University of California, USA.

Ana Lilia Campos-Manzo is Assistant Professor of Sociology at Connecticut College, USA.

Kevin Clay is Postdoctoral Associate at The Cornwall Center for Metropolitan Studies at Rutgers University–Newark, USA.

Rachel Garver is Assistant Professor of Educational Leadership at Montclair State University, USA.

Stacy Gherardi is Assistant Professor of Social Work at New Mexico State University, USA.

Ambra L. Green is Assistant Professor of Special Education at the University of Texas at Arlington, USA.

Grace Hall, BA, is affiliated with the Holleran Center for Community Action and Public Policy at Connecticut College and is working in New York City at a college counseling firm, helping high school students navigate the college admissions process.

Christina Ignatiadis is a graduate student with a concentration on clinical social work at the Columbia School of Social Work, USA.

Kyra Koehler has a master's in child life from the College of Charleston, USA.

Brittany Larkin was Assistant Professor in the Department of Educational Foundations at Auburn University, USA.

Jameson D. Lopez is Assistant Professor in the Center for the Study of Higher Education at the University of Arizona, USA.

Jennifer M. McKenzie is Assistant Professor in the College of Education and Human Development at Southern Utah University, USA.

Luis Enrique Ramos is affiliated with the Holleran Center for Community Action and Public Policy at Connecticut College and is an eighth-grade math teacher at Northbrook Middle School, USA.

Sophia Rodriguez is Assistant Professor of Educational Foundations at the University of North Carolina at Greensboro, USA.

Carlee Escue Simon is Assistant Professor of Educational Leadership at the University of Cincinnati, USA.

Maria Timberlake is Associate Professor of Inclusive Education in the Foundations and Social Advocacy Department at the State University of New York at Cortland, USA.

Catherine Kramarczuk Voulgarides is Assistant Professor in the Department of Special Education, City University of New York–Hunter College, USA.

James S. Wright is Assistant Professor of Educational Leadership at San Diego State University, USA.

1 Ambitious Imaginations and Education Policy

Swimming Upstream and Unsettling Neoliberal Enclosures

Miguel N. Abad, Socorro Cambero, Briana M. Hinga, Gilberto Q. Conchas and Kris D. Gutiérrez

> I was attracted to science fiction because it was so wide open. I was able to do anything and there were no walls to hem you in and there was no human condition that you were stopped from examining.
> —Octavia Butler, Interviewing the Oracle: Octavia Butler

During the 1980s, Margaret Thatcher, the conservative prime minister of Great Britain, deployed the notorious slogan "TINA", an acronym for "There Is No Alternative". For Thatcherites in England, and many others in the global north, the reigning liberal order signaled what scholars such as Francis Fukuyama (1992) proclaimed as the "end of history." The debate over what the future should look like seemed to be resolved as the Berlin Wall crumbled across television sets around the world. In its wake, Western liberal democracy and free-market capitalism were triumphant. TINA's ripple effects have touched every corner of the globe as formerly colonial states in Latin America, the Caribbean, Southeast Asia and the African continent continue to struggle for sovereignty and self-determination as they grapple with the disciplining power of international bodies of capital, such as the International Monetary Fund and the World Bank; such powerful institutions continue to adjudicate what "development" should look like through neocolonial, techno-euphemisms of "structural adjustment" (Hartman, 2008). Said differently, TINA is an example of the creative and destructive capacity of what Black radical scholars have referred to as *enclosure* (Woods, 2017). Enclosures set the terms of order, shape the horizons of what seem possible and render problems and solutions (il)legible. Moreover, they are made real through the ". . . historical contestations over power, resources, and ways of life that have ushered us to this present" (Sojoyner, 2016, p. xiii). As such, policy-making, especially as it relates to education, is a site where enclosures are created, reified and also refused, undermined and unsettled.

The Political Dimensions of So-Called Technical Problems

We offer this brief historiography for two reasons: First, educational research too often has been narrowly focused on the United States while not recognizing how educational policy is shaped not only by domestic issues but also by currents that transcend the artificial boundaries of modern nation-states. Globalization and financialization illustrate how markets, capital, gender and race are the global forces that sustain and reproduce our world systems. Moreover, what kinds of imagination are made possible under these end of history paradigms? Second, educational policies are embedded within larger political processes, conjunctures, conflicts and struggles for power. Educational interventions and policy should not simply be a matter of testing if a particular intervention "works" to produce a narrow range of outcomes (Gutiérrez & Penuel, 2014). The conventional perspective of educational policy—which is animated by researchers' and policy makers' narrow fixations on testing and achievement outcomes over everything else—reflects ideological projects consistent with technocracy (Brown, 2015; Danforth, 2016; Levine, 2007). Technocracy reflects a vision of the state "in which technically trained experts rule by virtue of their specialized knowledge and position in dominant political and economic institutions" (Fisher, 2009, p. 17). Moreover, this vision of the state and governance reduces sociopolitical issues as technical problems that are solvable by technical experts (Habermas, 1971).

Let us consider the case of anthropogenic climate change to illustrate the real-world limits of technocratic projects. Anthropogenic climate change is the most pressing existential threat to the United States and the rest of the world, and scientists who have devoted their careers to studying this phenomenon uncategorically agree on its existence, humanity's role in its development, as well as the need for collective action to prevent irreversible global temperature increases (Cook et al., 2013; Oreskes, 2004; Rosenzweig et al., 2008). While these conclusions enjoy a virtual consensus among climate researchers, the lack of political will has subverted many efforts to address this crisis (Intergovernmental Panel on Climate Change, 2018; Anderegg, Prall, Harold, & Schneider, 2010). While recent attempts by progressive politicians to put forth proposals to make structural changes to the country's economic and energy systems (Friedman, 2019), skeptics and deniers of anthropogenic climate change reflect powerful, organized political interests such as multinational energy corporations, conservative think tanks and politicians who have had success during the past few decades in undermining attempts at drastic action (Dunlap & Jacques, 2013; Dunlap & McCright, 2011; Latour, 2018; Norgaard, 2011). The point here is not to retreat to an idealized position where we attempt to extract politics and ideology from science but, rather, to understand how scientific practice and authority are entangled within competing social, political, economic and ideological projects (Callison, 2014; Gieryn, 1999). Efforts toward addressing so-called technical problems require a willingness and ability to skillfully recognize and operate within our political geography.

The heart of this book is focused on the ways in which empirical work and policy-making in education are always already situated within overlapping socio-political topographies and apparatuses. The collection of case studies in this book illustrate that while technical expertise is essential to solving educational and other social problems, it alone cannot resolve the political antagonisms and struggle that are concomitant to social problems. For all that empiricism has contributed to our understanding of our natural and social worlds, technical expertise alone is insufficient for addressing our most pressing domestic and global concerns. Although the comparison between educational problems and climate change cannot be very wide or deep, the issue of climate change illustrates how empirical and technical expertise is insufficient to social problems imbricated with political conflict. Policies—educational or otherwise—operate within larger assemblages where technical and scientific expertise are entangled within politics and ideology. Therein lies the complicated and fundamental tension outlined in this book.

Critical Bifocality and Swimming Upstream

Gutiérrez and Johnson's (2017) metaphor for a "river of struggle" seems useful here. "The river of struggle has many vibrant tributaries that connect people, connect us, to the larger river of struggle" (p. 247). The purpose of this volume is to present an offering to our colleagues who center educational policy within their research. This offering is an invitation for others to branch off into the other streams of this river—especially its historical, structural, ideological and political tributaries. Moreover, the editors and the authors of this volume find themselves swimming upstream against the current of hegemonic, technocratic perspectives of educational policy.

This effort symbolizes what Lois Weis and Michelle Fine (2012) have described as *critical bifocality*. *Critical bifocality* introduces a generative and healthy skepticism behind simplistic resilience narratives and popular "self-help" educational interventions that offer lofty promises of producing "equity." This standpoint encourages us to recognize

> the sinewy linkages or circuits through which structural conditions are enacted in policy and reform institutions as well as the ways in which conditions come to be woven into community relationships and metabolized by individuals . . . [and] h*ow* circuits of dispossession and privilege travel across zip codes and institutions, rerouting

resources, opportunities, and human rights upward as if deserved and depositing despair in low-income communities of color.

(p. 174)

Similarly, this book attempts to foreground a vision of education policy rooted in *critical bifocality*. This standpoint compels researchers to fully interrogate how even localized phenomena are entangled and shaped within larger political, economic and social projects and processes. Stories that focus only on one or the other produce incomplete pictures of inequality and marginalization, as well as contribute to the failure of education policies. Understanding educational problems—which are imbricated with racism, economic disparities and cultural homogeneity—also requires an understanding of the dynamics of structural formations animated through capitalism, anti-Blackness, White supremacy and settler colonialism. These systems shape how education is defined, what schooling institutions look like and what is taught in them and what kinds of relationalities are recognized, as well as our efforts toward institutional reform.

While policy can open up some possibilities for more desirable material realities, education policy can also be weaponized as a punitive tool to discipline educators, close schools and reinforce the most dehumanizing aspects of schooling. As such, this book is not simply guided by simplistic education policy discussions of "what works" but, rather, a desire to interrogate the questions that we ask, contextualize our attempts at generalization and make visible the forces that are the rebar of any policy endeavor (Gutiérrez & Vossoughi, 2010; Gutiérrez & Penuel, 2014). Educational policy-making is always already entangled within complex webs of political power and competing visions of society.

Peeking Beyond the Euphemisms

Drawing from Marxist theorist Louis Althusser, Zeus Leonardo (2012) described the ways in which science and ideology make up two sides of a Janus-faced coin:

> ... ideology itself, the opposite but complementary part of science. Ideology threatens science at every turn, as much as dark energy in the universe is the repelling force that may tear the galaxies apart from one another if it wins over the attractive force of gravity.
>
> (p. 37)

Indigenous scholars such as Linda Tuhiwai Smith (2012), have also illustrated how the history of Western science cannot be separated from its genealogical origins in collecting, categorizing, representing, and commodifying the "other" and attempting to speak into existence "truth" itself. In a commitment to being "good scientists", social scientists often attempt to distance themselves from this legacy through notions of neutrality and objectivity, which are key tenets within the Western archive (Simpson, 2014; Smith, 2012).

As researchers, we see this phenomenon play out within academic lexicons and how particular words are imbued with the authority to describe those powerful forces we often cannot see. "Structural" often becomes the go-to nomenclature for social scientists as they attempt to allude to those invisible forces that shape the lives, experiences and outcomes of communities and individuals. To deploy the phrase, "structural" suggests a larger cause of a phenomenon, yet what that cause is or can be implicates both science and ideology. Too often, social scientists allude to the "structural" but stop themselves—or are stopped by something else—when they attempt to articulate a source that deviates too far from the center, and hovers too close to the margins and risks being subject to the epithets of "critical", "biased" and "not rigorous". In other words, *structural* functions as a euphemism for the concepts, words and realities we want to express but without the heavy baggage of ideology. Yet, even when we replace words for other words—as when we displace the political for the neutral—its *trace* is always already there haunting both the writer and the reader (Derrida, 1998). Attending (or not) to this *trace* reflects the work of ideology (Žižek, 1989).

Many of the chapters within this book make gestures to maneuver beyond these common euphemisms. While the *structural* is a starting point, it can only be a placeholder for the word or words that we are afraid or reluctant to express. Said differently, the power of the "structural" is in its ability to index oppression, and oppression can only be made real by naming the interlocking systems that give it life: White supremacy, anti-Blackness, settler colonialism, capitalism and cisheteropatriarchy. While this short list is not an exhaustive representation of the matrices of domination that Black feminist theorists have taught us to recognize (Collins, 2002; Crenshaw, 1990; Combahee River Collective, 2014; Davies, 2007; Ransby, 2003), we offer it as a starting point to move beyond the comfort of our shared euphemisms. These projects cannot be fully understood through the mystified signifier of the "structural". Rather, we find a greater explanatory and interpretive power by naming the intellectual, political, cultural and material traditions that compose what we mean when we say "structural" in this historical moment.

Enclosures in the Neoliberal Era

All the chapters included in this volume highlight the ways in which neoliberal policy agendas and intellectual thought have shaped and informed attempted reforms throughout the United States' P-20 educational topography. Once relegated to the lines of obscure academic journals, neoliberalism currently finds itself injected within topical political debates among pundits and politicians. In order to deploy this concept with care and rigor, we draw from the work of scholars within the social sciences and the humanities as a way to understand the constellation of intellectual projects that have shaped our societies since the late 20th century, including modes of governance, political economy and cultural politics (Brenner & Theodore, 2002; Brown, 2015; Duggan, 2012; Hall, 2011; Harvey, 2007; Mbembe, 2012; Ong, 2006; Povinelli, 2011; Slobodian, 2018; Spence, 2015). Specifically, we lift up political scientist Lester Spence's formulation, which forwards an understanding of neoliberalism that eschews class reductionist or limited cultural interpretations. Spence (2015) presents a version that accounts for how race, cultural politics and political economy are braided in the context of the United States, which reflects Cedric Robinson's (2000) formulation of *racial capitalism*.

Spence and other scholars often situate the "neoliberal turn" in the United States within the 1970s starting with the Nixon administration and becoming fully realized during the 1980s as the Reagan administration fundamentally reconfigured the state's ideological and institutional assemblages. Even "liberal" American leaders such as Bill Clinton and Barack Obama furthered these projects. Clinton, for instance, mainstreamed "triangulation" as a tactic to "rise above" political antagonisms while spearheading attacks on public assistance as well as signing the Violent Crime Control and Law Enforcement Act—which facilitated the growth of the carceral state in the 1990s. Meanwhile, Obama consistently promoted the expansion of charter schools and school privatization agendas.

Spence (2015) describes neoliberalism as "the general idea that society works best when the people and the institutions within it work or are shaped to work according to market principles" (p. 3). In other words, it is a political and subject-making project that is produced by and produces market-oriented ideologies. Spence adds that "[w]e see this idea in seemingly non-political techniques designed to make individuals, populations and institutions more entrepreneurial" (2015, p. 3). This project reflects a move toward hyper-individualism and the fetishization of narrow forms of "freedom" and "choice" as defined by the market. Economism introduces markets into every conceivable sector of social life and constructs individuals as an index of "human capital" who are solely responsible or their own success and failures (Murphy, 2017). Within this conjuncture, anthropologist Elizabeth Povinelli (2011) has noted how the rhythms of the market become the natural determinant of our moral economies; the kinds of values that are of no use to the market are rendered illegible and outside of its moral framework.

For the past three decades, these threads have converged in the United States through corporate models of educational reform; teachers are demonized as scapegoats for failure, standardized testing regimes dominate curricular and pedagogical concerns, "choice" becomes a euphemism for privatization and school districts become more bifurcated and segregated across race and class (Ewing, 2018; Lipman, 2013). Government and social spending—especially those focused on supporting poor and racialized communities—are slashed through austerity politics, as they are seen as impediments and distortions to the will of the market.

> The public policy developed to deal with these populations becomes increasingly punitive, increasingly cordoning off these populations from the rest of society, increasingly reducing resources they have access to increasingly forcing them to undergo government surveillance and control in exchange for those few resources they receive and increasing leaving them to die when they are unable to behave "responsibly."
>
> (Spence, 2015, p. 24)

As such, the fates of "winners" and "losers" of late capitalism are naturalized, especially along the modalities of race (Hall, 1996). Social welfare policies are framed as "handouts" to poor and working-class Black, Indigenous, Latinx, Asian and Pacific Islander underclasses. Concurrently, what also arises are desires for policies that will instead regulate, police, incapacitate and incarcerate undeserving, surplus subjects (Camp, 2016; Gilmore, 2007). While security and defense spending has consistently been prioritized by both major political parties in the United States, public education has often been one of the primary casualties of divestment in the public sphere (Ali & Buenavista, 2018).

Even justice projects are vulnerable to rearticulation. Political scientist Adolph Reed (2018) has argued about how the state and capital are able to appropriate antiracism projects—such as neoliberal perversions of identity politics—and obfuscate the relationship between race and capitalism. Meanwhile, we are left with "diversity" projects that not only leave us unsatisfied, but they often also function as "moves to innocence" (Tuck & Yang, 2012) by institutions and undermine more radical projects for social transformation (Ferguson, 2012; Sexton, 2010; Walcott, 2019). As such, this logic stretches far and wide and illustrates not only a perspective for creating policy but also a specific vision of the state, social relations and political economy—and of education. Although we do not agree with Reed's relegation of antiracism as "a neoliberal alternative to the left," his argument underlines the need for critical education scholars to simultaneously grapple with racism and capitalism in order to understand how these intersecting systems continue to shape contemporary education policies (Brown & De Lissovoy, 2011). Today, even the most powerful applications of critical race theory in education research are often still unable to convincingly articulate the long lasting entanglements of these systems (Leonardo, 2013). Within this disjuncture, one rich source of theorizing we ought to turn to is the Black radical tradition. Within this long-standing intellectual current, the entanglement of capitalism and race has animated the character of modernity itself (Du Bois, 2001; Robinson, 2000; Gilmore, 2007). Said differently, how might racism and capitalism be understood not as inner angles (close but distinct), but as braided within the apparatus of the market and the racial state? This work will require a radical analytic that can apprehend the racialized and economic projects that are concomitant to our always already racialized paradigm of late capitalism.

Technocratic Realism and (Il)Legibility

Technocracy holds an important place within dominant approaches to policy-making where the fetishization of technical expertise promotes what political theorist Wendy Brown (2015) describes as the *de-democratizing* of the state. To elevate technocratic paradigms means to not only push aside political aspects of social problems but also to decouple politics from democracy. This project also reflects a particular kind of political-economic class politics, where capital and technical expertise find common ground as the rightful stewards of the state (Slobodian, 2018). Because there is no alternative within this framework, legitimate lines of inquiry are understood definitionally as depoliticized technical matters (Kiely, 2017). Said differently, social problems are only legible if they do not fundamentally unsettle capitalist realism (Fisher, 2009; Jameson, 1991) or invoke justice projects that are decolonial or abolitionist in quality (Stovall, 2018; Tuck & Yang, 2018). For example, the massive bifurcation of capital and political power between elites and nonelites in the United States illustrates a state configuration that eerily is coming to resemble an oligarchy (Gilens & Page, 2014). Technocracy positions fundamental social antagonisms as immaterial to the language of balanced budgets, means testing, cost–benefit analyses and other econometric techniques.

Unlike the *structural* euphemism, naming neoliberalism presents a more coherent picture of the political, economic and racial projects of this current historical juncture that maintain inequality and oppression in all realms of society, especially in relation to education. Moreover, identifying neoliberalism moves us past the technocratic standpoint of the "structural" and forces us to understand educational problems not only as technical concerns but also in terms of its concomitant political and ideological dimensions. Last, *neoliberalism* should not be equated as a synonym that is interchangeable with the "structural." While both terms can and do act as empty signifiers when deployed without care, neoliberalism stands apart in its ability to index relatively coherent intellectual, political, social, economic and racial projects. This book provides in-depth examples to how policies rooted in narrow technocratic perspectives are, at best, ineffective and, at worst, harmful to students, teachers, parents and nondominant communities.

Overview of Book

This anthology provides in-depth and nuanced interrogations of the consequences of educational reform policies. By highlighting issues of power, inequity and the political dimensions of reform, our contributors lay bare uncomfortable truths. The chapters in this volume help us make sense of how the technical failure of educational policies are always a function of hegemonic, political, racial and social problems and projects. The chapters cover policies related to school choice, school turnaround mechanisms, Upward Bound programs, American Indian education, racial integration, 1:1 computer programs, school closures and special education.

The contributors centered their analyses on this set of intertwined lines of inquiry:

1. How do deeply embedded structures, practices and beliefs shape policy reform to perpetuate educational inequity?
2. What patterns emerge across policy initiatives that unintentionally marginalize the most marginalized populations?
3. Who shapes the policies and their meaning in working toward justice? How are contradictions at the epistemological level navigated?

These case studies give witness to how equity driven policy is derailed when policy makers, educators and administrators elide the historical and localized roots of inequality. Moreover, the authors grapple with the ways in which neoliberal logics configure educational policy not as issues of social and political justice but as technical puzzles to be solved. The polyphony of voices within this volume offers a collective claim to the limits not only of narrow technical approaches to policy but also of the limitations and failures of the neoliberal imagination.

Book Road Map

In Section I, "False Choices", we take a journey into the consequences of the *longue durée* of school privatization efforts dating back to the late 20th century. Sophia Rodriguez, David Bonezzi and Kyra Koehler, in Chapter 2, illustrate how the language of diversity and multiculturalism within school choice policies function as a stand-in for actual changes that advance racial justice within a Southern community. Rodriguez, Bonezzi and Koehler address the considerably complex web of inequality produced out of neoliberal competitive school choice policies, illuminating the contradictory efforts between community members' advocations for racial balance in selective enrollment schools and the school board's desire not to address the racial inequalities and lack of diversity. As Jodi Melamed (2011) has noted, neoliberal multiculturalism substitutes substantive justice claims for symbolic language of inclusiveness. This case study reifies the need for future research to address racialized social structures in communities to track how communities are embedding inequality within policy and the effects of policy on individuals. Indeed, as these scholars posit, the critical perspectives from parent and youth activists are crucial when fabricating imaginative educational policies, as their "perspectives expose the lived realities of structural inequity."

Chapter 3, Kevin Clay's chapter on Upward Bound (UB) college preparation programs, highlights the ways in which being "college ready" was defined through hyper-individualistic forms of citizenship. Clay investigates the UB program across two main areas: (1) UB students' perceptions of justice-oriented action, specifically the utility of resisting structural and institutional inequality, and (2) UB staffs' positions regarding educating youth about racial injustice, including their evaluations of how their Black and Latinx students should navigate racism. Drawing on participant-observation data and interviews with UB staff and Black Latinx youth, this ethnographic study found that both staff and students embraced personal responsibility and participatory civic orientations. These findings point to an apprehension among staff and students in relation to justice-oriented approaches to civic action that focus on disruption and organizing against injustice, which Clay argues "leaves students unprepared to resist injustices." That is, while UB staff supported the idea that students should learn about racism and inequality, overwhelmingly, they viewed education around racial injustice as a matter of personal responsibility. This study is an example of the need for curriculum and educational programs to explicitly address structural inequality and prepare youth for justice-oriented civic engagement.

James S. Wright, in Chapter 4 on the political struggle over turnaround between Black school leaders and White district administrators in Connecticut, is illustrative of educational equity projects that are configured through neoliberal governmentality (Dumas, 2016). Culture-of-poverty tropes fundamentally shaped how district officials positioned Black and Latinx community members as unqualified and unequipped to know what a "good" and "successful" school should look like. Utilizing a life history methodology, Wright centers the perspectives of educators, local politicians and community activists from Waterbury's Black and Latinx communities to juxtapose the perspectives of schooling for children from nondominant community members to the perspectives of those within district leadership. This study evinces how the lack of cultural awareness and hegemonic leadership strategies on the part of the White leadership base—such as the removal of Walsh Elementary School's beloved Black principal—reflect a racially paternalistic policy agenda. Wright presents important implications regarding the need to address deficit depictions embedded in educational policy and the obligatory perspectives from communities that are impacted by power shifts between one group of Whites to another, which Wrights describes as "at the minimum, unethical, counterproductive and hegemonic".

Jameson D. Lopez and Evelyn C. Baca, in Chapter 5 on school turnaround in Whiteriver, an American Indian school district, highlight how settler colonial logics intersect with neoliberal education reforms. Guided by Tribal Critical Race Theory, Lopez and Baca illuminate the similarities of current school turnaround policies to previous federal policies that further problematize the discussion around American Indian/Alaska Natives (AI/AN) academic achievement. Through semistructured interviews and focus groups with district-level administrators, school principals, instructional coaches and teacher leaders, this case study revealed three prominent themes regarding how tensions between AI/AN sociocultural perspectives and mainstream assimilationist perspectives shaping school turnaround in Whiteriver regarding leadership, outcomes and sustainability. Lopez and Baca note that Whiteriver centered Apache culture in students' academic success, such as women's "coming of age" ceremonies, but these ideas were not always in sync with school turnaround values that gave precedence to academic measures when evaluating the school. Additionally, the outcomes of instructional improvement practices—specifically data-driven instruction—generated changes that lead to positive student outcomes; however, teachers and administrators reflected on the constraining influence of standardized curriculum that narrowed their ability to prioritize and sustain Apache cultural life within schools. Lopez and Baca encourage federal government, state government and local education agencies to "consider giving individual tribes opportunities to define academic success among their tribal students". Lopez and Baca's chapter provides a rich account of how tribal schools across Turtle Island continue to be sites of struggle for sovereignty and self-determination for Native peoples within the still-existing structures of settler colonialism (Grande, 2015; Lomawaima, 2000; Simpson, 2014; Tuck & Yang, 2012).

Section II, "Technical and Market Solutions for Issues of Justice", highlights the limitations of technocratic policy proposals that offer easy solutions to complex social and educational problems. In Chapter 6, Ana Lilia Campos-Manzo, Grace Hall, Luis Enrique Ramos and Christina Ignatiadis describe how racial and income-based integration fail to grapple with racial microaggressions and racial boundary policing in suburban and magnet integration programs in U.S. northwestern metropolitan areas dominated by a "school choice" culture. Drawing from conceptual frameworks of sociology of childhood and critical race theory to examine youth narratives, Campos-Manzo, Hall, Ramos and Ignatiadis suggest that White peer cultures use racial/ethnic microaggressions to police racial boundaries, but such practices vary in intensity and character across suburban and magnet schools. For example, young scholars of color enrolled in suburban schools' integration program faced an intolerant White adult culture and an aggressive White peer culture, which pinpoint the intersections of racial/ethnic micro-aggressions. Moreover, this study illustrates how school bussing programs, which aim to create "better" educational experiences for poor students of color may often overlook the experiences of gendered and racialized oppression from peers and teachers within "better" schools.

Stacy Gherardi, in Chapter 7 on a 1:1 computer program, reminds us that technology and access are by no means panaceas to racialized educational inequality. This chapter explores the ways in which factors such as culture, language, socioeconomics and school–family relationships interacted with a technology policy aiming to address social inequality facing students attending a midsized suburban school district serving predominantly low-income Latinx students. From internal measures, the program was successful in changing instruction, engaging students and providing new opportunities for diverse learners and suggests that 1:1 programs hold the potential to address economic inequities. However, further analysis revealed how the policy precluded teachers' voices, did not effectively address student opportunity gaps and increased gaps in parents' participation. Moreover, most decisions regarding the program implementation and message about the program were made largely at the level of district administration while not including input from the nondominant communities they served.

Brittany Larkin and Carlee Escue Simon, in Chapter 8, as well as Rachel Garver, in Chapter 9, illustrate how free-market schemes, school closures and accountability policies prove to be ineffective and even harmful to the people they are charged with serving. Larkin and Simon draw on a case study collected from 211 of 313 charter schools in Florida that closed within a 10-year period (2005–2015) to address the discrepancy in the variance among state policies that typically examine success as performance on graduation rates and standardized testing. This case study brings attention to how school failure can be identified in the rate of school closure and the "litigation" surrounding a few charter school management companies. Market logics frame charter school closures as proof of the self-regulating power of the market. However, Larkin and Simon reveal how these closures were often the result of mismanagement by profit-seeking charter organizations. Consequently, teachers were made into precarious laborers while students and families were regularly left scrambling to find new schools. Larkin and Simon's chapter troubles "commonsense" market logic when "the very notion of competition means someone fails".

Rachel Garver, in Chapter 9, explores teachers' and administrators' understanding of student performance, which ultimately shapes their response to subgroup accountability policy. This ethnographic study embedded within a racial and economically segregated school suggested that teachers' and administrators' data practices mediated the potential of subgroup accountability policy to promote equity based on (1) school demographics and (2) teachers' and administrators' perceptions of students. Indeed, as Garver notes, there is danger in assuming progression from data to practice is linear. For administrators and teachers, some "gaps" were worth investing time and resources into addressing (gender and racial), while other "gaps" were seen as unalterable (linguistic, disability). Ultimately, Garver's study reminds us "that subgroup accountability policy is unlikely to compensate for the inequities produced by economic and racial segregation".

In Section III, "The Legacy and Futures of Special Education", Jennifer M. McKenzie and Ambra L. Green, in Chapter 10; Catherine Kramarczuk Voulgarides, in Chapter 11; and Maria Timberlake, in Chapter 12, provide in-depth and richly historical accounts of special education policies. These final chapters are especially prescient as some prominent social scientists have begun to make claims that Black students and language-minority students are less likely to be identified as having learning and intellectual disabilities (Morgan et al., 2015), and therefore, districts and schools ought to make efforts to increase their representation in special education programs. Such conclusions are rooted in tired, "damage-centered" (Tuck, 2009) assumptions where youth with disabilities are seen by schools and researchers as naturally low achieving. Moreover, some researchers admit that it is still very difficult to determine to what extent "achievement gaps" can be attributed to disability versus educational disadvantage, as well as determine if special education provides the intended benefits (Collins, Connor, Ferri, Gallagher, & Samson, 2016). Ultimately, representation in special education is mediated by social, political, economic, individual and institutional factors, which require a thoughtful unpacking by researchers and educators (Porter & Walters, 2017; Skiba, Artiles, Kozleski, Losen, & Harry, 2016). The chapters within this section provide much-needed policy analyses and historiographies of special education that cut to the heart of contemporary debates.

Jennifer M. McKenzie and Ambra L. Green's chapter encapsulates the intentions behind the Individuals with Disabilities Education Act (IDEA) and the negative consequences of interpretation and implementation of federal law for students from nondominant backgrounds. Primarily driven by deficit paradigms, this chapter explores how students from nondominant backgrounds are systematically marginalized in educational spaces, despite equitable law implementation. McKenzie and Green argue how students from nondominant backgrounds are disproportionately overrepresented in special education categories, are placed in restrictive classroom spaces and are made vulnerable to exclusionary discipline practices. In addition, McKenzie and Green underlie how teacher preparation programs struggle to produce racially and culturally responsive special education teachers. Moreover, this current structure tends to silence the concerns of nondominant students and parents regarding their special education needs. This chapter ends with future state policy recommendations, situating the concerns of marginalized parents and community leaders as the backbone for a policy that strides toward creating more equitable spaces for nondominant students.

Catherine Kramarczuk Voulgarides, in Chapter 11, tackles the paradox between equity-based policies and the persistence of racial inequities in special education, despite the guarantee of free and appropriate education embedded in the IDEA. Voulgarides outlines the advocacy and legislative development of IDEA and its relation to current structures that monitor inequality within IDEA, noting that IDEA was not created to address interlocking identities such as race and disability; rather, the promises under IDEA are embedded with colorblind ideology. Voulgarides explicates the relationship between colorblind ideology and equal protection policies that generate a narrative that elides the racialized consequences and outcomes of special education and disability policies.

In Chapter 12, Maria Timberlake chronicles the triumphs and tensions of an assessment policy integration in Maine called Personalized Alternate Assessment (PAAP). PAAP, which first appeared in the authorization of IDEA and later expanded in No Child Left Behind, served as a special test with the intentions of increasing academic achievement to students previously considered unable to benefit from academic instruction and of holding schools accountable to the educational progress of students with disabilities. However, Timberlake poses imperative questions regarding why PAAP succeeded yet failed to change the marginalization of students with the most complex disabilities. The evidence expounded in this chapter is twofold: (1) The intentions behind the policy were not interpreted analogously by all people involved, and (2) the contradictions between a call for competency and inclusion were less powerful than existing norms defining ways to educate youth scholars with complex intellectual and physical disabilities. For example, teachers manifested disparate understandings of policy intent and were disappointed when the state was more interested in student progress toward standards than showcasing student work. Timberlake provides us with a notable viewpoint and foregrounds the perspectives of parents, caregivers and disability advocates as integral toward implementing education policy, noting that while the process would be logistically challenging, "the challenge is also the very reason to do so".

Chapter 13, the final chapter, concludes with a *testimonio* by Socorro Cambero, which illuminates the indispensability of both local knowledge and the theorizing that emerges from collective community action. Policy making and analyses that limit themselves to what Leigh Patel (2019) describes as the "achievement-measured desires" of the settler state ultimately privilege the interests of testing regimes above all other educational concerns. This conclusion also provides a conceptual reflection on how feminist, Indigenous, and other theories attend to the dimensions of power and justice that are often elided or illegible within conventional policy making and analyses. Theories, at their best, are rooted within legacies of social movements and struggles that unsettle the enclosures of policies, states, borders and hegemonic social projects.

The Need for Ambitious Imaginations in Educational Policy

Near the end of her life, trailblazing organizer, youth worker and political theorist Grace Lee Boggs noted, "I don't know what the next American revolution is going to be like, but you might be able to imagine it if the imagination were rich enough" (Rosen, 2015). Boggs's words unsettle the assumption that there is no alternative by pointing to the transformational and liberatory potential of our imaginations. A policy agenda that is transformational requires an ambitious imagination in partnership with technical prowess and the spirit for political struggle. In many ways, this book is a collection of stories that demonstrate what happens when policy is driven by timid imaginations that seek to tweak rather than transform and preserve rather than liberate.

As neoliberalism has driven much educational reform during the last three decades, educators, students and community members have stood in direct opposition to the encroachment of privatization and testing regimes. For example, Chicago's long legacy of movements for educational justice since the 1960s has served as a shining example for how organized movements by nondominant communities and educators can push back against corporate reform efforts, school privatization and school closures (Lipman, 2013; Todd-Breland, 2018). In 2018 and 2019, the country witnessed highly publicized teachers strikes in Los Angeles, Oakland and Denver, as well as cities in West Virginia, Oklahoma and Arizona. What is telling is that these strikes were not only focused on teacher compensation but also have been concerned with reducing class sizes, limiting standardized testing and increasing funding for wellness staff and mental health resources (Cowan, 2019; Li, 2019). These teachers, students, parents and organizers recognize that these shared working and learning settings are fundamentally intertwined. By offering an alternative vision for what their schools can and should look like, they remind us that these issues cannot be addressed solely through the technical solutions offered by academics and policy makers; equity projects also require organizing and the collective power of the communities that are often the subject of state policies. Mobilization and organizing efforts among classroom teachers, students, and youth activists—who have been agitating for Black life, queer life, Indigenous sovereignty and dignity for immigrant populations—demonstrate that solidarity is not a market exchange (Kelley, Amariglio, & Wilson, 2019) and that collective struggle is necessary to visioning and building forms of education that are aligned with liberation projects (Patel, 2019).

It is with this spirit of resistance and radical imagination that we offer this book with the hope of illuminating readers who already find themselves warm to the ideas found in these chapters. But just as important, we hope that skeptics find these works simultaneously generative and unsettling. Let us together swim upstream and imagine the unimaginable.

References

Ali, A. I., & Buenavista, T. L. (2018). Toward an antiwar pedagogy: Challenging materialism, militarism, and racism in education. In A. I. Ali & T. L. Buenavista, (Eds.), *Education at war: The Fight for students of color in America's public schools* (pp. 1–28). New York, NY: Fordham University Press.

Anderegg, W. R., Prall, J. W., Harold, J., & Schneider, S. H. (2010). Expert credibility in climate change. *Proceedings of the National Academy of Sciences*, 107(27), 12107–12109.

Brenner, N., & Theodore, N. (2002). Cities and the geographies of "actually existing neoliberalism". *Antipode*, 34(3), 349–379.

Brown, A. L., & De Lissovoy, N. (2011). Economies of racism: Grounding education policy research in the complex dialectic of race, class, and capital. *Journal of Education Policy*, 26(5), 595–619.

Brown, W. (2015). *Undoing the demos: Neoliberalism's stealth revolution.* Cambridge, MA: MIT Press.

Callison, C. (2014). *How climate change comes to matter: The communal life of facts.* Durham, NC: Duke University Press.

Camp, J. T. (2016). *Incarcerating the crisis: Freedom struggles and the rise of the neoliberal state.* Berkeley, CA: University of California Press.

Collins, K. M., Connor, D., Ferri, B., Gallagher, D., & Samson, J. F. (2016). Dangerous assumptions and unspoken limitations: A disability studies in education response to Morgan, Farkas, Hillemeier, Mattison, Maczuga, Li and Cook (2015). *Multiple Voices for Ethnically Diverse Exceptional Learners*, 16(1), 4–16.

Collins, P. H. (2002). *Black feminist thought: Knowledge, consciousness, and the politics of empowerment.* New York, NY: Routledge.

Combahee River Collective. (2014). A Black feminist statement. *Women's Studies Quarterly*, 42(3/4), 271–280. Retrieved from www.jstor.org/stable/24365010

Cook, J., Nuccitelli, D., Green, S. A., Richardson, M., Winkler, B., Painting, R., . . . Skuce, A. (2013). Quantifying the consensus on anthropogenic global warming in the scientific literature. *Environmental Research Letters*, 8(2), 024024.

Cowan, J. (2019, January 14). What to know about the L.A. teacher's strike. *New York Times*. Retrieved from www.nytimes.com/2019/01/14/us/california-today-los-angeles-teachers-strike.html

Crenshaw, K. (1990). Mapping the margins: Intersectionality, identity politics, and violence against women of color. *Stanford Law Review*, 43, 1241.

Danforth, S. (2016). Social justice and technocracy: Tracing the narratives of inclusive education in the USA. *Discourse: Studies in the Cultural Politics of Education*, 37(4), 582–599.

Davies, C. B. (2007). *Left of Karl Marx: The political life of black communist Claudia Jones*. Durham, NC: Duke University Press.

Derrida, J. (1998). *Of grammatology*. Baltimore, MD: Johns Hopkins University Press.

Du Bois, W. E. B. (2001). *Black reconstruction in America: Toward a history of the part which black folk played in the attempt to reconstruct democracy in America, 1860–1880*. New York, NY: Free Press.

Dumas, M. J. (2016). My brother as "Problem": Neoliberal governmentality and interventions for black young men and boys. *Educational policy*, 30(1), 94–113.

Duggan, L. (2012). *The twilight of equality? Neoliberalism, cultural politics, and the attack on democracy*. Boston, MA: Beacon Press.

Dunlap, R. E., & Jacques, P. J. (2013). Climate change denial books and conservative think tanks: Exploring the connection. *American Behavioral Scientist*, 57(6), 699–731.

Dunlap, R. E., & McCright, A. M. (2011). Organized climate change denial. In J. Dryzek, R. B. Norgaard, & D. Schlosberg (Eds.), *The Oxford handbook of climate change and society* (pp. 144–160). Oxford, UK: Oxford University Press.

Ewing, E. (2018). *Ghosts in the schoolyard: Racism and closings on Chicago's south side*. Chicago, IL: University of Chicago Press.

Ferguson, R. A. (2012). *The reorder of things: The university and its pedagogies of minority difference*. Minneapolis, MN: University of Minnesota Press.

Fisher, M. (2009). *Capitalist realism: Is there no alternative?* Winchester, UK: Zero Books.

Friedman, L. (2019, February 21). What is the green new deal? A climate proposal explained. *New York Times*. Retrieved from www.nytimes.com/2019/02/21/climate/green-new-deal-questions-answers.html

Fukuyama, F. (1992). *The end of history and the last man*. New York, NY: Free Press.

Gieryn, T. F. (1999). *Cultural boundaries of science: Credibility on the line*. Chicago, IL: University of Chicago Press.

Gilens, M., & Page, B. I. (2014). Testing theories of American politics: Elites, interest groups, and average citizens. *Perspectives on Politics*, 12(3), 564–581.

Gilmore, R. W. (2007). *Golden gulag: Prisons, surplus, crisis, and opposition in globalizing California*. Berkeley, CA: University of California Press.

Grande, S. (2015). *Red pedagogy: Native American social and political thought*. Lanham, MD: Rowman & Littlefield.

Gutiérrez, K. D., & Johnson, P. (2017). Understanding identity sampling and cultural repertoires: Advancing learning in justice pedagogies. In D. Paris & H. S. Alim (Eds.), *Culturally sustaining pedagogies: Teaching and learning for justice in a changing world* (pp. 247–260). New York, NY: Teachers College Press.

Gutiérrez, K. D., & Penuel, W. R. (2014). Relevance to practice as a criterion for rigor. *Educational Researcher*, 43(1), 19–23.

Gutiérrez, K. D., & Vossoughi, S. (2010). Lifting off the ground to return anew: Mediated praxis, transformative learning, and social design experiments. *Journal of Teacher Education*, 61(1/2), 100–117.

Habermas, J. (1971). *Toward a rational society: Student protest science and politics*. Boston, MA: Beacon Press.

Hall, S. (1996). Race, articulation, and societies structured in dominance. In H. A. Baker, Jr., M. Diawara, & R. H. Lindeborg (Eds.), *Black British cultural studies: A reader* (pp. 16–60). Chicago, IL: University of Chicago Press.

Hall, S. (2011). The neo-liberal revolution. *Cultural Studies*, *25*(6), 705–728.
Hartman, S. (2008). *Lose your mother: A journey along the Atlantic slave route*. New York, NY: Farrar, Strauss and Giroux.
Harvey, D. (2007). *A brief history of neoliberalism*. Oxford, UK: Oxford University Press.
Intergovernmental Panel on Climate Change. (2018). *Global warming of 1.5° C* (Report No. 1). Retrieved from www.ipcc.ch/sr15/
Jameson, F. (1991). *Postmodernism, or, the cultural logic of late capitalism*. Durham: NC: Duke University Press.
Kelley, R. D., Amariglio, J., & Wilson, L. (2019). "Solidarity is not a market exchange": An RM interview with Robin DG Kelley, part 2. *Rethinking Marxism*, *31*(2), 152–172.
Kiely, R. (2017). From authoritarian liberalism to economic technocracy: Neoliberalism, politics and "de-democratization". *Critical Sociology*, *43*(4–5), 725–745.
Latour, B. (2018). *Down to earth*. Cambridge, UK: Polity.
Leonardo, Z. (2012). The race for class: Reflections on a critical raceclass theory of education. *Educational Studies*, *48*(5), 427–449.
Leonardo, Z. (2013). *Race frameworks: A multidimensional theory of racism and education*. New York, NY: Teachers College Press.
Levine, P. (2007). Education policy and the limits of technocracy. *Philosophy and Public Policy Quarterly*, *27*(3/4), 17–21.
Li, R. (2019, February 16). Oakland teachers plan to go on strike Thursday. *San Francisco Chronicle*. Retrieved from www.sfchronicle.com/bayarea/article/Oakland-teachers-will-walk-out-on-strike-Thursday-13622490.php
Lipman, P. (2013). *The new political economy of urban education: Neoliberalism, race, and the right to the city*. New York, NY: Routledge.
Lomawaima, K. T. (2000). Tribal sovereigns: Reframing research in American Indian education. *Harvard Educational Review*, *70*(1), 1–23.
Mbembe, A. (2012). At the centre of the knot. *Social Dynamics*, *38*(1), 8–14.
Melamed, J. (2011). *Represent and destroy: Rationalizing violence in the new racial capitalism*. Minneapolis, MN: University of Minnesota Press.
Morgan, P. L., Farkas, G., Hillemeier, M. M., Mattison, R., Maczuga, S., Li, H., & Cook, M. (2015). Minorities are disproportionately underrepresented in special education: Longitudinal evidence across five disability conditions. *Educational Researcher*, *44*(5), 278–292.
Murphy, M. (2017). *The economization of life*. Durham, NC: Duke University Press.
Norgaard, K. M. (2011). *Living in denial: Climate change, emotions, and everyday life*. Cambridge, MA: MIT Press.
Ong, A. (2006). *Neoliberalism as exception*. Durham, NC: Duke University Press.
Oreskes, N. (2004). The scientific consensus on climate change. *Science*, *306*(5702), 1686–1686.
Patel, L. (2019). Fugitive practices: Learning in a settler colony. *Educational Studies*, *55*(2), 1–9.
Porter, K., & Walters, N. M. (2017). Disability, disadvantage, or discrimination? In T. Torres & C. R. Barber (Eds.), *Case studies Special education: A social justice perspective* (pp. 74–92). Springfield, IL: Charles C Thomas.
Povinelli, E. (2011). *Economies of abandonment: Social belonging and endurance in late liberalism*. Durham, NC: Duke University Press.
Ransby, B. (2003). *Ella Baker and the Black freedom movement: A radical democratic vision*. Chapel Hill, NC: University of North Carolina Press.

Reed, A. (2018). Antiracism: A neoliberal alternative to a left. *Dialectical Anthropology*, 42(2), 105–115.

Robinson, C. J. (2000). *Black Marxism: The making of the Black radical tradition.* Chapel Hill, NC: University of North Carolina Press.

Rosen, Z. (2015, October 5). Remembering Detroit's Grace Lee Boggs. *Michigan Radio*. Retrieved from www.michiganradio.org/post/remembering-detroits-grace-lee-boggs

Rosenzweig, C., Karoly, D., Vicarelli, M., Neofotis, P., Wu, Q., Casassa, G., . . . Imeson, A. (2008). Attributing physical and biological impacts to anthropogenic climate change. *Nature*, 453(7193), 353.

Sexton, J. (2010). People-of-color-blindness: Notes on the afterlife of slavery. *Social Text*, 28(2), 31–56.

Simpson, A. (2014). *Mohawk interruptus: Political life across the borders of settler states.* Durham, NC: Duke University Press.

Sojoyner, D. M. (2016). *First strike: Educational enclosures in Black Los Angeles.* Minneapolis, MN: University of Minnesota Press.

Skiba, R. J., Artiles, A. J., Kozleski, E. B., Losen, D. J., & Harry, E. G. (2016). Risks and consequences of oversimplifying educational inequities: A response to Morgan et al. (2015). *Educational Researcher*, 45(3), 221–225.

Slobodian, Q. (2018). *Globalists: The end of empire and the birth of neoliberalism.* Cambridge, MA: Harvard University Press.

Smith, L. T. (2012). *Decolonizing methodologies: Research and Indigenous peoples.* New York, NY: Zed Books.

Spence, L. K. (2015). *Knocking the hustle: Against the neoliberal turn in Black politics.* Brooklyn, NY: Punctum Books.

Stovall, D. (2018). Are we ready for "school" abolition?: Thoughts and practices of radical imaginary in education. *Taboo: The Journal of Culture and Education*, 17(1), 6.

Todd-Breland, E. (2018). *A political education: Black politics and education reform in Chicago since the 1960s.* Durham, NC: University of North Carolina Press.

Tuck, E. (2009). Suspending damage: A letter to communities. *Harvard Educational Review*, 79(3), 409–428.

Tuck, E., & K. W. Yang (2012). Decolonization is not a metaphor. *Decolonization: Indigeneity, education & society*, 1(1), 1–40.

Tuck, E., & Yang, K. W. (2018). Introduction: Born under the rising sun of social justice. In E. Tuck & K. W. Yang (Eds.), *Toward what justice? Describing diverse dreams of justice in education* (pp. 1–17). New York, NY: Routledge.

Walcott, R. (2019). The end of diversity. *Public Culture*, 31(2), 393–408.

Weis, L., & Fine, M. (2012). Critical bifocality and circuits of privilege: Expanding critical ethnographic theory and design. *Harvard Educational Review*, 82(2), 173–201.

Woods, C. (2017). *Development arrested: The blues and plantation power in the Mississippi Delta.* New York, NY: Verso.

Žižek, S. (1989). *The sublime object of ideology.* New York, NY: Verso.

Part I
"False Choices"

2 How Long Do We Have to Wait?

Examining School Choice, Selective Enrollment Schools, and the Reproduction of Racial Inequality in a Southern Community

Sophia Rodriguez, David Bonezzi, and Kyra Koehler

Introduction

This chapter addresses the considerably complex web of inequality produced out of current neoliberal competitive school choice policies and practices that govern contexts of education and negatively impact minoritized communities (Fabricant & Fine, 2012; Frankenberg & Orfield, 2013; Harvey, 2005; Lipman, 2011; Lipman, Vaughan, & Guiterrez, 2014; Rodriguez, 2016, 2017). While this chapter addresses how educational policy perpetuates inequality, we focus specifically on what we perceive to be a lack of policy related to diversity in selective enrollment schools in Brownview Community School District (BCSD).[1] In other words, the word *diversity* was used in the local discourse, that is, at school board meetings and other town halls related to this incident, but as a keyword, it contains so many meanings and parlays an aura of legitimacy for the mostly white school board[2] to use even though it was not clearly defined. As researchers, we learned that local minoritized community members and youth activists meant racial diversity or associated the word *diversity* with race or race issues, and the school district refused to name the challenges in the district as relating to race. The result of those in power not naming racial issues allowed them to sustain inequity in selective enrollment admissions policies. Thus, when the community was fighting for racial equity, which to them meant racial balance in the best schools in the district, the school board used the colorblind language of a "diversity policy" to shun them. By not defining or acknowledging the lack of diversity in the best schools in the district, the school board superficially attempted to create what it called a diversity policy, which yielded further racial antagonism and inequity in the community and further marginalized minoritized community members and youth.

This chapter documents the contradictory efforts between what the community was fighting for, a desire for racial balance in selective enrollment schools, and the school board's desire not to address the racial inequities and a lack of diversity in selective enrollment schools. We discuss the arguments and efforts brought forth by the community for a diversity policy and ultimately what the district actually decided as part of the diversity policy, which did not align with what the community called for, nor did it address racial inequity writ large in the community. Due to the struggle between the desire of minoritized community members and youth for racial equity and the school board's disregard for racial inequity, the attempts at a diversity policy from its inception were problematic. The outcome of what would become the district's diversity policy gave the impression that the policy-makers addressed diversity issues; however, the diversity policy ultimately fails to address the structural, systemic issues that prevent access for racial minorities to selective enrollment schools.

The Context of Brownview

Brownview is situated in a historical context that promoted slavery as well as other forms of servitude and exclusion toward the black community (Blackmon, 2008; Walker, 2000). The community maintains a rich legacy of segregationist practices, being a city that did not integrate schools for nearly a decade after *Brown v. Board* (1954).[3] Importantly, it is enshrined in the state constitution to only provide a minimally adequate public education,[4] which disproportionately affects impoverished communities of color. This historical context embeds structures similar to other districts across the country such as meritocratic school choice as well as selective enrollment admissions' policies. These structures and practices along with the ideological beliefs in this particular community related to colorblindness and meritocracy perpetuate inequity. Furthermore, using structures to perpetuate inequity is called stratification, and specifically, the opportunistic school choice policy and selective enrollment schools as part of public education function as mechanisms to stratify a capitalist society (Bourdieu & Passeron, 1990; Bowles & Gintis, 2003; Willis, 1977). Within public schools, we commonly observe other practices of stratification that produce unequal outcomes for racial minorities. For instance, it is widely noted that an example of "structural" processes that reproduce class inequality beyond schooling include the practice of tracking with advanced placement courses and gifted programs as well as other hidden curricula (Morris, 2006; Oakes, 2005; Staiger, 2006). This chapter connects to this literature and advances the conversation about how selective enrollment schools in a historically segregated southern city reproduce racial inequality.

This chapter describes the specific stages of policy in a unique way because it traces how local community members, including youth activists and parents, struggled with the school board to generate equitable school choice policy. They did so by drawing attention to the lack of racial balance in Brownview's selective enrollment schools and the backlash they experienced in their struggle. Using case study design (Yin, 2014) and data sources such as school board meeting minutes, field notes from participant observations at youth and parent advocacy meetings, observations at school board meetings, and interviews with parents and youth affected by the lack of racial balance and the lack of transparency, we unravel how these various actors challenged the district to generate an equitable policy. The specific stages of policy development include how the diversity discussion escalated at various school board meetings and how youth and parents reacted to these discussions and responded with ideas for change. Our focus here is to emphasize the perspectives of minoritized community members as they persistently raised issues of racial inequity, or what was referred to by the school board as a lack of diversity. We highlight the voices of community members because they are the ones deeply impacted by the lack of attention to racial inequity in Brownview. So, while this chapter addresses how a lack of policy impacts minoritized groups, we focus on what was really a lack of policy that is race-conscious on the part of the school district and how the colorblindness and ignorance of the school board maintains inequality for minoritized community members. The data that follow show how parents and youth made sense of and called for social, systemic change. We conclude with a discussion of the implications of colorblind diversity policies as part of school choice on communities of color.

To be clear, when this study began, there was no policy related to equity in the selective enrollment admissions process. Instead, selective enrollment schools maintained approximately 98% white populations and a very flexible school choice policy so that white, middle to upper middle-class families could send their children to the best schools. Meanwhile, the public schools in the district were serving predominately African American and Latinx populations and were largely abandoned in terms of resources. Our point here is to focus on how minoritized community members raised issues of racial inequity after a series of racially charged incidents were published in local media (Rodriguez, 2017).

Review of Literature

This section reviews literature related to historical intentions of school choice, which includes magnet schools and selective enrollment schools like those in Brownview, and the effects of school choice on minoritized groups. Previous scholarship discusses the historical perspectives on school choice, specifically the development of selective enrollment and magnet schools as part of desegregation efforts across the United States.[5] Post 1960s and the passage of the landmark *Brown* (1954) case, magnet programs were placed in poor, racially segregated neighborhoods as a way to attract middle-class, white families to these neighborhoods

(Orfield & Frankenberg, 2013; Siegel-Hawley, 2014). The legacy of magnet and other "choice" options has failed to reduce racial isolation and low-quality schools in areas of poverty because the burden of achieving racial balance in once-segregated school districts falls on local school authorities to ensure nondiscriminatory practices for admissions (Rossell, 2010). The local context of Brownview provides an interesting place to understand connections to this history of "choice," particularly with the aforementioned long history and struggle with racial isolation, marginalization, and delayed desegregation.

Recent discussions on school choice have focused on how it perpetuates inequality in the current context of neoliberalism. Specifically, scholars explain how the proliferation of school choice and privatization of public schools negatively impacts on communities of color (Cucchiara, 2013; Fabricant & Fine, 2012; Garcia, 2007; Lipman, 2011; Parker, 2001; Pattillo, 2015; Scott & Holme, 2016). Additionally, scholarship on school choice posits that where families live in urban cities often determines where kids attend school and the types of schools that kids attend, with impoverished minoritized families experiencing less useful social networks and residential mobility (Rhodes & Deluca, 2014). This research also observes the advantage that parental knowledge of choice provides for middle- to upper middle-class families while lower income families, often racial minorities also, struggle to navigate the opaque choice policies and unclear selective enrollment processes. Researchers argue that middle-class parents are able to "use their social and cultural capital to work the system" (Cucchiara, 2013, p. 107) and, as such, are often able to make more meaningful, informed choices for their kids (Posey, 2012; Posey-Maddox, 2014; Rhodes & Deluca, 2014). This research comments on the persistent racial disparities in school choice practices and discusses the specific ways that low-income communities of color face barriers to navigating the choice process with regard to transportation, access to information about options, and a lack of understanding about the process made worse by a district's lack of outreach in the case of Brownview. While it is important to highlight the negative effects of school choice (Garcia, 2007), the analysis in the Brownview study sheds light specifically on families from minoritized backgrounds, an often-silenced perspective in the current scholarship, to humanize their experiences of meritocratic, opportunistic white-privileged practices of choice.

Conceptual Orientation

Given this exploratory case study's intention to address the gap in the literature by examining how school choice policies—selective enrollment schools—reproduce inequality and inhibits diversity from the perspectives of minoritized community members, our conceptual framework was informed by Milem, Chang, and Antonio's (2005) concept of diversity,

Bonilla-Silva's (1997) concept of structural racism, and, most critically for our work, Leonardo's (2007) explanation of colorblindness as it relates to policy-making. Taken together, this conceptual orientation informs our critique of the current ways "diversity" work is ineffective, particularly in discussions of increasing diversity in selective enrollment schools in Brownview; it also calls attention to how we might think of structural or institutional mechanisms that promote or inhibit diversity in practice.

The concept of diversity is both key to this literature and key to the study. The normative definitions and conceptualizations of diversity are often leveraged by policy-makers without criticality or attention to how antiblackness and racism inform policy-making (Dumas, 2016). In other words, Brownview school board members, for example, refused to relate diversity with race or to put forth a race-conscious definition of it. As such, the claims of "diversity policy" from the structural, bureaucratic perspective of the school board were contradictory to the perspective of the community in the study because community members held a race-conscious understanding of diversity.

Furthermore, *diversity* evokes ideas of multiculturalism, and often the metaphor of the melting pot in American society emerges (Rumbaut, 2011). In addition, the term *diversity* can be used to describe the composition of a student body in numerical terms, referring explicitly or implicitly to racial balance. Both of these common understandings for the term *diversity* are inadequate and distract from the meaning of diversity that believes in "opposing unfair forms of exclusion, prejudice, and discrimination" (Milem et al., 2005, p. 5), which is the perspective of the community members in Brownview. Milem and colleagues (2005) conceptualized diversity as "engagement" across racial and ethnic lines, whereby school campuses employ an "intentional and coherent process of planning, developing, and implementing institutional policies and practices" in order to address racial imbalance and improve the racial climate of school campuses (p. 19). In order to achieve "diversity" within and across racial lines, schools must examine the organizational and structural policies and practices and think through how they include and exclude racial minorities explicitly; then, diversity work can address barriers to social mobility and opportunity in America's racialized social system (Bonilla-Silva, 1997).

To elaborate, Bonilla-Silva (1997) defines a racially organized social system as a society that places actors into racial categories and structures economic, political, and social levels along a racial hierarchy. The race that is placed in the superior position is entitled to greater social rewards from the racialized social system and holds the power to draw physical and social boundaries between themselves and other races. Within the field of education, selective enrollment admissions policies act as a mechanism that limits the life chances of racial minorities by perpetuating a racially organized social system. Understanding society as a racialized social system allowed us to consider the processes and practices that once again seek to draw boundaries between racial groups, often giving more access to opportunity and resources for the dominant groups in society, i.e. white, middle- to upper middle-class groups, while groups lower on the racial hierarchy receive less access and resources (Lewis, 2003).

Furthermore, much of the discourse surrounding educational policy reflects a colorblind ideology that masks rather than exposes and dismantles structural racism (Bonilla-Silva, 1997; Leonardo, 2007). Leonardo (2007) attempts to problematize the colorblind ideology embedded within educational policy discourse and reframes it as an

> act of whiteness that perpetuates the innocence of whiteness as a system of privilege. Its white common sense deems racial disparities as unfortunate outcomes of group competition, uneven social development, or worse, as stubborn cultural explanations of the inferiority of people of color.
>
> (p. 261)

Too often in the school choice literature we see commentary that capitalizes on colorblind, meritocratic choice ideology, or simply points out the 'either you have it or you don't,' with regard to the cultural transmission of capital. This further assigns the burden of disadvantage to be a problem of the individual rather than shifting focus to the structural, institutional dimensions of social problems. In the context of our study, the diversity policy discourse within BCSD employs a similar colorblind, meritocratic ideology. Guinier (2004) argues that structures in society, such as meritocratic choice policies, engender racialized hierarchies that are durable and maintain racial inequity, shaping the public. Colorblind ideologies that underlie educational choice policy make it difficult to understand the failure of *Brown* and the post-*Brown* desegregation efforts. Guinier's (2004) research makes visible the ways in which society is racialized and ordered in a way to benefit those in power by stratifying resources and excluding minoritized groups from decision-making and policy-making. And, as we demonstrate, the colorblind stance of the school board and the diversity policy that the school board ultimately arrived at fails to address structural racism as a compelling social force that hinders opportunities for students of color in the district.

To this end, we maintain a two-pronged argument that links the previous scholarship to our exploratory case study in Brownview: (1) The normative definition of *diversity*, which is colorblind and held by the school board in Brownview, needs to be problematized within a critical framing, and (2) colorblind ideologies that are ever present in normative definitions of diversity perpetuate inequity in Brownview's and the challenges associated with choice and racial balance in the top schools in the community.

Context and Methodology

Context for the "Diversity" Issue in Brownview

In January 2015, a local news source published a "diversity chart" that showed the number of students of color enrolled in the high-status selective enrollment schools in BCSD. The local community learned that Brownview Magnet, the top high school in the district, only enrolled 16 African American students out of the 644 total students at the school despite the large number African American students in the district. For instance, during the 2015–2016 academic year, the district contained approximately 49,000 students. White students made up approximately 45% of the district while African American students make up 46%, yet Brownview Magnet contains fewer than 1% of African American students. This contextual information shows the disproportionate number of white students at the highest status school in the district. These numbers, along with the other selective enrollment schools with low populations of minorities, reflect the precarious nature of selective enrollment schools in providing access to high-quality education for all students. In other words, students of color from marginalized communities are not attending these schools, and BCSD is not actively reaching out to low-income, minoritized groups to help navigate admissions processes—this aligns with past studies showing that "choice" is an "educational delusion" and manifests in the Brownview study with the lack of racial balance in selective enrollment schools (Orfield & Frankenberg, 2013).[6] While this information in the local news was not earth-shattering, it compelled local youth and parents, in particular, to form advocacy groups and to push for dialogue on the racial disparities and issues of "diversity" in Brownview. In Brownview, issues of diversity connect with larger structural inequalities embedded in school choice, which are not even debated or considered problematic by the school board because, again, school choice policies enable segregation in selective enrollment schools to persist.

Research Questions and Study Design

Connected to the purpose of this book, we examine how deeply embedded structures, practices, and beliefs shape policy reform to perpetuate educational inequity. The research questions for the study included, What are the ideologies of minoritized community members, and how do they conflict with dominant ideologies of the school board in the context of Brownview? How does a community, including school board policy makers, parents, and youth, respond to a lack of diversity at selective enrollment schools? We document the process of how minoritized community members challenge the deeply embedded structures, practices, and beliefs of the school board, whose members' perspectives did not support a race-conscious, equity-driven diversity policy. We also document how community members' call for an equitable selective enrollment admissions policy that reflected the racial diversity in Brownview rather than the current one in place that maintains a lack of racial balance at the best selective enrollment schools. This process called for what became known as a "diversity policy" despite the fact that the school board never articulated an actual policy or stance on a race-conscious diversity policy during the yearlong study. After several concessions, the school board did develop a diversity policy called the "Top Two Diversity Policy," which did not reflect community desires for equitable choice policy. We unravel the different meanings of diversity and the contradictory perspectives on what *ought* to be an equitable diversity policy from the perspectives of minoritized community members as they conflicted with the colorblind beliefs and agenda of the school board.

To pursue answers to the research questions, we employed an exploratory case study design (Yin, 2014). Yin (2014) instructs us to design case studies with parameters in mind in order to bound the case (p. 33). For us, this meant that we specifically targeted youth and parents in locally formed advocacy groups. The youth- and parent-founded groups had the same name in the community, Youth Advocating for Diversity (YAD, pseudonym) and Parents Advocating for Diversity (PAD, pseudonym). These groups were formed in Brownview following several instances of racial violence in the community without attention by the school board (see Rodriguez, 2017). Youth and parent groups met separately, and the first author attended youth- and parent-group meetings between 2015–2016. Guided by our conceptual framework we explored the intersection of structures (selective enrollment admissions' processes), ideologies (colorblindness in the community), and the lived experiences (youth and parents impacted by the lack of diversity and transparency).[7]

Research Role and Reflexivity

The research team consisted of one biracial Cuban American female faculty member and two graduate research assistants. The faculty member conducted the interviews and participant observations. One graduate research assistant was a white female, studying Child Life, which is a specialty area that works with chronically ill children in health care settings, with no prior knowledge or course work on structural racism. The other graduate research assistant was a white male who has four years teaching experience in a Title I school that predominately serves African American students from a low-income community and is pursuing a graduate degree with a specific focus on race, class, and gender inequities in education. Given our differences in background, experiences, and commitments to racial justice, we had several discussions, thinking through the definition of *diversity*, in particular, in order to engage in our data analysis. Given that the normative definition of diversity was at play by the school board, we intentionally took a race-conscious definition of *diversity*, which is what the community members did as well.

Data Sources and Collection

The data sources for this chapter include school board meeting minutes, field notes from observations and parent and youth advocacy group meetings, and interviews with parents and youth ($n = 20$). The first author, Sophia, conducted ethnographically oriented participant observations (Emerson, Fretz, & Shaw, 2011; LeCompte & Schensul, 2010) at monthly advocacy meetings led by youth and parents and at school board meetings (April 2015–June 2016) and conducted semistructured interviews with parents and youth, using purposive sampling and recruiting participants from the specific advocacy groups (Merriam, 2009). These semistructured interviews asked questions related to why the youth and parents formed the advocacy groups, their observations of district policies, and challenges they faced as activists seeking change from the district.

Data Analysis

To analyze the data, the first phase of analysis included open coding to identify emergent themes, that is, diversity, access, equality, policy, and class. The research team engaged in both independent and collective analytic coding using the emergent themes as well as themes generated by the conceptual framework, that is, structural racism, diversity, and colorblindness (Saldaña, 2013). Having three researchers involved in independent coding at various stages, as well as coming together at research team meetings to determine consensus around the codes, helped mitigate bias in the findings and address validity and reliability (Armstrong, Gosling, Weinman, & Martaeu, 1997; Kirshner, 2009). For example, upon completion of coding these documents independently, we found 111 instances across 13 documents, meaning the data sources listed earlier, in which diversity was discussed either explicitly or implicitly. In other words, diversity was a code for us, but during coding, we endeavored to understand what diversity meant to the various community actors. After discussion, we narrowed this to 76 instances. We repeated this process with each code, continually comparing data to each other and narrowing the instances of the various codes (Glaser, 1965). This constant comparative method enabled a critical, interpretive data analysis procedure, helping to clarify the eventual themes we describe in the following: *diversity climate*, *systemic inequality*, and *diversity as policy*. Next, we address each of these themes with evidence from the data sources listed earlier.

Findings

The Diversity Climate: "You Have to Be Willing to Accept Diversity"

The data revealed three key findings as to how minoritized parents and youth interpreted the diversity climate at selective enrollment schools in BCSD. First, minoritized youth described a negative racial climate on selective enrollment campuses that do not support diversity. Second, minoritized parents and youth describe that teachers at selective enrollment schools often believe that racial minorities lack the ability to achieve academically. Third, minoritized youth indicated that principals and teachers are reluctant to improve the diversity climate on selective enrollment campuses. The findings related to the theme of diversity climate indicate that the stakeholders at BCSD who hold the power to draw physical and social boundaries between themselves and other races are unwilling to "accept diversity" (Field notes, 8/28/15).

To begin, the theme of diversity climate emerged across youth comments. Youth struggled with identifying factors that contribute to the dwindling enrollment of students of color over the last 5 to 10 years at selective enrollment schools across BCSD. One member of the youth activist group YAD asked, "If watermelon incidents are occurring, would that deter students from applying?" (Field notes, 3/8/15).[8] Youth explained the lack of racial balance and the presence of racial violence, coupled with a lack of administrative action signal that diversity, are unwelcome. Across the data, minoritized youth described other acts of racial violence that further contextualize the negative racial climate on selective enrollment campuses that support this notion. During a parent meeting, they reported there was an incident where a picture of a group of African American girls was posted on a social media site that addressed the young ladies as the "N word" (Field notes, 3/8/15). During a YAD meeting, youth described an incident where a "white student called a gay black student a gay N word" (Field notes, 12/4/15). Another youth described an incident where the racial slur "Bindi" was directed at a student of Indian cultural background who "fell asleep and had a red blotch on his head from sleeping hard" (Field notes, 12/4/15). When incidents like the ones described previously happen often, the school is slow or negligent to respond to or address the issue; one youth explained, "Usually nothing happens" (Field notes, 12/4/15). Another youth indicated with regard to the social media post, "That's all that was heard because the principal has not addressed this at all" (Field notes, 3/8/15). Furthermore, when consequences for racial violence do occur, students feel they are at best inconsistent: "I know what teachers will say instantly and which ones won't" (Field notes, 12/4/15).

Aside from the outright acts of racial violence described earlier, more subtle messages were present within the racial climate of selective enrollment schools in BCSD. Minoritized parents and youth described a tacit belief among teachers that racial minorities lack the ability to meet the academic demands of selective enrollment schools. During a diversity panel at one selective enrollment school, a concern was expressed that increasing diversity meant that schools would have to lower the rigor of their academics. One parent illustrated her perception of this sentiment by explaining that when minoritized students are admitted into selective enrollment schools, teachers "already have an attitude that you're less than" (Field notes, 2/2/16). This statement indicates that teachers perceive minoritized students' academic ability differently from white students attending selective enrollment schools. This is especially true of minoritized students who had previously attended Title I elementary or middle schools. For example, the same parent described an incident where the band teacher from a selective enrollment school told her son that "a 98% at Title I middle school in Brownview is not going to be good enough. You're gonna have to work a lot harder" (Field notes, 2/2/16). This notion that minoritized students are unable to meet the academic demands of high-level course work was perceived by the youth attending selective enrollment schools as well. Often the few minoritized youth that attend selective enrollment schools are not placed in high-level course work on entering a selective enrollment school. As one youth explained, advanced placement (AP) and honors courses at her school have "extremely, extremely low minority representation" and that she is "either the only, or one of two," minoritized youth taking AP or honors courses (Interview, 12/21/16). In order to be placed in AP or honors classes at selective enrollment schools, students need a teacher recommendation, which, as she believes, also accounts for the lack of minority representation in AP or honors classes. Echoing the perception of the earlier parent, this youth explained, "If a teacher doesn't think that we are capable of it . . . you're probably led to believe that you aren't capable and you should be in a lower class" (Interview, 12/21/16). The data suggest that minoritized parents and youth perceive a belief among teachers at selective enrollment schools that youth of color lack the ability to achieve academically. This belief hints toward a racial hierarchy with regard to academic performance, which makes selective enrollment policies justifiable to the white majority fighting to uphold them.

Parents and youth believe the lack of diversity present at selective enrollment schools is to blame for the negative racial climate and acts of racial violence that are occurring. As such, they urge that increasing diversity at selective enrollment schools would foster tolerance and respect for different cultures and, in turn, would reduce instances of racial violence. One youth responded, "If you are not exposed, or if you are convinced of your racial superiority, or if you have no peers to shake that, then stuff like this happens" (Interview, 12/21/16). In this sense, diversity becomes a sort of check and balance for racial prejudice. Improving the racial climate would be a step in the right direction for increasing diversity at selective enrollment schools by sending the message to marginalized youth that diversity is appreciated in the community. Indeed, parents and youth advocates have called for just that. For example, during a diversity panel held at one selective enrollment school, youth expressed that "a lot of people want to see some sort of teacher diversity training. We still have some teachers at my school and at a lot of schools across the district who need to really learn how to work with students of color" (Field notes, 12/14/15).

Despite arguments from parents and youth to increase diversity, there is little evidence throughout the data that indicates BCSD is making strides to improve the racial climate at these schools with specific policy formation and implementation on the part of BCSD. Instead, issues related to diversity and racial violence persist, and parents and youth indicated that a negative racial climate on campus sends the message that diversity is not valued at selective enrollment schools. The data also highlight the ways in which minoritized youth are often deterred from even applying to selective enrollment schools and explain why minority students chose not to apply to selective enrollment schools. And if they do manage to enter a selective enrollment school, they are "forced out" through social isolation and a lack of belonging to the school, as one student noted (Field notes, 1/25/15).

Systemic Inequality: "These Systems Are So Big That They Take on a Life of Their Own"

The quote in this section's title is emblematic of another key finding revealed in the data. The lack of diversity at selective enrollment schools can be explained by structural and institutional racism. Specifically, parents and youth point to the admission process as a barrier for racial minorities. As one youth activist pointedly remarked, the admission process is "Jim Crow-esque" (Field notes, 3/11/16). Parents and youth described the admission process and the curious arrangement of selective enrollment schools at BCSD as a system that designates educational winners and losers. In reference to the competitive arrangement of the school system, one parent made it clear that "[h]ere everybody wants a piece of the pie" (Field notes, 2/2/16). Another parent echoing the same sentiment stated, "The adults who have arranged the pie to look like this are not helping you" (Field notes, 12/2/15). Here, parents are connecting the imbalance of power embedded in the social arrangements of the school system and the ways in which the admission process continues to reproduce inequality due to the lack of clarity about what the process actually is. Furthermore, parents described how systemic issues, that is, transportation, access to information, quality of schools, and tracking in low-performing schools, set up additional barriers to an already-unclear admissions process for selective enrollment schools. These barriers place undue burdens on racialized minorities. During a meeting, one parent proclaimed, "These issues need to be addressed because it's not that black children are not getting smarter" (Field notes, 3/08/15). This statement highlights a keen awareness that the community needs to name and address structural and institutional racism as a factor that denies diversity and racial balance in some of the best schools in the community.

Speaking to additional structural barriers, parents and youth illustrated the burden of transportation and the lack of access to information about the enrollment process as mechanisms that make it difficult for racial minorities to apply, be accepted into, and attend selective enrollment schools. For example, one parent described her experience contacting the district office to inquire about choice options for her son. She was informed that "we [BCSD] have school choice and you can decide where you send your children" (Field notes, 2/02/16). However, she also learned that school choice comes with one little caveat: "you will be responsible for transportation" (Field notes, 2/02/16). In BCSD, many selective enrollment or magnet schools are outside of the attendance zone where youth live. As this parent explained, providing her son with transportation to school "would be a bind because we have one vehicle" (Field notes, 2/02/16). Thus, if a parent is unable to provide transportation for his or her child because of his or her financial situation, then enrolling in select schools is not an option.

In addition to lack of transportation, the nebulous admissions process is a factor that excludes racial minorities from attending selective enrollment schools. During the diversity panel discussion held at Brownview Magnet, it was asked how the admissions process was communicated to parents of color. One parent bluntly indicated, "It's not communicated," while a student added, "I sorta applied to this school. I don't know how the admissions process worked" (Field notes, 3/08/15). Another youth described that information about selective enrollment middle or high schools is privy to students who attend selective elementary schools, stating that the kids attending selective elementary schools know about Selective Art School "'cause it's an art school [. . .] a lot of the kids who went to the selective art elementary school also go to the selective art school" (Interview, 12/21/16). This comment points to how young people are part of the network as elementary school students, they are more likely to know about "*THE ART SCHOOL*" in Brownview (Interview, 12/21/16) since the information is not readily available by the district nor does the district do outreach.

Along with transportation issues and accessing information as described earlier, the data also indicated that BCSD is not providing an equal opportunity for all students to attend selective enrollment schools—lack of resources and preparedness at the "regular" public schools. Parents and youth explain that their children lack access to quality schools that prepare them to attend selective enrollment schools and that the district fails to invest in all schools equally. One student explained that it's like "feeding communities that are full and starving the ones that are not" (Field notes, 1/25/15). This comment speaks to how youth understand the most resources are poured into the selective schools while the nonselective schools, particularly at the elementary and middle levels, are left with features of high-poverty schools that reproduce inequality such as weak organizational coordination and coherence, dire facilities, low teacher quality and retention, a lack of resources and guidance and counseling, and underdeveloped curricula (Ingersoll, 2003). It is widely known in the community that selective enrollment schools are better resourced, and thus, students have an array of experiences. Given that the district fails to address this systemic inequity, the selective enrollment school waiting lists are markedly long, ranging from 500 to 3,000 students each year.

Responses from parents and youth alike confirm the unique experiences that are available at selective schools, which is another example of the unequal access to preparedness and opportunity in elementary and middle selective schools. One youth described her experience at Selective Art School, stating, "I am in the piano program. We attend music festivals and travel out of state. We have gone to colleges. Just being able to perform is an opportunity I would not have had otherwise" (Interview, 12/21/16). A student from Brownview Magnet explained, "I went to a Selective Elementary Art School. I was given the tools for success. A lot of kids aren't told they are able to come here and don't have the same opportunities to get here" (Field notes, 12/02/15). These types of experiences are completely different from the schooling that is offered to racial minorities attending Title I schools in the district. One parent who had a daughter attending Selective Elementary Art School and a son attending Title I middle school depicted stark contrast between the experiences at these two schools: "Title I middle school was built to give low-income students discipline. Over half of its student body was suspended. People assume they are on drugs or whatever" (Field notes, 2/02/16).

Youth also described how certain schools, typically ones attended by racial minorities, do not offer course work that is required for the application to selective enrollment schools, which is another example of the systemic nature of inequality. Many children attending Title I nonselective elementary schools are excluded from selective enrollment high schools due to the fact that their schools do not offer the required prerequisite coursework to even apply to a selective enrollment high school. For example, many Title I middle schools do not offer algebra. In order to get into Brownview Magnet or Selective Art School, students must have taken algebra in middle school. Additionally, there is a rubric that rates a student's previous course load and that is used for determining eligibility when applying to selective enrollment schools. One youth activist inquired about the subjective ways that youth are scored on tests that then matter for admission to selective enrollment schools (Field notes, 3/11/16). A second student lamented, "[W]e can put a forensic science [in our selective school] but why can't we have a basic class [put into the Title I middle schools]? Why is it not a requirement to offer it, but it's a requirement to get into our [selective] high school?" (Field notes, 3/11/16).

Moreover, when minoritized youth do make it into select schools often they are tracked out of higher level course work because of their previous educational opportunities. One parent shared how her son, who started at a Title I middle school but still was accepted into Selective Art School, was tracked into the lowest math class. It was explained to her that "there was a rubric [as part of admissions and entrance to the Selective Art School] and you get points for Gifted and Talented [at the elementary or middle level], you get points for honors [at the elementary or middle level], and honors wasn't offered at Title I middle school where he came from" (Field notes, 2/02/16), so even though he was accepted to Selective Art School primarily due to his audition, his rubric scores were low given that he had attended a Title I middle school, so he was placed in a lower track at Selective Art School. This made her feel as if the arrangement of the school system was stacked against her son. Many parents and youth perceive the selective enrollment process in the same light. They are adamant that the selective enrollment process prevents racial minorities from accessing the best schools.

Diversity as Policy: "Nothing Is Going to Happen and Nothing Is Happening"

This third theme points to what we found to be an "absence" of a policy. The theme highlights the contradictions between the normative view of the white stakeholders and the minoritized groups. The absence of a policy indicates from the white normative perspective that a diversity policy isn't necessary, while the voices of the minority youth and parents indicate that, based on the absence of diversity at selective enrollment schools, that a diversity policy is necessary. While we found a wealth of data from parents and youth, examining BCSD's policy documents revealed a lack of discussion and policy implementation related to diversity. Given the nearly two-year effort of parents and youth to raise awareness of the diversity issues at school board meetings and local protests, our document analysis of BCSD school board meeting revealed a colorblind policy discourse on the part of policy makers that ignored issues of structural and institutional racism. We examined eight months of school board meeting minutes and found zero instances in which the board formally discussed a diversity policy in the public record. This, coupled with the disappearance of the Diversity Task Force, left us to wonder how the board would address diversity issues in policy formation and implementation.

During a board meeting, attended by the first author, the discussion on improving diversity at choice schools was focused on two policies: standardizing the application process and creating an ad hoc committee for improving diversity. Parents challenged the board to begin a discussion about the lack of racial diversity in selective enrollment schools. What unraveled was another contradiction between what the community members desire, more diversity, and how the board intercepted their request, which was to form an ad hoc committee and to generate a standardized application. One district policy-maker explained the proposed application policy for selective enrollment schools: "This just looks to standardize as many elements as possible with the 27 schools" (Field notes, 10/26/15). She continued to talk about the benefits of making the application completely online without any regard for issues of access for racial minorities: "We feel like we can serve our families better with the user-friendly online application" (Field notes, 10/26/15). Here, the focus remains on the application process and making it "user-friendly" online without attention to issues raised by parents and youth earlier not to mention the potential access issues to the online application. Despite the failed attempt of the initial Diversity Task Force, the board discussed the purpose of a newly created ad hoc committee. The Diversity Task Force was supposed to "look at diversity," in order to "increase diversity in the student population" by including "three members from the school improvement council, the principal or assistant principal, two community business partners, two teachers from the respective schools, and one constituent board member from the district in which the schools are located" (Field notes, 10/26/15). From later board meetings, we learned that the ad hoc committee was in place, but the specifics of the ad hoc committee remained out of the public record.[9]

What is absent from both of these policy discussions is the acknowledgment of racial inequality, as well as structural and institutional barriers that prevent racial minorities from accessing selective enrollment schools. The policy discourse from the data analyzed supports the premise that policy makers espouse a colorblind ideology when discussing "diversity" issues in the district by proposing to "standardize the application" and "look at diversity." When policy-makers talk about "diversity" in colorblind terms they mask the discussion of racial imbalance and inequality. This further supports the claims by parents and youth that nothing is going to happen from a policy standpoint that will adequately address the present diversity issues in BCSD.

In the face of the board's lack of diversity policy, parents and youth continued to voice their frustration with BCSD at protests before and during school board meetings and during public comments at the meetings. Despite the persistent protests of community members and parents, the board failed to initiate a policy to address racial imbalance and access to educational opportunity. When explaining the lack of action on the part of the school district, parents and youth speak of issues related to power and the distribution of resources. One youth activist explained, "They close out every voice. They don't want to hear what people have to say. They don't want a reason to increase diversity or make change" (Interview, 12/21/16). One of the founding members of YAD expressed disappointment with BCSD in addressing diversity issues: "I often hear it said that the district promotes more minority representation and more diversity, but I haven't seen it happening. I have been super disappointed by their efforts to increase diversity. I don't see anything happening" (Interview, 12/21/16). Similarly, a parent critical of the district's diversity policy, or lack thereof, claimed, "It's not diversity how we want it; they want diversity so long as they can control it" (Field notes, 3/8/15). Here, parents and youth expressed frustration with policy-makers who are unwilling to accept that there are diversity issues in the district, and more specifically that selective enrollment policies are producing racial inequality. Parents and youth remained unheard as policy-makers refuse to acknowledge that selective admission policies have racial implications and are excluding racial minorities from attending the best schools.[10]

We continued to see the board denying racial equity and diversity in selective enrollment schools with colorblind educational policy. All the data presented show the persistent struggle of parents and youth to voice their desires for equity and the dismissal of their desires by the school board, resulting in sustained inequity. The data also reveal quite vividly how minoritized communities' desire for equity is ignored consistently and despite their best efforts to show up at multiple school board meetings at that. To illustrate this, it is of note that as of June 2016, the board announced it would reinstate a lottery to be implemented in the fall of 2016, signaling a compromise to parent and youth requests for systemic change and more access and transparency. Following the board after the study concluded, we know that on January 23, 2017, the board called for "The Top Two Admissions Protocol," to increase diversity at Brownview Magnet (not all selective enrollment schools). This plan helps identify the top two students in BCSD's eighth-grade programs with the highest grade point average and they must score a minimum number on the subjective rubric that is currently used at Brownview Magnet (email correspondence, 1/23/17). The "Top Two" diversity policy resulted after two years of parent and youth dissent. This "Top Two" diversity policy, according to the minoritized community members, exemplifies colorblind educational policy in that it ignores structural and institutional racism. Furthermore, this policy fails to address diversity climate issues on selective enrollment campuses since merely placing potentially different races on campus does not guarantee a positive racial climate. A strong diversity policy, from the perspective of community members it is intended to benefit, would address racial climate issues, inclusionary practices, and systemic access to such opportunity. Knowing the unequal resource distribution across public eighth grades and within school stratification mechanisms like tracking, it is unlikely that most minoritized youth, especially at the Title I schools would satisfy the requirements for the "Top Two" diversity policy.

Discussion and Implications

The data have broader implications for the policy-making process. The few instances that the board discussed diversity issues and possible policy solutions, parent and youth concerns of structural issues were not acknowledged or addressed through the intended "Top Two" diversity policy. Given this, the selective enrollment admissions policy coupled with the powerful discourses of colorblindness and the ideological climate of diversity continue to perpetuate inequality. Diversity work in schools is challenging to be sure, but this chapter revealed the multiple voices and stakeholders most impacted by a lack of policy or by a policy that perpetuates inequality. Returning to our conceptual orientation, we consider some implications for selective enrollment processes as well as the consequences of colorblind diversity work as part of school choice.

The divergent views on diversity and equity along with the consistent ways that community voices were silenced or ignored compel us to argue there is a need to address structural, systemic processes such as selective enrollment admissions requirements and resource distribution across all public schools. We also argue there is a deep need to identify colorblind policy discourse. While BCSD saw its "Top Two" diversity policy as a plausible solution, data from parent and youth suggest that it is an act of whiteness (Leonardo, 2007) because it recenters the diversity work within the merit-based feature of choice and selective enrollment, that is, the belief that the playing field is level and the students at Brownview Magnet worked hard and deserve to be there. The "Top Two" diversity policy fails to address systemic inequity and segregation. Instead, this policy is guided by what Leonardo (2007) calls an "ideology of whiteness" that "depends on the continuation of racial differences as part of a logical, rather than social, outcome (pp. 268–269). Instead, colorblind, merit-based policies like the "Top Two" ensure the continuation of racial structures (by refusing to address them) rather than abolishing those structures. The poignant theme "Nothing is happening; nothing will continue to happen" speaks to the power of colorblindness and the intensification of racial disparity despite the ways it is masked (p. 266).

The implications of this work point to the need for future research to address racialized social structures in communities and to track how communities are embedding inequality within policy and practice. Many school choice studies reiterate the competition, market-based explanations, or a natural hierarchy in a capitalistic society without calling attention to the ways in which colorblind ideology is linked to institutional mechanisms and policies. More recent scholarship discusses how racial disparities persist without attention to their impact on the lived experiences of racialized minorities. Similar to Scott and Holme (2016), our research called attention to the grassroots, social movements in a local community because these instances seek to revitalize urban education and transform oppressive systems. We have examined the policy stages alongside the intersection of parent and youth voices. We found that despite the disappointment parents and youth endured, the emphasis on their voice and effort contributes distinctly by including those often marginalized in the policy formulation and implementation processes. In addition, minoritized parents and youth help elucidate to those in power the systemic, delayed opportunity and access to educational equity in the process that we have documented. Future research demands attention to groups that are impacted by colorblind policy. Eventually, we hope that continued pressure on districts will result in much more than BCSD's archaic "Top Two" diversity policy that harkens to W. E. B. Dubois's (1903) "Talented Tenth" and Thomas Jefferson's (1779) "Natural Aristocracy," both perpetuating meritocratic, bootstrap discourses that reproduce stratified racialized social systems in which racial minorities are the losers in the competition.

Conclusion

This chapter addressed how one case of a community, saddled with a legacy of segregation and inadequate facilities for racial/ethnic minorities, grappled with diversity and inequity in the choice, selective enrollment policies in the district. We demonstrated the (un)intended consequences of colorblind education policies. We also documented the community efforts to resist persistent educational stratification through selective enrollment admissions' processes and institutionalized racism. As suggested earlier, the diversity policy is really a lack of a diversity policy, and the attempts to address it did not advance the hopes of community members. We argued here that parent and youth activists offer a critical perspective for researchers and policy-makers in the face of neoliberal competitive school choice policies because their perspectives expose the lived realities of structural inequity.

Notes

1. All names in this chapter are pseudonyms.
2. At the time of this study (2015–2016), the school board was composed of eight white members and two African American members. One of the eight was a white female superintendent. But more important, the new school board superintendent was a white female who came in after a highly charged racial incident that led to the forced resignation of an African American superintendent. For research related to this incident, see Rodriguez (2017).

3. Brownview technically desegregated in 1963, with full-scale desegregation by 1971; however, there were many efforts to thwart desegregation, particularly through the privatization movement and local attempts to structure inequality in the school district (Hale & Cooper, 2017).
4. Various educational groups have discussed the dire conditions that African American children attend school in the state Brownview is in. In fact, the documentary *Corridor of Shame* details the problematic nature of the "minimally adequate" component of the state's constitution. For more information on the "right to minimally adequate education," see Fogle, 2000; Hale & Cooper, 2017). Additional efforts to thwart desegregation included the state's "Segregation Committee," which recommended ways to support privatization and choice for white parents. The state passed a bill in May 1963 to provide funding to parents who chose not to enroll their children in public schools, encouraging parents to choose private schools. This is did not include religiously affiliated schools (Hale & Cooper, 2017).
5. Frankenberg and Lee (2003) discuss the original intentions of school choice, including magnet and selective enrollment schools, and the unintended consequences of such policies as a result of *Brown* and desegregation efforts. They argue that "[m]ost educational choice options (such as magnet schools) arose from desegregation plans. In 1973 the U.S. Supreme Court extended desegregation requirements to northern and western cities. However, just a year later, the court rejected the lower Detroit court's proposition that integrating minority students in heavily minority and rapidly changing districts required including the suburbs to produce long-lasting desegregation. Big cities looking at demographic facts and seeing the conflict over mandatory reassignments of students in cities such as Boston looked for a way to accomplish desegregation through voluntary choice. The problem was that very few whites had ever voluntarily chosen to attend black schools or to transfer for integration purposes. The idea of the magnet schools' movement was to create specialized schools that could offer unique opportunities that would create a demand for voluntary transfers from both white and minority students and result in a student population that would meet desegregation standards. By establishing special programs and curricular offerings in inner-city areas, school systems used magnet schools and programs to attract white students to predominantly minority schools" (p. 6).
6. In Brownview, larger structural inequities that result from school choice were not even discussed due to the legacies of segregation here that we mentioned previously. As part of integration efforts in the South a decade after *Brown v. Board* (1954), Brownview strategically used school choice to sustain racial segregation. The legacy of desegregation and the efforts to thwart it are ever present in southern cities such as Brownview (Grundy, 2017; Rodriguez, 2017).
7. Related to the setting, in Brownview, there are three selective enrollment high schools in Brownview that are considered the cream of the crop. We assigned pseudonyms to these later, Brownview Magnet (the school that had the diversity chart published about it), Selective Art School, and Selective Prep.
8. The "watermelon incident" refers to when the mostly white football team at Brownview Magnet selective enrollment engaged in a postgame ritual of drawing a caricature of an African American on a watermelon and smashing it into the ground as they chanted and made monkey-like noises and engaged in what YAD members called a "culturally insensitive ritual" (Rodriguez, 2017). The school board was compelled to fire the coach after the community created uproar over this racially charged incident and what some community members deemed to contain racial undertones while others in the community did not see this as a race issue. However, after the white, middle-class community engaged in a battle, the coach was reinstated and

9. The first author was initially invited to be part of this Diversity Task Force, but after it was dismantled, she attempted to follow up with those in charge to no avail. It was stated to the first author by a special consultant to the school district on matters of diversity that the original Diversity Task Force was challenging because "too many voices were involved." The first author inquired about what this meant, specifically asking if "too many community members voices were challenging the dominant white, middle-class norms in the community." The first author was not invited back to whatever ad hoc committee did manifest.
10. During this study the Diversity Specialist position at the district office was eliminated, and the Diversity Task Force that had initially been formed after the publication of the "diversity chart" was disbanded after one meeting. The stated rationale was that the district was unclear on the purpose of the Task Force. The superintendent formed the Task Force in the spring of 2015 to address the diversity issues. This task force was loosely defined and configured. This means, community members, parents, teachers, and principals were a part of the task force that came together to identify the most pressing issues related to diversity in the district. The first author was also invited to attend the task force because of her expertise at one point. She attended one meeting in the spring of 2015, and the task force was dismantled by August 2015. Her attempts to ask why this happened were unsuccessful. It was noted that the task force had too many competing voices and ideas were involved. The district has since formed a new "diversity council" and sent out emails to former task force members asking for their continued involvement, but information regarding the new council has been sparse, resulting in a continued gap in community input on diversity issues.

References

Armstrong, D., Gosling, A., Weinman, J., & Martaeu, T. (1997). The place of inter-rater Reliability in qualitative research: An empirical study. *Sociology, 31*(3), 597–606.

Blackmon, D. A. (2008). *Slavery by another name: The re-enslavement of Black Americans from the Civil War to World War II*. New York City, NY: Anchor Publishing.

Brown *v.* Board of Education, 347 U.S. 483 (1954).

Bonilla-Silva, E. (1997). Rethinking racism: Toward a structural interpretation. *American Sociological Review, 62*(3), 465–480.

Bourdieu, P., & Passeron, J. C. (1990). *Reproduction in education, society and culture*. London, UK: Sage Publications.

Bowles, S., & Gintis, H. (2003). Schooling in capitalist America twenty-five years later. *Sociological Forum, 18*(2), 343–348.

Cucchiara, M. (2013). *Marketing schools, marketing cities: Who wins and who loses when schools become urban amenities*. Chicago, IL: University of Chicago Press.

Dubois, W. E. B. (1903). *The Negro problem: A series of articles by representative American Negroes of today*. New York: James Pott and Co.

Dumas, M. (2016). Against the dark: Antiblackness in education policy and discourse. *Theory into Practice, 55*(1), 11–19.

Emerson, R. M., Fretz, R. I., & Shaw, L. L. (2011). *Writing ethnographic field notes*. Chicago, IL: University of Chicago Press.

Fabricant, M., & Fine, M. (2012). *Charter schools and the corporate makeover of public education: What's at stake?* New York, NY: Teachers College Press.

Fogle, J. L. (2000). Abbeville county school district v. state: The right to a minimally adequate education in South Carolina. *South Carolina Law Review, 51.*

Frankenberg, E., & Lee, C. (2003). Charter schools and race: A lost opportunity for integrated education. *Education Policy Analysis Archives, 11*(32). Retrieved April 2019, from http://epaa.asu.edu/epaa/v11n32/

Frankenberg, E., & Orfield, G. (2013). *The resegregation of suburban schools: A hidden crisis in American education.* Cambridge, MA: Harvard Education Press.

Garcia, D. R. (2007). The impact of school choice on racial segregation in charter schools. *Educational Policy, 22*(6), 805–829.

Glaser, B. G. (1965). The constant comparative method of qualitative analysis. *Social Problems, 12*(4), 436–445.

Grundy, P. (2017). *Color and character: West Charlotte High and the American struggle over educational equality.* Chapel Hill, NC: University of North Carolina Press.

Guinier, L. (2004). From racial liberalism to racial literacy: Brown v. Board of education and the interest-divergence dilemma. *The Journal of American History, 91*(1), 92–118.

Hale, J., & Cooper, C. (2017, forthcoming). Lowcountry, high demands: The struggle for quality education in Charleston, South Carolina. In V. Showers Johnson, G. Graml, & P. Williams Lessane (Eds.), *Deferred dreams, defiant struggles: Critical perspectives on blackness, belonging and civil rights.* Liverpool, UK: Liverpool University Press.

Harvey, D. (2005). *A brief history of neoliberalism.* Oxford, UK: Oxford University Press.

Ingersoll, R. (2003). *Who controls teachers' work? Power and accountability in America's schools.* Cambridge, MA: Harvard University Press.

Jefferson, T. (1779, June 18). *A bill for the more general diffusion of knowledge.* Retrieved July 2019, from https://founders.archives.gov/documents/Jefferson/01-02-02-0132-0004-0079

Kirshner, B. (2009). "Power in numbers": Youth organizing as a context for exploring civic identity. *Journal of Research on Adolescence, 19*(3), 414–440.

LeCompte, M. D., & Schensul, J. J. (2010). *Designing and conducting ethnographic research: An introduction.* Lanham, MD: AltaMira Press.

Leonardo, Z. (2007). The war on schools: NCLB, nation creation and the educational construction of whiteness. *Race Ethnicity and Education, 10*(3), 261–278.

Lewis, A. (2003). Everyday race-making: Navigating racial boundaries in schools. *American Behavioral Scientist, 47*(3), 283–305.

Lipman, P. (2011). *The new political economy of urban education: Neoliberalism, race, and the right to the city.* New York, NY: Routledge.

Lipman, P., Vaughan, K., & Guiterrez, R. R. (2014). *Root shock: Parents' perspectives on school closings in Chicago.* Chicago, IL: University of Illinois, Collaborative for Equity and Justice in Education.

Merriam, S. B. (2009). *Qualitative research: A guide to design and implementation.* San Francisco, CA: Jossey-Bass.

Milem, J. F., Chang, M. J., & Antonio, A. L. (2005). *Making diversity work on campus: A research-based perspective.* Washington, DC: Association American Colleges and Universities.

Morris, E. W. (2006). *An unexpected minority: White kids in an urban school.* New Brunswick, NJ: Rutgers University Press.

Oakes, J. (2005). *Keeping track: How schools structure inequality*. New Haven, CT: Yale University Press.

Orfield, G., & Frankenberg, E. (2013). *Educational delusions: Why choice can deepen inequality and how to make schools fair*. Berkeley, CA: University of California Press.

Parker, W. (2001). The color of choice: Race and charter schools. *Tulane Law Review*, 75(3), 563–630.

Pattillo, M. (2015). Everyday politics of school choice in the black community. *Du Bois Review: Social Science Research on Race*, 12(1), 41–71.

Posey, L. (2012). Middle- and upper-middle-class parent action for urban public schools: Promise or paradox? *Teachers College Record*, 114(1), 1–43.

Posey-Maddox, L. (2014). *When middle class parents choose urban schools: Class, race, & the challenge of equity in public education*. Chicago, IL: University of Chicago Press.

Rhodes, A., & DeLuca, S. (2014). Residential mobility and school choice among poor families. In A. Lareau & K. Goyette (Eds.), *Choosing homes, choosing schools* (pp. 137–166). New York City, NY: Sage Publications.

Rodriguez, S. (2016). "We need to grab power where we can": Teacher activists' responses to neoliberal policies during the Chicago teacher's strike of 2012–2013. *Workplace: A Journal for Academic Labor*, 26, 74–88.

Rodriguez, S. (2017). "My eyes were opened to the lack of diversity in our best schools": Re-conceptualizing competitive school choice policy as a racial formation. *The Urban Review*, 49(4). 529–550.

Rossell, C. (2010). *The carrot or the stick for school desegregation policy: Magnet schools or forced busing*. Philadelphia, PA: Temple University Press.

Rumbaut, R. (2011). Assimilation's bumpy road. In M. Chowkwanyun & R. Serhan (Eds.), *American democracy and the pursuit of equality* (pp. 184–219). Boulder, CO: Paradigm Publishers.

Saldaña, J. (2013). *Coding manual for qualitative researchers + qualitative data analysis: A methods sourcebook*. Thousand Oaks, CA: Sage Publications.

Scott, J., & Holme, J. J. (2016). The political economy of market-based educational policies. *Review of Research in Education*, 40(1), 250–297.

Siegel-Hawley, G. (2014). Race, choice and Richmond public schools: New possibilities and ongoing challenges for diversity in urban districts. *Urban Review*, 46(4), 507–534.

Staiger, A. D. (2006). *Learning difference: Race and schooling in the multiracial metropolis*. Redwood City, CA: Stanford University Press.

Walker, V. (2000). Valued segregated schools for African American children in the South, 1935–1969: A review of common themes and characteristics. *Review of Educational Research*, 70(3), 253–285.

Willis, P. E. (1977). *Learning to labour: How working class kids get working class jobs*. Farnham, UK: Ashgate.

Yin, R. (2014). *Case study research: Design and methods* (5th ed.). Thousand Oaks, CA: Sage Publications.

3 Education for What and Whom?

The Paradoxical Nature of an Upward Bound Program

Kevin Clay

Introduction

Over the past decade, high-profile instances of racial terror, including attacks on Black and Latinx teenagers' civil rights and personal safety, both on and off college campuses, offers some indication of the challenges for which college-bound youth from this generation must prepare (e.g., Dried & Najmabadi, 2016; Hinton, 2017; Jaschik, 2016; Tate, 2017; *CBS News*, 2017; Fernandez & Perez-Pena, 2015). While some consider college admission an entry point into self-determination, it is all the more critical that youth of color from the most divested neighborhoods are prepared to navigate the world (including higher education) from their specific social positionality as many of them transition into independent legal adult status. Although scholars identify "cultural" preparation as a necessity in any college access curriculum (e.g., Corwin, Colyar, & Tierne, 2005), programs that formally prepare youth of color from marginalized communities tend to overlook this kind of cultural preparation in their college access curriculum.

This chapter focuses on the complex relationship between college preparation, civic development, and Upward Bound (UB). Despite UB's success in college admissions for its population of White students, there are areas where questions remain, and data are thin regarding its role in preparing youth of color for life after high school. These gaps are of critical importance considering that UB tasks itself with college access *and* retention for a population of young people that overwhelmingly represent historically marginalized backgrounds (National Trio Clearinghouse, 2000) and whose rates of college enrollment and completion lag their counterparts from middle-class and affluent backgrounds (Myers, Olsen, Seftor, Young, & Tuttle, 2004; Butrymowicz, 2015).

Among other areas in its broad curriculum that ranges from science, technology, engineering, and mathematics; foreign language; and literature to mentoring and financial aid literacy, UB identifies "cultural enrichment" as one component of advancing its mission toward increasing the rate of postsecondary enrollment and retention for students whose families are "low-income" and neither parent holds a bachelor's degree.[1]

I argue that disparate outcomes between UB students from Black and Brown communities and their White counterparts in the program suggest challenges in the area of cultural enrichment; challenges that require UB to clarify and perhaps expand its notion of cultural enrichment at the site level to best serve its largest population—Black and Latinx youth (National Trio Clearinghouse, 2000).

I argue that a college preparation for these particular young people must consider the importance of a critical, action-oriented, political education to support their secondary educational pursuit, college enrollment, *and* attainment. To that end, this ethnographic study investigates an Upward Bound program across two main areas: (1) UB students' perceptions of justice-oriented action, specifically the utility of collective action to address societal inequality, and (2) UB staff's positions regarding educating youth about racial injustice, including their evaluations of how their Black and Latinx students should navigate racial inequality. These considerations ultimately drive at unpacking the underexamined "cultural enrichment" component of college preparation for Black and Latinx youth, specifically within the context of Upward Bound.

This chapter presents findings from the first several weeks of 16 months of sustained ethnographic fieldwork within a UB program housed in a community college in the Mid-Atlantic region. To begin, I briefly review the policy context surrounding the creation of UB—a federal TRIO program and appendage of the Higher Education Act of 1965 (HEA). I utilize a critical race theory (CRT) critique of liberalism to frame the context that foregrounds the advent of the HEA and Upward Bound (HEA UB). I then move into empirical analysis of UB staff and youth's views around questions of civic orientation in relation to issues of race/ism and other injustice, theoretically grounded in Westheimer and Kahne's (2004) framework regarding "the politics of educating for democracy." Specifically, I situate how UB youth and staff grapple with notions of ideal citizenship within the three modes of citizenship theorized by the authors—these are *personally responsible*, *participatory*, and *justice-oriented citizenship*. While *participatory* citizenship and *personally responsible* citizenship are models of citizenship in which the citizen holds it as his or her private responsibility to promote the public good either through personal acts like paying taxes (personally responsible) or organizing a group to pick up trash (participatory), *justice-oriented* citizenship involves challenging systems and institutions that reproduce inequitable outcomes and working to change those systems through forms of advocacy or activism.

From Recompense to Self-Help: The HEA

The advent of HEA UB is best analyzed through CRT's critique of liberalism which rejects the ahistorical premise on which race-blind law and policy argue that selective consideration of race/ethnicity in the shaping of any social policy, particularly as a remedy to past injustices against communities of color, is inherently unjust (Delgado & Stefancic, 2012). I argue that HEA UB was founded in a *neoliberal* ethos that carries over to and ultimately backfires at the site level, undermining the program's ability to achieve its stated altruistic aims for youth from underserved communities. In this section, I review President Johnson's inconsistent framing of Great Society reforms, including HEA UB, to provide a backdrop for empirically analyzing the unreconciled dissonance and paradoxical nature of one particular UB program.

Early formulations of Great Society reforms as presented to the public, found Lyndon Johnson engaging a discourse that *professed* a commitment to the pursuit of justice; that is, through these reforms, eliminating structures that make race and class highly predictive of life chances. However, as actual social policies were unveiled, Johnson's tone made a neoliberal transformation—elevating the primacy of reform beneficiaries' personal effort. President Johnson's Great Society speech given at the University of Michigan's commencement on May 22, 1964, confirm his acknowledgment of the federal government's responsibility for addressing race and class disparities. He says, "The Great Society rests on abundance and liberty for all. It demands an end to poverty and racial injustice, to which we are totally committed in our time."[2] He decried "The Ugly American"—a reference to the 1958 political novel of the same name that characterized American soldiers as bombastic, hedonistic, and racist, while he also highlighted *structural impediments* to the realization of social equality, continuing,

> In many places, classrooms are overcrowded and curricula are outdated. Most of our qualified teachers are underpaid and many of our paid teachers are unqualified. So, we must give every child a place to sit and a teacher to learn from. Poverty must not be a bar to learning.

At Ohio University on May 7, 1964, he continued elevating racial justice and the state's responsibility in bringing about change when he stated, "We want to bring equal justice to all our citizens.... We must end open bias and active bigotry."[3] Great Society reforms would eventually target fair and affordable housing, health care for the poor and elderly, voting rights for African Americans, and increased commitment of financial resources for minoritized K–12 and higher education populations, among several other areas. Although acknowledgment of the *structural* disparities between the lives of the rich and poor, and Blacks and whites, was a touchstone of the rhetoric around Johnson's Great Society platform, the language by which actual means-tested policies were later introduced was noticeably de-racialized, and hinged heavily on personal responsibility, and preemptively warned against giving away handouts.

In this new discourse, Great Society reforms were merely scaffolding for individual mobility for those who were willing to make something of themselves. Allusions to reforming systemic inequities were replaced by a call to individual persons to be responsible, work hard and take advantage of opportunities. For example, at the signing of the 1964 Economic Opportunity Act (EOA), Johnson articulated the perspective that reforms were a stepping-stone for the truly hardworking, stating that EOA would help young men and women have "productive lives, not wasted lives. . . ." He continued:

> [W]e will reach into all the pockets of poverty and *help our people find their footing for a long climb* [emphasis added] toward a better way of life. . . . Our American answer to poverty is not to make the poor more secure in their poverty but to reach down and to help them *lift themselves* [emphasis added] out of the ruts of poverty.[4]

This shift in tone was also apparent at the rolling out of the 1965 HEA.

Among other things, HEA dedicated billions of federal funds to Pell grants that covered most if not the full tuition cost of public college for students from low-income households and created TRIO programs (one of which being UB) that supported students from low-income backgrounds in developing their academic competencies, financial aid literacy, and offering extracurricular opportunities (Glater, 2016). Upon signing, Johnson stated, "To thousands of young men and women, this act means the path of knowledge is open *to all that have the determination to walk it*" [emphasis added]. It means a way to deeper personal fulfillment, greater personal productivity, and increased personal reward."[5] This oscillation between a policy ethos of neoliberal personal responsibility and one of commitment to remedying injustice that characterizes the foundation of HEA UB, I argue, undermines its effectiveness at reducing educational disparities.

Although Black and Latinx youth represent 63% of UB, the most recent data show that they lag significantly behind their White counterparts in the program (National Trio Clearinghouse, 2000; Myers et al., 2004). Statistical analysis of UB's impact on college enrollment comparing a control group of demographically comparable UB *eligible* students (i.e., low income and/or would-be first generation in their family to attend college) to UB students finds that UB increased the enrollment of white students from 58% to 69%, while Latinx students—for whom UB made the greatest impact—only enrolled at 50% (Myers et al., 2004). There was no significant difference between rates of enrollment for Black students in UB compared to those who fit the demographic criteria of UB eligibility. Additionally, for students who were both low income and first generation, UB held no statistically significant difference in rates of four-year enrollment.

These outcomes are a far cry from Johnson's stated vision of the Great Society and point to issues that I argue, in part, rest with the unresolved tension of whether HEA UB is ultimately a neoliberal bootstrap policy program for "low-income students" or one that is chiefly committed to the advancement of justice for communities historically locked out of resources and access higher education. Specifically, considering the disparate outcomes between marginalized UB students and White participants, it is critical to raise the question, "Who is this program for?" Answering this question is the first step in resolving *what* kind of education this program should provide.

Johnson's vision and UB's stated mission are broader frameworks that require site-level staff at UB to interpret and execute. The explicit and implicit messages that staff communicate to students relay important information to them about how they are understanding what UB is (and is not) as a policy program dedicated to "low-income" youth's college admission and retention. In turn, students relay information about what their potential needs are in relation to the UB program, particularly as it relates to college enrollment and retention—needs that might reach beyond what the UB curriculum currently offers. Although UB students enroll in four-year institutions, limited data have been reported about their higher education experience and retention.

I take the position that a political education is crucial preparation for college-bound youth (Duncan, 1996). The experiences of Black and Latinx youth both in and outside of PK–12 schooling are historically and deeply embedded in systems of racial inequality, and research and current events demonstrate that this does not change when youth move on to higher education (Solórzano, 2000; Milkman, Akinola, & Chugh, 2015). Additionally, as scholars have identified that marginalized youth thrive academically when exposed to a political education (e.g., El-Amin et al., 2017), it stands to reason that an intervention like youth participatory action research (YPAR) in the UB curriculum would prove useful toward bolstering positive academic outcomes in line with UB's stated goals.

What Did I Study?

This study investigates the questions, How are Black and Latinx UB students conceptualizing what actions are appropriate in response to inequality and injustice? How does UB staff frame *responsibility* for educating Black and Latinx youth about inequality? and What ways do they consider ideal for their college-bound youth to approach these issues? To answer these questions, this research draws on field experience between July 2015 and November 2016 with high school students enrolled in a UB precollege program. This UB grant is located in a historically divested urban community that I call Milton whose population is 50% Black and 37% Latinx and where the poverty rate is nearly 27%. The population of the rising 9th through 12th graders in UB and those who participated in YPAR reflects this racial/ethnic breakdown. Participants in this study are the 14 consenting of 21 total students in my elective 'research' course that I created to facilitate YPAR. Critical YPAR is an approach to youth organizing, research, and resistance that centers both the use and production of young people's indigenous knowledge to actively address some local force of inequity. Although the empirical goal of this research was to study youth researchers' political identity development over the course of 16 months, I engaged a YPAR approach to educate youth about legacies of structural racism that produced and exacerbated social and economic inequalities felt across many Black and Brown communities (including theirs), to lead young folks toward more radical political orientations, and to prepare them to empirically research community issues as a foundation to enact local change.

Participants also include the three full-time UB staff members whom I interviewed in relation to capturing how institutional spaces may play a role in shaping youth's politics. The UB program was the most consistently reported place after high school in which youth spent the most time. I interviewed each staff one time in the last three months of 2016. Staff consisted of the program director, Mrs. Pryce, a Jamaican woman in her early forties who immigrated to the U.S. in her childhood, grew up in the city, and attended the very program she now directs; Mr. Chesnutt, the assistant director/counselor, a middle-aged Black American man

Table 3.1 Youth Researcher Background Information

Name	Grade	Race/Ethnicity	Gender	School
Kumar	11	Black	M	Excelsior Charter
Shante	11	Black	F	Milton West (Public)
Beauty	11	Black	F	Milton West (Public)
Justice	12	Black	M	Milton High School (Public)
Selena	10	Honduran and Mexican	F	STEM Charter
Jonae	12	Black	F	Milton Day/Night (Last Chance School)
Ebony	12	Black	F	Milton High School
Rosada	10	Puerto Rican	F	Milton High School/ Visual and Performing Arts (Public)
Faylah	12	Black	F	Private Catholic
Cindy	12	Black	F	Private Catholic
Gustavo	9	Mexican American	M	Traditional Public (nearby suburb)
Maria	9	Latina	F	Milton High School/ 9th Grade Academy (Public)
Salim	9	Egyptian (identifies as African)	M	Milton High School/ 9th Grade Academy
Hector	12	Mexican American	M	Milton High

originally from Harlem, New York; and Ms. Brown, a Black American woman in her late twenties who also grew up in the city and went through this very UB program as a high school student. Staff members consistently demonstrated a deep care for the UB students and their futures in the warmth they showed toward young people. They showed up in important ways when, oftentimes, the work was exhausting, pulled them in multiple directions, and required significant patience on their part to deal with students of varying personality types with myriad private circumstances.

I draw on participant observation data from my first several weeks facilitating YPAR during which I examined how young people talked about race/ism, class, and social change. I focus on the beginning stage of YPAR because it is during these weeks that I probed young people for their political views without offering any instruction or critical reaction. After these weeks, I provided direct instruction on issues of structural inequity, and I offered my perspectives with much less reservation. Within this time frame, I audio-recorded eight YPAR meetings and wrote six days of field notes on my observations.

I also rely on interview data with UB staff. Interviews with staff focused on how staff understood the role UB played in preparing its youth for college and their reflections on young people's learning in relation to issues of race/ism and injustice, broadly defined. Coding and memoing using qualitative research software allowed me to identify patterns in the data related to the aforementioned research questions and within Westheimer and Kahne's (2004) framework of civic orientations.

What Do the Data Tell Us?

Data analysis revealed that several UB students held tenuously the value of *justice-oriented citizenship* and promoted *participatory* and *personal responsibility* models (Westheimer & Kahne, 2004). It also revealed that program staff positioned learning about racism and inequality as students' private responsibility—a responsibility that they felt students fell short in fulfilling. Much like Johnson, the UB staff pivoted between recognizing their students' as struggling against structural inequality and emphasizing the imperative that they exercise independent initiative to manage these issues on their own. Recognizing that students did and would encounter inequity and racism, the staff championed approaches for dealing with such issues that involved personal resilience and other forms of strategic accommodation.

UB Youth's Perspectives on Inequality and Action

Early in the YPAR process, young people (each of whom elected to be a part of the research) communicated that they were very interested in having conversations about racism and inequality, even if only because those topics were rarely approached in their classrooms at school, which signaled to many of them that talking about racial injustice was taboo in formal learning settings. One student even remarked that a teacher told him it was "illegal" to discuss current events around police shootings in school. Amid the summer of 2015, several high-profile cases of police killing and assaulting unarmed Black victims were still active in the news cycle. These cases involved victims like Freddie Gray, Sandra Bland, and Walter Scott. Despite their interest and desire to unpack the circumstances of these deaths, several youth showed ambivalence toward responses that took on various forms of *justice-oriented citizenship*. This was evidenced succinctly in part of a conversation we had about police violence that summer.

We read a think piece that related the Baltimore riots following the death of Freddie Gray to the *Hunger Games*.[6] The piece questioned the fleeting empathy of those who would side with "The District" in the movie but would critique the civil disobedience in Baltimore the days after Gray's death at the hands of law enforcement. I began the lesson by inviting students to relay the events that led to the death of Freddie Gray and asked them about the news coverage related to the protests and rioting; Shante discussed the one-sided coverage of "rioters," and Rosada describes her feeling that citizens have no power to disrupt police violence:

SHANTE: It was a cover-up. The news only puts—I believe that the news only shows what everybody in Baltimore was doing instead of what was going on with the cops that caused Freddie Gray's injuries because they know that the cops was wrong and they don't like putting that out there; "Oh, the cops was wrong so we just gonna show what the other people are doing to the cops."
CLAY: Ok so, how do you feel about the rioting; do you think the rioting served any purpose? Do you think it was valuable in any way? Do you think it was a bad thing? Do you think it hurt the cause ultimately? How do you feel about rioting?
ROSADA: So, with the whole riot thing, I think for me it was a waste of time, because I think at the end of the day, *they know that police are gonna do what they want and the government is not gonna stop them. It's just—there's no point. You can try and keep trying, but then again, these are policeman, they're not gonna do anything* [emphasis added].

Rosada's feelings about the hopelessness of resistance were justified considering that between 2013 and 2016, there was a preponderance of reports documenting cases of unarmed Black men, women, and youth who have died at the hands of law enforcement without police facing any charges or convictions (Funke & Susman, 2016). After we read the piece, I asked students to reflect on parallels between the *Hunger Games* and real life. Like Rosada, Justice and Faylah expressed some hesitations about the merits of organized civic action in their community:

CLAY: When we look back at something like the Hunger Games, what do you think it would take for the people in the District to get equality?
FAYLAH: Not do nothing. Cause they supply the government. So, if they don't do anything, the government can't happen.
JUSTICE: I think that's gonna hurt you and the government. 'Cause let's say . . . let's put it to real life: if we were to stop, like, going to stores and stop, you know, just buying stuff in general, you're going to have a . . . let's say grocery stores, for example: you stop buying food from there—the business isn't getting money to give to the government and at the same time, you're not getting any food from them.
CLAY: Faylah, so what do you think about that, how would you respond to what Justice said?
FAYLAH: I was just going off of the *Hunger Games*. [All laugh.] The Capital don't know what to do but the people know how to fend for themselves.
CLAY: So, if you had to apply that to real life, do you think that model would work?
FAYLAH: No, not now. No. It might, but I don't know how it would.

I responded to the Faylah and the other youth researchers by asking them if they were familiar with the Montgomery bus boycotts during the civil rights movement and explaining to them the effect it had on public busing and desegregation efforts in the South under Jim Crow. Conversations and interviews that followed in the succeeding days of YPAR illuminated many students' limited exposure to successful (or partially successful) revolutionary and reformatory movements for human rights and liberation both in the U.S. and abroad. Westheimer and Kahne (2004) confirm the lack of attention given to this kind of learning as programs like The Character Counts! Coalition, promoting personally responsible citizenship, and others that promote community service and service learning enjoy widespread support and funding from the educational establishment. The most telling part of the preceding exchange was Faylah's comment, "It might, but I don't know how," in response to my question about the real-life utility of boycotting a public or private institution, as it suggests a gap in her civic knowledge that, I argue, calls for UB's curriculum to offer young people opportunities to reflect on and learn about activist work. This absence in UB's curriculum is paradoxical considering that HEA UB is a policy program that exists in part due to youth activism during civil rights movement (Glater, 2016; Franklin, 2014; Glater, 2011; Perlstein, 2008). Not only that, but campus reforms and larger advents in academia that made schools more inclusive to Black and Brown youth also owe credit to Black and Brown college-student activism (Murch, 2010).

Several students' uncertainty about justice-oriented activism was accompanied by their adherence to principles of *personally responsible* and *participatory citizenship*. For instance, during one YPAR meeting, I asked the group, "Why are whole communities poor and not just individuals?" considering that poor whites are much more likely than poor Black folks to find affordable housing in mixed-income or higher income communities (Troutt, 2013). After a brief pause and some overlapping debate amongst students over structure versus agency, Ebony's voice emerged, saying,

> I don't necessarily think it's the government's fault. I mean, you know, well, we know for *our* communities, they're not going to do anything, so why not try to do something yourself, as a community. Like, this is where you live, this is where you lay your head at night, so, if you don't like the way it's looking or if it's poor then you should try to make it better. You can't just blame it on the government.

Ebony communicated a valid perceptive on government apathy in relation to Black and Latinx communities specifically. Her comments suggest that she recognized structural racism manifest in government inaction; however, her grievance in this regard did not rest with the government. The argument that government is not responsible for addressing local poverty and that this burden is ultimately one that residents must themselves fix reflects a politics of *neoliberal governmentality*—or the government's outsourcing of its responsibility for addressing public problems into the hands of citizens or the private sector (Kwon, 2013; Spence, 2015). Following up, Faylah takes Ebony's view that community poverty doesn't reflect a problem at the government level, saying, "It's kind of our fault because government sends out the census to see how many people are in the town and people don't fill it out. They don't know how much money to give." Faylah's personally responsible view of citizenship suggests that residents' failure to perform basic civic duties, like filling out a census survey, undermines their own community vitality.

These findings demonstrate some youth's proclivity toward personally responsible and participatory forms of citizenship. They also allude to some of their reservations about particular forms of activism. While being prepared for college is not typically thought to include preparation for political engagement, it is useful to consider the history of Black and Latinx college youth's activism and the ways in which their activism reformed higher education by spearheading the creation of the very first Black and Chicano Studies programs and Black Student Unions (Murch, 2010). Black and Latinx youth activism has created culturally sustaining spaces on college campuses for Black and Brown students today. It stands to reason, then, that education around activism would be in line with UB's college admission and retention goals.

Our 16 months of following these initial weeks in YPAR offered an opportunity for our action research group to participate in learning about structural inequality and organizing for justice. Although the research course gained popularity among the students and eventually generated a lot of interest from the UB staff, their perspectives about youth in relation to political education diverged significantly from the justice-oriented ethos of our YPAR group.

Black Resilience Neoliberalism in the UB Pipeline

My interviews with UB staff during the closing days of my research revealed insights about how they viewed *responsibility* for educating youth around racism and injustice and what they thought that education should look like. Although UB staff supported the idea that students should learn about racism and inequality, overwhelmingly, they viewed education around racial injustice as students' personal responsibility. Much like Johnson, the UB staff pivoted between recognizing their students' as struggling against structural inequality and emphasizing the imperative that they exercise human capital in resolving or enduring these issues. This view reflects a politic that I call Black Resilience Neoliberalism (BRN; Clay, 2019). BRN is an ideology that places a premium on Black Americans accommodating structural racism by normalizing their human capital efforts to "overcome" or endure racism, ultimately obscuring or ignoring the suffering they are made to endure. Findings from the previous section suggest that these messages were not lost on young people like Ebony and Faylah who subscribed to similar ideas about personal responsibility in relation to dealing with structural racism.

Mrs. Pryce, the program director, held strongly to the idea that UB's curriculum was divided into two strands—the academic component and a cultural component, which was couched in terms of activities such as museum trips, college tours, theme parks, and general socialization with peers. Her concern was that many students were not as invested in the academics as they were in the cultural experience of UB.

Pryce responded favorably to my request to facilitate YPAR as an elective, understanding that it was an experience in which the class would explore issues of race/ism and inequality and where our group would eventually engage in community work around these issues; however, when we met in May 2015 to go over the details of this work, she voiced concerns about the political nature of the language I used to describe the class, and we brainstormed how to strategically reframe *the description* of YPAR into something that spoke to more traditional subject-area college preparation (Baldridge, 2014). (She did not request a curriculum change.)

When I asked Mrs. Pryce what UB students should be learning about racism and injustice, she emphasized her disappointment in students lack of Black history knowledge. She went on to say,

> Our students need to read more. They need to read more. They need to research more. They need to pay close attention to these movies that are coming out highlighting some of the struggles that African Americans and the [Native] Americans have gone through. They need to begin to focus on those things. Not just on Black History Month, you do a presentation on Martin Luther King . . . [pauses, squints her eyes, then speaks in a very deliberate voice] *I'm so tired of every time Black History month comes and you ask them to do research, the first person they pick out is Martin Luther King.* There's other folks out there that have made a difference, that have done something that I shouldn't have to see six different projects on Martin Luther King. You know? Because that's all they know. If they open up their minds and they read more and they research more and they know more, when you say Black History Month, they could come up with other individuals other than Martin Luther King.

Mrs. Pryce expressed dismay about the depth of students' grasp of Black history knowledge and argued that they needed to take more initiative to learn this history on their own; however, she is the director of the college preparation program with authority over curriculum. Similarly, Mr. Chesnutt described his position that learning about injustice was something students should do on their own, especially considering their access to technology. Mr. Chesnutt responds to the question, "Who do you feel is primarily responsible for teaching students about racism and injustice?" by saying,

> I think you could teach yourself. [Teaching] yourself is more important. One of the things you could do? Research. Nowadays, you can research anything; smartphone, YouTube, computer. You can research anything. You know, but that's, you should look at yourself. You know, look in the mirror and say, "Do I want better or do I want to be in the same situation as my parents or something like that?" You gotta have somebody to motivate you. But, I think it's yourself.

Personal responsibility remained at the forefront of the full-time staff's evaluations of student learning about these issues. Even when students expressed dismay about the quality of education they received in school, the staff presented this as a personal problem to overcome with self-motivation. For example, Mr. Chesnutt elaborates on a common complaint of students in the program about their schooling and relays his typical response:

> They try to blame [their low GPAs] on the teachers, but it could go both ways. You've got to motivate yourself. A lot of teachers don't want to teach. A lot of teachers give out handouts instead of teaching

them so they run into that too, but I feel like you know . . . you got to motivate yourself and do well.

Here Chesnutt engages a BRN discourse: recognizing a pattern of banal teaching practices in Milton schools and placing the burden on students to overcome this systemic issue by motivating themselves. Ms. Brown took a similar stance with regard to students overcoming systemic inequalities. Responding to the question, what should UB students know about racism and injustice, Ms. Brown answers,

> They should know . . . I guess, the world's perception of them because growing up when . . . or growing up in a community that's majority black, we tend not to see color, and that's because everyone pretty much looks like us. . . . [For me], leaving high school and then going into the real world and seeing how people treat you once you get there, not everyone is like that group of people that I was able to enjoy my high school experience with. Then that made it all the more clear about how I had to carry myself in order to not be judged as an angry black woman or as a woman that puts her career before everything else or whatever the other stereotypes are that come along with being black.

Brown believed that students should learn about anti-Black stereotypes in order to evade them. She told a story that alluded to her view that young folks should respond to this bias by *code-switching* or engaging in self-management and performative acts that align with supposed "white middle-class" ways of being (Carter, 2008). Her comments suggest that students need to change themselves (even if temporarily) in ways that would help them to get by in a context that was systemically inequitable.

UB staff regarded students learning about racial injustice as a personal responsibility. They acknowledged that their students did and would encounter structural inequality and other challenges beyond young people's control and offered recommendations for youth to navigate these issues in ways that asked them to work hard academically or just cope to navigate those barriers. Accommodating approaches to racism like the ones promoted by UB staff are rooted in a history of survival within a society built on the death and exploitation of Black, Native, and Latinx peoples. Staff's views about youth's navigation of structural racism suggested a belief that change was intractable. Accordingly, their views on how youth should deal with these challenges centered on student resilience rather than *student resistance.*

Discussion and Conclusion

The definition of *cultural enrichment* in college preparation scholarship is elusive and often implies that culture is to be understood as value added to an overall positive self-regard in youth of color and should be championed through practices that invoke ethnic or racial pride (Villalpando & Solórzano, 2005). Cultural enrichment is also held as acclimating young people to the norms and expectations of higher education and helping them to "acculturate" (i.e., assimilate; Corwin et al., 2005). To a much lesser extent is cultural enrichment conceptualized as a set of critical practices to confront structures of racial oppression. This study examined an Upward Bound program in relation to how staff and students reflected on navigating issues of racism and injustice, finding that both staff and students embraced personal responsibility and participatory civic orientations, and were much less drawn to justice-oriented models.

Ultimately, UB must reexamine for what and whom its educational program is devised. Is it for youth from communities both historically and structurally locked out of access to educational opportunities or simply "low-income, first-generation youth"? Although this may appear to be merely a question of semantics, the latter conception circumspectly adheres to a liberal colorblind standard, passively overlooking needs and challenges specific to Black and Latinx youth, which may help to explain, in part, why white students—who do not confront structural racism—experience better outcomes in the program. However, if UB positions itself as a program for students whose communities and schools have been shaped by processes of structural racism, then a broader kind of education is in order—a critical political education that prepares young people to challenge the inequities they experience in divested communities and are likely to confront in higher education and beyond. Inviting critical political education into the curriculum through YPAR offered UB youth the opportunity for learning critical capacities that have in some cases been shown to bolster achievement. Moreover, as Black and Latinx youth transition onto college campuses increasingly more hostile to them, the research and advocacy skills and the civic and political knowledge cultivated in YPAR are likely to support their capacity to shape institutions in ways that facilitate their retention. To this end, I argue that "cultural enrichment" in UB's curriculum must, in part, include preparing youth for justice-oriented civic engagement.

Notes

1. U.S. Department of Education. *Programs: Upward Bound.* Retrieved June 2019, from www2.ed.gov/programs/trioupbound/index.html.
2. Lyndon B. Johnson: "Remarks at the University of Michigan," May 22, 1964. Online by Gerhard Peters and John T. Woolley, *The American Presidency Project.* www.presidency.ucsb.edu/ws/?pid=26262.
3. Lyndon B. Johnson: "Remarks in Athens at Ohio University," May 7, 1964. Online by Gerhard Peters and John T. Woolley, *The American Presidency Project.* www.presidency.ucsb.edu/ws/?pid=26225.
4. Lyndon B. Johnson: "Remarks Upon Signing the Economic Opportunity Act," August 20, 1964. Online by Gerhard Peters and John T. Woolley, *The American Presidency Project.* www.presidency.ucsb.edu/ws/?pid=26452.

5. Lyndon B. Johnson: "Remarks at Southwest Texas State College Upon Signing the Higher Education Act of 1965," November 8, 1965. Online by Gerhard Peters and John T. Woolley, *The American Presidency Project*. www.presidency.ucsb.edu/ws/?pid=27356.
6. Ashley Nicole Black: *Why Protestors Turn Violent*. ATTN, May 5, 2015. Retrieved from www.attn.com/stories/1554/empathy-for-black-protestors.

References

Baldridge, B. J. (2014). Relocating the deficit: Reimagining black youth in neoliberal times. *American Education Research Journal*, 51(3), 440–472.

Butrymowicz, S. (2015, September 24). An unprecedented look at Pell Grant graduation rates from 1,149 schools. *The Hechinger Report*. Retrieved from http://hechingerreport.org/an-unprecedented-look-at-pell-grant-graduation-rates-from-1149-schools/

Carter, P. (2008). Teaching students fluency in multiple cultural codes. In M. Pollock (Ed.), *Everyday antiracism: Getting real about race in school* (pp. 107–111). New York, NY: The New Press.

CBS News. (2017, September 13). DACA student targeted by classmate says university has done nothing to help. *CBS News*. Retrieved from www.cbsnews.com/news/outed-daca-student-kentucky-pleads-help-transylvania-university/

Clay, K. L. (2019). "Despite the odds": Unpacking the politics of black resilience neoliberalism. *American Educational Research Journal*, 56(1), 75–110.

Corwin, Z. B., Colyar, J. E., & Tierney, W. G. (2005). Introduction: Engaging research and practice-extracurricular and curricular influences on college access. In W. G. Tierney, Z. B. Corwin, & J. E. Colyar (Eds.), *Preparing for college: Nine elements of effective outreach* (pp. 29–48). New York: SUNY Press.

Delgado, R., & Stefancic, J. (2012). *Critical race theory: An introduction*. New York, NY: New York University Press.

Dried, N., & Najmabadi, S. (2016, December 13). Here's a rundown of the latest campus climate incidents since the Trump's election. *The Chronicle of Higher Education*. Retrieved from www.chronicle.com/blogs/ticker/heres-a-rundown-of-the-latest-campus-climate-incidents-since-trumps-election/115553

Duncan, A. G. (1996). Space, place and the problematic of race: Black adolescent discourse as mediated action. *The Journal of Negro Education*, 65(2), 133–150.

El-Amin, A., Seider, S., Graves, D., Tamerat, J., Clark, S., Soutter, M., Johnnsen, J., Malhotra, S. (2017). Critical consciousness: A key to student achievement. *Phi Delta Kappan*, 98(5), 18–23. https://doi.org/10.1177/0031721717690360

Fernandez, M., & Perez-Pena, R. (2015, March 10). As two Oklahoma students are expelled for racist chant, Sigma Alpha Epsilon vows wider inquiry. *The New York Times*. Retrieved from www.nytimes.com/2015/03/11/us/university-of-oklahoma-sigma-alpha-epsilon-racist-fraternity-video.html

Franklin, S. M. (2014). *After the rebellion: Black youth, social movement activism, and the post-civil rights generation*. New York: New York University Press.

Funke, D., & Susman, T. (2016, July 12). From Ferguson to Baton Rouge: Deaths of black men and women at the hands of police. *Los Angeles Times*.

Glater, J. D. (2011). The other big test: Why congress should allow college students to borrow more through federal aid programs. *NYU Journal of Legislation and Public Policy*, 14(1), 11–73.

Glater, J. D. (2016). Debt, merit, and, equity in higher education access. *Law and Contemporary Problems*, 79(3), 89–113.

Hinton, J. (2017, April 11). Salem College students conduct sit-in protest, allege racism, sexism and elitism. *Winston-Salem Journal*. Retrieved from www.journalnow.com/news/local/salem-college-students-conduct-sit-in-protest-allege-racism-sexism/article_bfe4dbfd-7f47-574c-bcf3-2490a1bd694a.html

Jaschik, S. (2016, October 26). Backlash to anthem protests. *Inside Higher Ed*. Retrieved from www.insidehighered.com/news/2016/10/24/alabama-and-greenville-backlash-anthem-protests-black-students

Kwon, S. A. (2013). *Uncivil youth: Race, activism, and affirmative governmentality*. Durham: Duke University Press.

Milkman, K. L., Akinola, M., & Chugh, D. (2015). What happens before? A field experiment exploring how pay and representation differentially shape bias on the pathway into organizations. *Journal of Applied Psychology, 100*(6), 1678–1712.

Murch, D. J. (2010). *Living for the city migration, education, and the rise of the Black Panther Party in Oakland, California*. Chapel Hill: University of North Carolina Press.

Myers, D., Olsen, R., Seftor, N., Young, J., & Tuttle, C. (2004). *The impacts of regular upward bound: Results from the third follow-up data collection* (Report by Policy and Program Studies Services Prepared for U.S. Department of Education Office of the Under Secretary). Washington, DC: Mathematica Policy Research, Inc.

National TRIO Clearinghouse. (2000). Racial and ethnic diversity in the federal TRIO programs. *National TRIO Clearinghouse*. Retrieved from www.pellinstitute.org/trio_clearinghouse.shtml

Perlstein, D. (2008). Freedom, liberation, accommodation: Politics and pedagogy in SNCC and the Black Panther Party. In C. M. Payne & C. S. Strickland (Eds.), *Teach freedom: Education for liberation in the African American tradition* (pp. 75–94). New York: Teachers College Press.

Solórzano, D. (2000). Critical race theory, racial microaggressions, and campus racial climate: The experiences of African American college students. *Journal of Negro Education, 69*(1/2), 60–73.

Spence, L. (2015). *Knocking the hustle: Against the neoliberal turn in black politics*. Brooklyn, NY: Punctum.

Tate, E. (2017, January 24). Protest of blackface incidents at Oklahoma State. *Inside Higher Ed*. Retrieved from www.insidehighered.com/quicktakes/2017/01/24/protest-blackface-incidents-oklahoma-state

Troutt, D. D. (2013). *The price of paradise: The costs of inequality and a vision for a more equitable America*. New York: New York University Press.

Villalpando, O., & Solórzano, D. G. (2005). The role of culture in college preparation programs: A review of the research literature. In W. G. Tierney, Z. B. Corwin, & J. E. Colyar (Eds.), *Preparing for college: Nine elements of effective outreach* (pp. 29–48). New York: SUNY Press.

Westheimer, J., & Kahne, J. (2004). What kind of citizen? The politics of educating for democracy. *American Educational Research Journal, 41*(2), 237–269. https://doi.org/10.3102/00028312041002237

4 Turnaround, Mayoral Control, Minoritized Communities, and Dirty Water

School Reform in an Urban District in Connecticut

James S. Wright

Introduction

This study investigates a complex web of inequality occurring in the Waterbury Connecticut school district. During the height of the industrialization and manufacturing period, from the early to mid-nineteenth century, Waterbury was a magnet for immigration (Brooke, 1985; Ryan, 1992). James Brooke (1985) of the *New York Times* recalled, Waterbury "was the 19th-century version of today's Silicon Valley" (Brooke, 1985). Today, Waterbury is an urban city ravaged by deindustrialization and economic divestment in the urban areas, in spite of some the highest tax rates in Connecticut—a state among the highest tax rates in the country. As a result, poverty and a debilitating drug epidemic have led to a sweeping mass incarceration phenomenon in Waterbury (Wright, 2017).

Geographically, Waterbury is in a southwest corner of the state and is part of New Haven County and about 50 miles northwest from New York City. Waterbury has a history of well-documented political malfeasance: recurring and widespread political and institutional investigations of city officials, notably within city hall (Associated Press, 2014; Leduff & Herszenhorn, 2001). This study is about an entanglement with the mayoral-led Waterbury public schools and this relationship to minoritized[1] communities, mostly Black and Latinx, which make up more than 85 percent of the Waterbury school district (Naples, 2014; Wright, 2017). This study centers the perspectives of educators, local politicians, and community activists from Waterbury's Black and Latinx communities as well as other minoritized perspectives. Educators and community members from Waterbury's Black and Latinx communities are concerned with turnaround policy application and mayoral led educational strategies and practices. This is an inquiry of school leadership and the implementation of the *turnaround* policy under a mayoral controlled Waterbury school district that began in 2011.

I was born and raised in Waterbury and experienced K–12 schooling in Waterbury public as well as parochial schools. My relationship to the city of Waterbury is established as to proclaim my relationship and ties to the sociopolitical discourses and practices in Waterbury; particularly from the perspective of minoritized communities. I chose the life history methodology to conduct this inquiry as to make explicit my positionality in this study. The framework used in this study relies on a critical analysis of educational policy studies. This critical policy analysis uses Sandra Stein's (2004) Culture of Education Policy framework to highlight discourses and language used to *frame* individuals and groups.

Framing the Culture of Education Policy

Conventional policy analysis is rooted in the belief that policy serves as a mechanism to solve problems and produce better outcomes (Ng, Stull, & Martinez, 2019). For example, policy analysis in education are typically focused on inputs such as school leadership initiatives, like training, evaluation, resource allocation and on outputs like the quality of school leadership, and student achievement (Gates, Baird, Master, & Chavez-Herrerias, 2019; Herman et al., 2017; Wang et al., 2018). However, recent engagements with policy studies are challenging the conventional methods. These challenges encourage critical analyses of discourses, narratives, and symbols that undergird and define policy (e.g., Diem, Young, Welton, Mansfield, & Lee, 2014; López, 2003; Stein, 2004; Wright, Whitaker, Khalifa, & Briscoe, 2018). Thus, critical policy analysis suggests that policy should be understood for its potential to reproduce and replicate much of the inequity it seeks to dispel.

In accord with this critical perspective on policy, the concept of culture of education policy (or culture of policy) frames this study. Culture is recognized as the epistemologies: norms, values, practices, and ways of knowing specific to particular groups (e.g., Curry, 2017; Ishimaru et al., 2016; Khalifa, 2018; Mignolo, 2012). Stein (2004) argues that culture of policy is useful for critically examining the assumptions built into policy and by challenging "the ways in which policies shape institutional and individual perceptions and treatments of those they aim to serve" (p. 12).

Dirty Water: A Life History

> Indeed, since the 1980s, it has been common practice for qualitative researchers in general to 'write themselves' into their research, on the grounds that personal, background information will enhance the rigour of their work by making potential biases explicit.
> —Goodson and Sikes (2001, p. 35)

Waterbury is known across Connecticut and throughout the region as "The Dirty Water." The Dirty Water moniker originated in Waterbury's

North End neighborhoods, where the focus school of this study, Walsh Elementary, is located. Inner-city hip-hop artists from Waterbury created the infamous Dirty Water moniker. A local Waterbury DJ at WZMX Hot 93.7, a popular radio station in the region, began referencing Waterbury as the Dirty Water during live broadcasts (Wright, 2017). As a result, many throughout the Northeast came to know of Waterbury as the Dirty Water. Dirty Water is, in part, a reference to recurring, widespread political and institutional misconduct on the part of city officials. Within a decade, two Waterbury mayors, Mayor Joseph Santopietro in 1992 and Mayor Philip Giordano in 2002, were imprisoned following investigations during their tenures as mayor (Associated Press, 2014; Cowan, 2003; Hays, 1992). These arrests and convictions were followed by the investigation and eventual imprisonment of Connecticut's governor John J. Rowland in 2004, also a Waterbury native (Cowan, 2017; Zielbauer, 2004). In addition, many of Waterbury's inner-city and minoritized residents have, for decades, lamented about police brutality and misconduct as rampant federal investigations haunted many rank-and-file city officials (Leduff & Herszenhorn, 2001; Mahony, 2016; Press, 2012). There always appeared to be a dark cloud over the city and something in the *water*, as local residents commonly suggested.

Insights From the People

In this inquiry, I analyzed policy discourses through document analysis and conducted interviews with school leaders and prominent voices from Waterbury's minoritized communities. The document analysis included Waterbury board of education meeting minutes, local media stories, court records, and social media content. Specifically, the board of education meeting minutes propelled me to various other school leaders, board members, community members, parents, students, and activists impacted or otherwise concerned with turnaround school policies and mayoral controlled educational strategies and practices in Waterbury. I collected and analyzed these documents from the time turnaround was implemented at Walsh elementary in 2011. Content analysis and interviews were collected and conducted between 2015 and 2018. Participants all self-identified as Black or African American. This purposive sampling selection was intentional (Palys, 2008).

The blowback from turnaround in the Waterbury school district garnered much attention regionally and nationally to some degree. However, urban, Black and Latinx communities, culture, and students in the district at large were deficitized, framed negatively, and depicted as problems in much of the media content. These deficitized and negative frames are indicative of what was found in the *Connecticut State Law Tribune*. The popular and influential legal publication framed Walsh Elementary

School as in a "rough part" of the city full of "blighted homes" and poor families whose students struggled speaking English and were in need of special education (Spicer, 2016, para., 1). Thus, communities and perspectives that were largely marginalized in dominant discourses and platforms are centered in this chapter. This study is positioned around an analysis of discourses and practices of the mostly White educational leadership in Waterbury, in contrast to the perspectives of Black/Latinx and minoritized community members in Waterbury.

Life History Methodology as a Counterculture

This inquiry is conducted using a life history methodology. The focus years of this life history was from 2011 through 2018. I utilized the life history methodology as an antithesis to traditional educational research methods. Some scholars call life history methodology a counterculture (Wright, 2019). A divergence from traditional educational research methods—the ways we come to know including the strategies, paradigms, research models, grammar, and theories in educational research (Dhunpath, 2000; Goodson & Sikes, 2001).

The particular epistemological position of the life history methodology values the subjective, emic, and ideographic, wherein objective generalizations are not the goal (Goodson & Sikes, 2001). "Life history data disrupts the normal assumptions" and "forces a confrontation" with subjective perceptions and claims of objectivity (Goodson & Sikes, 2001, p. 7). Thus, this inquiry centered and amplified, oftentimes contrasting, perspectives and insights from minoritized communities, their culture, and students and educational leadership personnel in the district. My approach to the life history method is to humanize the experiences of African Americans, Latinx, and other minoritized communities and groups in Waterbury by chronicling a sample of their experiences and their insights. Such experiences and insights contrast with powerful discourses and practices driving schooling in Waterbury, led by a powerful mayor. Moreover, this approach works to fill gaps in educational history and in research on Black and Latinx/urban education in the United States, specifically Connecticut.

Connecticut is often thought of for its affluence and wealth. Rarely do people associate Connecticut cities and neighborhoods with Black and Brown families and impoverished, failing schools (Wright, 2017). Life history studies are designed to not only add shape to some feature of life experience but to bring to the front marginalized identities and perspectives (Goodson & Sikes, 2001; Munro, 1998; Wright, 2019). This life history study centers and amplifies voices of people living in the shadows of Connecticut's affluence. This study highlights how the Waterbury school district implemented the turnaround policy, and how the minoritized community members responded.

Turnaround in Dirty Water

In 2011 Walsh Elementary School in the Waterbury school district was cited for turnaround. Funding for the turnaround policy is granted through Title I. Although 60 percent of the City of Waterbury's budget is allocated for education; millions of additional funds were poured into the district as a result of turnaround (State of Connecticut, 2010). The criterion for turnaround was that schools needed to be in the lowest 5 percent on standardized test scores in math and reading. In 2011 two schools in the Waterbury school district met these criteria, one elementary and one high school. The elementary school, Walsh Elementary school, is a main focus of this inquiry. An African America male, Erik Brown, was the principal at Walsh at the time of turnaround. The student population at Walsh was around 95 percent Latinx (a majority of whom were Puerto Rican and African American), and nearly 90 percent of Walsh students received free and reduced-priced lunch (Wright, 2017). Implementation of turnaround occurred through an integrated governance model: mayor control (State of Connecticut, 2010; Waterbury Minority Teachers, 2015; Wright, 2017).

Mayoral Control in Education

Large urban schools and districts with large populations of minoritized students are those most likely to be taken over or cited for mayoral control (Morel, 2018; Wright et al., 2018). Wong and Shen (2013) reported a strong correlation between mayoral governance and enhanced student achievement (test scores) in many large urban districts and cities. Thus, business leaders, politicians, and school unions are leading the charge for mayoral control of schools (Kirst & Wirt, 2009; McDermott, 2013; Wong, 2007). Henig (2013) rightly acknowledged that there are "proponents arguing that it [mayoral control] catalyzes reform and opponents complaining that it marginalizes parent and community groups" (p. 178). Thus, mayoral control is perhaps most noted for the hard lines that it draws between its proponents and opponents.

Critiques of Mayoral Control

Arguments for successful outcomes of mayoral control are vague and blurry (Morel, 2018). Davis (2013) argued that "governance structures too often allow politics to play an overwhelming role in education, sometimes blocking innovation" (p. 74). Lipman (2011) posits that "mayoral control is a critical tool to restructure school systems from the top with minimal public 'interference'" (p. 47). Kirst and Wirt (2009) described the integrated governance strategy of mayoral control as an underexamined "bully pulpit" (p. 287). Hess (2008) noted that those who study the idea of mayoral control are generally equivocal about it. Kirst and Wirt (2009) noted that "the overwhelming evidence is inconclusive" that mayoral control is as effective as it is branded (p. 163). Much research on mayoral control cites the potential and possibility for success in mayoral-led school districts; however, successful outcomes are scant and mostly idealistic (Morel, 2018).

What Mayoral Control Means for Waterbury

Lipman (2011) reminds us that mayoral control is designed for minimal interference and can silence concerns and inquiries raised by individuals and groups. Per Connecticut's 2017 state budget, Waterbury was one of 52 cities cited for an education budget increase (Rabe Thomas, 2017). Waterbury was to receive a $38 million increase, raising its total educational budget to a staggering $174 million, one of the state's highest (Rabe Thomas, 2017). The state issued total autonomy to local municipalities on how to spend that money. This has caused alarm for some in the state because as Patrice McCarthy, the deputy director of the Connecticut Association of Boards of Education, warned, "it will be up to the municipalities to determine whether to actually spend it on their schools—or use it to close their own local budget shortfalls or make up for other state budget cuts" (Rabe Thomas, 2017). Furthermore, McCarthy noted that "it's not going to go to support student needs in most communities. . . . It's important that people understand that education grants might not be being spent on education" (Rabe Thomas, 2017). McCarthy was concerned that federal funds designated for urban schools could be diverted elsewhere.

Ex Officio as Mayoral Control

The City of Waterbury's charter grants the mayor ex officio status, which means the mayor is a board of education member. Although a board member (ex officio), the mayor is not allowed to vote, but in the event of a tie, the mayor breaks the tie (Wright, 2017). Ex officio status was not a new development that emerged with turnaround. Ex officio dates back at least to the 1902 City of Waterbury charter (Electors of the City of Waterbury, 1902, 2002). Since 2011, Waterbury mayor Neil O'Leary has used the legislative language in the city's charter to control the board of education and influence educational decisions throughout the school district (Wright, 2017). O'Leary, a White male member of the Democratic Party, was born in Waterbury and began serving as a member of the city police department in 1980. In 2004, he became chief of police and then stepped down from that post when he was elected as mayor of the city in 2011 (Wright, 2017). During his tenure as police chief, O'Leary was also a member of the board of education. By virtue of the city charter, the mayor was a member of the board of education (Electors of the City of Waterbury, 1902, 2002). However, historically, mayors in Waterbury left matters of education to the district's educational leaders, the board of education, the superintendent, and the central office or the local education administration (Wright, 2017).

Erik Brown versus the Waterbury Board of Education

By multiple accounts coming from the Latinx and Black communities, including many educators that I interviewed or quoted from archived documents, Erik Brown was beloved by students and parents and the broader minoritized communities in Waterbury (Waterbury Board of Education Meeting Minutes, 2013; Wright, 2017). I interviewed Athena Wagner, an unapologetic minoritized community advocate and activist, member of the local National Association for the Advancement of Colored Peoples and the president of the School Governance Council (SGC) at Walsh during Erik Brown's tenure as principal. SGC was a bridge organization between parents and school administrators during the time of turnaround (Wright, 2017). I asked Wagner her perspective of Mr. Brown as a principal and as a school leader, she said,

> he's a good educator, he's fair, he knows his craft. And in an urban district he is *culturally competent*. So when it comes to teachers, he tries to help develop them if they are weak or if they fall short in a certain area. With the children, he becomes very familiar with parents and the community. So the parents know him they come to love him; because they know that he loves the kids. He cares about them. He's not going to do anything to hurt them; he's not malicious, there's no malicious intent when it comes to discipline. . . . And usually the parents are on the same page with him.
>
> (Wright, 2017, p. 125)

When turnaround was implemented in 2010–2011, the Waterbury school superintendent Kathleen Ouellette addressed community members' concerns at a board of education meeting regarding what would happen to Erik Brown once turnaround was implemented. Superintendent Kathleen Ouellette was quoted as saying that "this principal [Erik Brown] will stay in place, I will make sure of it" (Waterbury Board of Education Meeting Minutes, 2013, p. 16). However, in 2013, Walsh Elementary School principal Erik Brown was removed from Walsh and demoted to vice principal at another school within the district. Brown appealed his demotion and was eventually vindicated by an arbiter and was reinstated as a head principal in the Waterbury school district but not at Walsh (Wright, 2017). The arbiter determined that Brown's demotion occurred without due process (Puffer, 2015).

At the board of education meeting on July 31, 2013, a significant amount of time was dominated by parents and community members addressing their displeasure at the removal of Erik Brown from Walsh (Wright, 2017). At that board of education meeting, Athena Wagner presented to the board of education a petition of 60 signatures from Walsh School parents that wanted Brown reinstated as principal at Walsh (Waterbury Board of Education Meeting Minutes, 2013). In addition to Wagner, Joshua, a Walsh school student addressed the Waterbury Board of Education at the July 31, 2013 board of education meeting. Joshua proclaimed, "I want Mr. Brown back at Walsh school" (Waterbury Board of Education Meeting Minutes, 2013, p. 17). Ramona Diaz, a Latina (Puerto Rican) parent, addressed the board, stating that the removal of Erik Brown from Walsh was like a "punishment" to the kids—who were never asked their perspective of Erik Brown by turnaround auditors (Waterbury Board of Education Meeting Minutes, 2013, p. 18). The only Black board of education member, Karen Harvey, said to me in an interview that, overwhelmingly, parents and students wanted Brown at Walsh. She stated, "I am a big fan of Erik (Brown) I believe in listening to what the kids want and what the parents want" (Wright, 2017, p. 163). Harvey believed Erik Brown was wrongly removed as Walsh Elementary School principal. She noted the complexity of being deeply involved in Waterbury's minoritized communities, stating that "the community has my ear but the other commissioners (9 of 10 were White) can care less" (Wright, 2017, p. 164). As the only African American on the board of education when Erik Brown was removed from Walsh, Karen Harvey offered insight and a unique perspective.

The Ghosts of City Hall, Ex Officio, and Turnaround

I interviewed Reginal Beamon, Sr., a retired Connecticut state legislator. Mr. Beamon is an African American and respected local politician, community organizer, and political science professor at a local community college in Waterbury. I sought Beamon's political perspective and assessment of what was occurring in the Waterbury school district. He said this:

> I will put it this way: all politics [are] local and all local politics [are] about one thing—money. And the bottom line here is . . . Walsh as a turnaround school . . . you had the purse strings coming from the State [Connecticut] with special grants of which principals had autonomy to hire, and to implement what they felt their schools needed in order to succeed. There's no way, in the city of Waterbury, with all that kind of money coming in, they [City Hall/Waterbury's mayor] were [going to] allow non-political players [Erik Brown-Walsh school principal] and those who look like 'us' [Black/minoritized community members] to control those purse strings. That's from a political standpoint.
> (Wright, 2017, p. 109)

Mr. Beamon was alluding to the notion that turnaround would have given the principal, Erik Brown, autonomy to make decisions about his school. The idea of Erik Brown, who looked like "us" African American, controlling the purse strings for funds designated for Walsh Beamon deemed unallowable according to his insight into Waterbury politics.

Lisa Lessard, a White female community activist and a parent of a special needs student in the Waterbury school district, raised concerns about corruption at the board of education meeting on July 31, 2013 (Waterbury Board of Education Meeting Minutes, 2013). Lessard indicated that Stefan Pryor, the State of Connecticut Board of Education commissioner at that time, informed her that "the Waterbury educational system is on [his] educational radar because he saw past fiscal mistakes" (Waterbury Board of Education Meeting Minutes, 2013, p. 4). Karen Harvey, the longest tenured Waterbury board of education member, described the complexities of being on the board thusly: "yea I'm on the board but it's very difficult being a Black [person] on the board" (Wright, 2017, p. 164). With the infamous history of Waterbury mayors in mind (Waterbury mayors have been involved in political corruption, including graft, which led to the indictment and convictions of two Waterbury mayors in 1992 and 2002), I asked Karen Harvey about mayoral control respective to the scandalous history of Waterbury's City Hall and its connection to what was happening in education. After a long pause and a deep breath, she stated:

> I think as long as you keep the mayor's position as ex officio; that [corruption] will always exist in the education system. 60 percent of our [City of Waterbury] budget is in education. Which means we control a lot of money. And with a mayor like this mayor that has his hands in everything, I mean he has done some good, but some things he needs to keep his hands out of . . . and let the school system, those that have been educated and trained to run the school system, run it. So as long as that ex officio position is in place the political part of it; that corruption will always exist until we remove that.
> (Wright, 2017, p. 108)

In contrast to the accusations by members of various communities in Waterbury at the Waterbury Board of Education meeting on July 31, 2013, the mayor, arguably the most powerful White male in Waterbury, who oversees a majority Latinx and Black school district, offered a much different assessment of what was occurring in the district (Wright, 2017). According to board of education meeting minutes, the mayor described himself as being "sea-sick" by all of the back and forth and "cynical comments" being made by community members who came to the public board of education meetings in defense of Erik Brown (Waterbury Board of Education Meeting Minutes, 2013). Furthermore, the mayor contested that from his "numerous meetings and conversations" with the

State of Connecticut Board of Education commissioner Stefan Pryor and the State of Connecticut governor Dannel Malloy, "they both have enormous respect for what's happening in this district" (Waterbury Board of Education Meeting Minutes, 2013, p. 31). These comment by the mayor speaks volumes about the cultural disconnects and misunderstandings he has of the minoritized communities and their concerns, along with much broader and deeper systemic disconnects related to policy application.

Racial Tension and Its Day in Court

Between 2013 and 2017, Erik Brown was battling a racial discrimination suit against the Waterbury Board of Education and its superintendent. In 2013 the Waterbury Board of Education and its superintendent demoted Brown for alleged misconduct. Brown was transferred to vice principal at another school within the district. In 2015, an arbiter determined that Brown's demotion occurred without due process (Puffer, 2015). Brown later filed a federal racial discrimination suit against the superintendent of Waterbury and the board of education (Spicer, 2016; United States District Court & District of Connecticut, 2016). On March 11, 2016, a district court judge in Connecticut found merit in Brown's racial discrimination claim and allowed the case to proceed to trial (Puffer, 2015; Spicer, 2016; United States District Court & District of Connecticut, 2016). As a result, in 2016, 62 years after the original *Brown v. Board of Education* case in 1954, there is another landmark *Brown v. Board of Education* in federal court centered on racial discrimination. In late 2017, an undisclosed financial settlement was reached in Brown's racial discrimination suit against the Waterbury Board of Education and its superintendent, and presently (2019), Brown holds a head principal position in Waterbury (Gagne, 2017). To some extent, these key court rulings lend credibility to many of the minoritized community members' claims that Brown was a great principal, that he was beloved by them, and that he was treated unfairly by the Waterbury school district and its leadership.

Conclusion and Implications

The Waterbury, Connecticut, school district found itself in a complex web of inequity as indicated in this inquiry beginning in the 2011 school year. In 2011, Walsh Elementary School, the focus school in this inquiry, was cited for the turnaround policy. Of the City of Waterbury's budget, 60 percent is designated to the Waterbury school district, which consists of more than 85 percent Black and Latinx students. The turnaround policy, through Title I, infused millions more dollars into the Waterbury school district. This study found that mayoral control of the Waterbury school district coincided with the implementation of turnaround. Mayoral control, however, occurred not due to new legislation but through a reinterpretation of the city's charter. The mayor's position as ex officio board member was utilized to strategize and determine the trajectory of schooling in Waterbury. Waterbury's infamous mayoral history raised credible concerns and exacerbated racial tensions. The removal of Walsh Elementary School's beloved Black principal, Erik Brown, outraged many throughout Waterbury's minoritized communities. Community members and parents were concerned that funds, designated for the district's most needy schools, were diverted elsewhere. Imposing leadership discourses and practices by educational leaders, the mayor, board of education members, and the superintendent intensified racial and cultural disconnects and misunderstandings, in which the 85 percent of the Latinx and Black students in the district were adversely affected.

The culture of education policy calls into account a history of discourses and practices that shaped educational policy by crafting deficit depictions of policy beneficiaries. The district not only did not display a welcoming environment of parents and minoritized community members; the mayoral-led district was also hostile toward the Black, Latinx, and minoritized communities and its educators who disagreed with its educational agenda. Perhaps the most unfortunate outcome in this study was the removal of a principal who Black and Latinx community members admired and respected and who students were drawn to. Yet, the leadership decisions, which were overwhelmingly handed down by Whites either failed to see or ignored these connections and their potential for student growth and success. Important implications in this study are that if we intend for sustained educational reform in urban communities or in minoritized communities, we need to address deficit depictions embedded in educational policy and practices by leaders that are indifferent to and condescending toward the culture, epistemologies, values, and norms inherited by students from their broader communities.

Note

1. I refer to the Black and Latinx community members in this study as minoritized, a verb meaning an action that is happening to them. They are not minor or minority, a noun, a fixed state or object. Furthermore, they are the majority in the district, composing 85 percent of the students. And last, they do not refer to themselves as minor or minority.

References

Associated Press. (2014, June 6). *Woman convicted in former Waterbury Mayor Giordano case resentenced*. Retrieved from www.nhregister.com/general-news/20140606/woman-convicted-in-former-waterbury-mayor-giordano-case-resentenced

Brooke, J. (1985, March 6). For the brass city, an era has ended. *The New York Times*. Retrieved from www.nytimes.com/1985/03/06/nyregion/for-the-brass-city-an-era-has-ended.html

Cowan, A. L. (2003, March 14). Prostitute recounts ex-mayor's trysts with 2 girls. *The New York Times*. Retrieved from www.nytimes.com/2003/03/14/nyregion/prostitute-recounts-ex-mayor-s-trysts-with-2-girls.html

Cowan, A. L. (2017, December 21). Rowland name endures on Connecticut public buildings, despite convictions. *The New York Times*. Retrieved from www.nytimes.com/2014/10/14/nyregion/rowland-name-endures-on-connecticut-public-buildings-despite-convictions.html

Curry, T. J. (2017). *The man-not: Race, class, genre, and the dilemmas of black manhood*. Philadelphia: Temple University Press.

Davis, M. R. (2013). *Education governance for the twenty-first century: Overcoming the structural barriers to school reform* (P. Manna & P. J. McGuinn, Eds.). Washington, DC: Brookings Institution Press.

Dhunpath, R. (2000). Life history methodology: "Narradigm" regained. *International Journal of Qualitative Studies in Education*, *13*(5), 543–551. https://doi.org/10.1080/09518390050156459

Diem, S., Young, M. D., Welton, A. D., Mansfield, K. C., & Lee, P.-L. (2014). The intellectual landscape of critical policy analysis. *International Journal of Qualitative Studies in Education*, *27*(9), 1068–1090. https://doi.org/10.1080/09518398.2014.916007

Electors of the City of Waterbury. *Charter and Ordinance of the City of Waterbury*. Pub. L. No. 1C-1, 125 (1902).

Electors of the City of Waterbury. *Charter of the City of Waterbury*. Pub. L. No. 1C-1, 125 (2002).

Gagne, M. (2017, August 16). *Waterbury principal Brown, city reach a settlement*. Retrieved April 8, 2018, from Republican-American website www.rep-am.com/post/2017/08/16/waterbury-principal-city-reach-a-settlement/

Gates, S. M., Baird, M. D., Master, B. K., & Chavez-Herrerias, E. (2019). *Principal pipelines: A feasible, affordable, and effective way for districts to improve schools*. Santa Monica, CA: RAND.

Goodson, I., & Sikes, P. (2001). *Life history research in educational settings: Learning from lives* (1st ed.). Buckingham, UK and Philadelphia, PA: Open University Press.

Hays, C. L. (1992, April 3). Former mayor of Waterbury found guilty of corruption. *The New York Times*. Retrieved from www.nytimes.com/1992/04/03/nyregion/former-mayor-of-waterbury-found-guilty-of-corruption.html

Henig, J. R. (2013). *Education governance for the twenty-first century: Overcoming the structural barriers to school reform* (1st ed., P. Manna, Ed.). Washington, DC: Brookings Institution Press.

Herman, R., Gates, S., Arifkhanova, A., Barrett, M., Bega, A., Chavez-Herrerias, E., . . . Wrabel, S. (2017). *School leadership interventions under the every student succeeds act: Evidence review: Updated and expanded*. https://doi.org/10.7249/RR1550-3

Hess, F. M. (2008, May). *Looking for leadership: Assessing the case for mayoral control of urban school systems*. Retrieved April 4, 2017, from Frederick M. Hess website www.frederickhess.org/5127/looking-for-leadership

Ishimaru, A. M., Torres, K. E., Salvador, J. E., Lott, J., Williams, D. M. C., & Tran, C. (2016). Reinforcing deficit, journeying toward equity: Cultural brokering in family engagement initiatives. *American Educational Research Journal*, *53*(4), 850–882. https://doi.org/10.3102/0002831216657178

Khalifa, M. (2018). *Culturally responsive school leadership*. Retrieved from http://hepg.org/hep-home/books/culturally-responsive-school-leadership

Kirst, M., & Wirt, F. (2009). *The political dynamics of American education* (4th ed.). Richmond, CA: McCutchan Pub Corp.

Leduff, C., & Herszenhorn, D. M. (2001, August 1). Mayor's arrest hits Waterbury harder than past corruption. *The New York Times*. Retrieved from www.nytimes.com/2001/08/01/nyregion/mayor-s-arrest-hits-waterbury-harder-than-past-corruption.html

Lipman, P. (2011). *The new political economy of urban education: Neoliberalism, race, and the right to the city*. New York: Routledge.

López, G. R. (2003). The (racially neutral) politics of education: A critical race theory perspective. *Educational Administration Quarterly*, *39*(1), 68–94. https://doi.org/10.1177/0013161X02239761

Mahony, E. H. (2016, September 26). Ex-Gov. Rowland reports to Prison [Hartford Courant]. Retrieved September 11, 2017, from courant.com website www.courant.com/news/connecticut/hc-rowland-prison-0927-20160926-story.html

McDermott, K. (2013). Interstate governance of standards and testing. In *Education governance for the twenty-first century: Overcoming the structural barriers to school reform* (p. 26). Washington, DC: Brookings Institution.

Mignolo, W. (2012). *Local histories/global designs: Coloniality, subaltern knowledges, and border thinking*. Princeton, NJ: Princeton University Press.

Morel, D. (2018). *Takeover: Race, education, and American democracy*. New York, NY: Oxford University Press.

Munro, P. (1998). *Subject to fiction: Women teachers' life history narratives and the cultural politics of resistance*. Buckingham, England and Philadelphia: Open University Press.

Naples, K. (2014, September 25). *Waterbury school district to discuss student arrests* [CBS 46 Atlanta]. Retrieved March 27, 2017, from www.cbs46.com/story/26630360/waterbury-school-district-to-discuss-student-arrests

Ng, J. C., Stull, D. D., & Martinez, R. S. (2019). What if only what can be counted will count? A critical examination of making educational practice "scientific". *Teachers College Record*, *121*(1), 1–26.

Palys, T. (2008). Purposive sampling. In L. Given (Series Ed.), *The SAGE encyclopedia of qualitative research methods* (1st ed., Vol. 2, pp. 697–698). Thousand Oaks, CA: Sage Publications.

Press, T. A. (2012, September 24). Former Waterbury state's attorney John Connelly dies. Retrieved August 15, 2017, from New Haven Register website www.nhregister.com/news/article/Former-Waterbury-State-s-Attorney-John-Connelly-11450854.php

Puffer, M. (2015, October 13). *Mayor: Waterbury should comply with arbitrator's order Republican American* [Local Newspaper online]. Retrieved April 3, 2016, from Waterbury Republican American Online website www.rep-am.com/articles/2015/10/13/news/local/913979.txt

Rabe Thomas, J. (2017, February 8). *Some education aid increases might not be spent on schools*. Retrieved March 28, 2017, from The CT Mirror website https://ctmirror.org/2017/02/08/some-education-aid-may-not-be-spent-on-schools/

Ryan, B. (1992, December 6). Wounded Waterbury: No place to go but up. *The New York Times*. Retrieved from www.nytimes.com/1992/12/06/nyregion/wounded-waterbury-no-place-to-go-but-up.html

Spicer, M. (2016, March 15). *Judge Allows black school principal's discrimination Lawsuit to move forward*. Retrieved April 1, 2016, from Connecticut Law Tribune website http://m.ctlawtribune.com/?AspxAutoDetectCookieSupport=1#/article/1202752281233/Judge-Allows-Black-School-Principals-Discrimination-Lawsuit-to-Move-Forward?_almReferrer=
State of Connecticut. School Improvement Grants Application: Section 1003 (g) of the Elementary and Secondary Education Act. Fiscal Year 2010. CFDA Number 84. 377A. State of Connecticut. Pub. L. No. CFDA Number: 84.377A, § OMB Number: 1810-0682, Section 1003(g) School Improvement Grants (2010).
Stein, S. J. (2004). *The culture of education policy*. New York: Teachers College Press.
United States District Court, & District of Connecticut. *Erik Brown, Plaintiff v. Waterbury Board of Education and Dr. Kayhleen Ouellette*. Pub. L. No. 3:15-cv-00460 (MPS), 18 (2016).
Wang, E. L., Gates, S., Herman, R., Mean, M., Perera, R., Tsai, T., . . . Andrew, A. (2018). *Launching a redesign of university principal preparation programs: Partners collaborate for change*. Santa Monica, CA: Rand.
Waterbury Board of Education Meeting Minutes. (2013). *Waterbury board of education*. Waterbury Board of Education Minutes~Rescheduled Meeting, Waterbury Arts Magnet School.
Waterbury Minority Teachers. (2015). *Waterbury public school district action plan to increase representation of Black and Latino educators* [Plan of Action]. Waterbury, Connecticut: State of Connecticut Department of Education. Retrieved from https://www.cga.ct.gov/ed/tfs/20150622_Minority%20Teacher%20Recruitment/20151216/FINAL%20ACTION%20PLAN%20-%20WATERBURY.pdf
Wong, K. K. (Ed.). (2007). *The education mayor: Improving America's schools*. Washington, DC: Georgetown University Press.
Wong, K. K., & Shen, F. X. (2013, March 22). *Mayoral governance and student achievement*. Retrieved April 3, 2017, from Center for American Progress website www.americanprogress.org/issues/education/reports/2013/03/22/56934/mayoral-governance-and-student-achievement/
Wright, J. S. (2017). *School leadership in dirty water: Black and minoritized perspectives on mayoral control and turnaround in Waterbury, CT 2011–2016* (PhD). East Lansing, MI: Michigan State University. Retrieved from ProQuest LLC.
Wright, J. S. (2019). Re-introducing life history methodology: An equitable social justice approach to research in education. In K. Strunk and L. A. Locke (Eds.), *Research methods for social justice and equity in education* (pp. 177-189). Cham, Switzerland: Palgrave Macmillan.
Wright, J. S., Whitaker, R. W., Khalifa, M., & Briscoe, F. (2018). The color of neoliberal reform: A critical race policy analysis of school district takeovers in Michigan. *Urban Education*, 0042085918806943. https://doi.org/10.1177/0042085918806943
Zielbauer, P. von. (2004, June 22). Connecticut's governor steps down: The governor: A cockiness that wore down opponents, colleagues and, at last, himself. *The New York Times*. Retrieved from www.nytimes.com/2004/06/22/nyregion/connecticut-s-governor-steps-down-governor-cockiness-that-wore-down-opponents.html

5 The Influence of School Turnaround Leadership[1]
An American Indian School District Case Study

Jameson D. Lopez and Evelyn C. Baca

Introduction

In the last hundred years there have been several attempts to improve the state of American Indian/Alaska Natives (AI/AN) education through federal policies. Many of these education policies started in the 1800s to colonize and assimilate AI/AN students through boarding schools. The boarding school era would be commemorated by Captain Richard J. Pratt's infamous quote, "Kill the Indian, Save the Man." The idea was to replace AI/AN values with the dominant White Christian values. During the 1920s, it became more evident that these policies toward AI/AN education were not working, as many Indian reservations remained in poverty. The U.S. government often disregarded AI/AN perspectives as holding knowledge and relied heavily on the assimilationist perspectives of the government to inform the policy process evident in the Merriam Report.

The Meriam Report documented the insufficient education provided by the U.S. government to AI/AN schools (Meriam, 1928) that later lead to the Indian Reorganization Act to reverse the previous federal assimilation policies. Despite some necessary changes in AI/AN education, the new policies were equally ineffective, which was evidenced by the continual academic struggles that AI/AN students experienced when required to adhere to non-Native academic performance standards. In 1969, AI/AN education was again addressed at the federal level after a report from the U.S. Senate subcommittee titled "Indian Education: A National Tragedy, A National Challenge" (Sharpes, 1979). The report, similar to the Merriam Report, documented the failures of federal efforts to educate American Indians. The Indian Education Act of 1972 passed, which sought to recognize that AI/AN have unique educational and culturally related academic needs and reaffirms the federal government's responsibility to the education of AI/AN students. The trend of federal education policies to improve AI/AN achievement would continue in the ensuing decades.

In 2001, Congress passed the Native American Education Improvement Act as part of the No Child Left Behind act to raise the academic achievement of AI/ANs (U.S. Department of Education [USDOE], 2001). Furthermore, the reauthorization of No Child Left Behind (NCLB) (USDOE, 2001) introduced a federal system of high stakes accountability that regulated the Nation's lowest achieving schools. As a part of this close regulation, the U.S. Department of Education (USDOE) required the lowest performing schools to adopt school improvement models, not only for AI/ANs but also for all students in struggling K–12 schools. These policies took a punitive "one size fits all" approach to school improvement by giving our nations struggling schools four restructuring options, one of which was *school turnaround*. In addition to outlining specific instructional and accountability standards, the turnaround model required the dismissal of principals and up to 50% of school staff. Other restructuring options included reopening as public-charters, closing the school entirely and sending students to other schools in the LEA, or a school transformation option that was limited to fewer than 10% of the schools designated for restructuring. While the government eventually reformed NCLB under the Every Student Succeeds Act, the federal Race to the Top program continued to concentrate on improving our nation's chronically lowest achieving schools competitive grants. The approximate $3.5 billion in Title I School Improvement Grants (SIG) the USDOE made available in 2009 went to state education agencies and local education agencies in order to help *turn around* the educational outcomes of youth in schools classified by the state as underperforming, where many AI/ANs students attend.

However, through all these policies, there has yet to be significant increases in AI/ANs standardized student achievement (Reyhner & Eder, 2015). It is important to point out these government policies are deeply rooted in viewpoints that place value on increased competition, a winner-versus-loser mentality, and the problematic nature of standardized achievement. These assimilationist perspectives became even more evident in the culture-blind nature of the polices and the disheartening reality that there was little collaboration with the 567 federally recognized tribal Nations, which each have varying needs and educational goals for their respective youth.

In looking more specifically at *school turnaround*, we draw from the verbiage of Mass Insight to define *school turnaround* as a process that "requires dramatic changes that produce significant achievement gains in a short period (within two years), followed by a longer period of sustained improvement" (Calkins, Guenther, Belfiore, & Lash, 2007, p. 4). According to this same publication, school turnaround is a complex process of targeted "professional discipline that requires specialized experience, training, and support" in order to be effective (Calkins et al., 2007, p. 4). As a part of this project, we investigated the results of one such school turnaround initiative that was implemented in Whiteriver Unified School District on the White Mountain Apache Indian Reservation through a partnership between the WestEd West Comprehensive Center and Partnership for Leaders in Education Program.

Relevant Literature

The amount of literature on school turnaround focusing on AI/AN populations is severely limited. The following is a brief overview of studies from peer-reviewed journal articles and dissertations on school turnaround from schools in urban, rural, and one reservation district. Reports on school turnaround suggest that the degree to which schools implement certain turnaround practices influences student achievement and outcomes, but there has yet to be widespread evidence of successful school turnaround (Peck & Reitzug, 2014). In this section, we provide a description of school turnaround practices and approaches, including school leadership, school culture, instructional practices, and sustainability efforts (Cucchiara, Rooney, & Robertson-Kraft, 2015; Willis, 2014). Additionally, this section includes a short overview of the literature that critiques school turnaround policies.

Strong leadership is essential to guide a school through the changes needed to implement turnaround. There is no single school turnaround formula as the circumstances contextually vary by school site; however, the literature on school turnaround does point to the need for innovative and supportive school leaders to oversee school improvement efforts (Buckrham, 2016; Cucchiara et al., 2015; Willis, 2014). School leadership is imperative because it influences the school culture. School culture refers to the environment, attitudes, learning structures, classroom productivity, innovation, improvement, and habits of students, staff, and faculty. Schools in turnaround consistently approach improvement by addressing school culture (Cucchiara et al., 2015; Jacobson, Brooks, Giles, Johnson, & Ylimaki, 2007). However, the approaches used to influence school culture frequently vary in practice and degree of implementation (Cucchiara et al., 2015; Willis, 2014). Some schools in school turnaround established positive school cultures by pursuing organizational stability with regard to administration and teachers, focusing on classroom instruction and supporting teachers (Cucchiara et al., 2015). While schools described as having negative school cultures had teachers who were frustrated by constant changes to programs and schedules and treated disrespectfully by school leaders (Cucchiara et al., 2015). In addition to attempting to improve school culture, school leaders sought to implement instructional improvements.

Schools in some instances tried to improve instruction by implementing new curriculum, establishing professional learning communities, or employing new systems to track academic progress (Mette & Stanoch, 2016; Willis, 2014). Other schools hired instructional coaches to work with teachers to improve their instructional practices (Willis, 2014).

However, the sustainability of school turnaround is a concern given the reality that educators involved in school turnaround frequently experienced burnout (Von der Embse, Pendergast, Segool, Saeki, & Ryan, 2016). With burnout comes turnover of staff, faculty, and administrators. Furthermore, some schools that implemented school turnaround policies and practices achieved underwhelming results and found that the aspects of the programs were unsustainable over the long term (Mette & Stanoch, 2016). As a result, a number of critiques on school turnaround policies emerged.

One of the critiques of school turnaround is that the policies disregard the participation of diverse constituencies (Peck & Reitzug, 2014; Trujillo & Renee, 2015). Some researchers suggest that turning around persistently low-achieving AI/AN schools requires community involvement, and current evidence indicates that school turnaround policies disregard the importance of community (Mette & Stanoch, 2016; Peck & Reitzug, 2014). The fact that AI/AN achievement has remained nearly constant over the course of the last decade has intensified calls to incorporate more AI/AN community-rooted perspectives (The Education Trust, 2013). Paris' (2012) culturally sustaining pedagogy (CSP) and McCarty and Lee's (2014) culturally sustaining/revitalizing pedagogy (CSRP) further explains the necessity for community involvement in educational programming. Specifically, Paris (2012) explains the role of CSP in sustaining native languages and incorporating nonstandardized literacies and cultures into the curriculum as a means to contribute to democratic schooling efforts. CSRP is rooted in CSP and extends these notions to further emphasize that AI/AN schooling involves the goal of transforming legacies of colonization, reclaiming and revitalizing that lost from colonization, and community-based accountability. The evidence further exemplifies the need for community and demonstrates the problematic goals of assimilation through previous (and current) federal education policies. In the subsequent section is an overview of Tribal critical race theory that addresses the problematic goal of assimilation that permeates federal education policy affecting AI/AN students.

Theoretical Framework

Tribal critical race theory (TribalCrit) emerged as a theory to allow Indigenous peoples to address the complicated relationship between AI/ANs and the U.S. federal government and describe AI/ANs liminality as racial and legal/political groups and individuals (Brayboy, 2006). TribalCrit has nine different tenants that guide the theory. However, for this study we focus on the first and sixth tenant for the analysis: Colonization as endemic and governmental policies and educational policies toward Indigenous peoples are intimately linked to the problematic goal of assimilation. Colonization refers to European American thought, knowledge, and power structures that dominate present-day society in the United States (Brayboy, 2006). Assimilation refers to adopting the characteristics of a particular group, most often the dominant group.

The problematic goal of assimilation is evident in the previous failed federal policies that imposed traditional European education models on AI/ANs (Meriam, 1928; The Education Trust, 2013). These past policies called for AI/ANs to abandon their traditional form of education, adopt and assimilate into formal European education, replace Native language with English, and follow federal policies based on the goal of increasing AI/AN academic achievement according to non-Native standards. Through a TribalCrit lens, we aim to illuminate the similarities of current school turnaround policies to previous federal policies and further problematize the discussion around AI/ANs academic achievement.

Colonization as endemic demonstrates why AI/ANs need to challenge federal school turnaround and other assimilationist policies. Brayboy (2006) wrote that:

> the colonization has been so complete that even many American Indians fail to recognize that we are taking up colonialist ideas when we fail to express ourselves in ways that may challenge dominant society's ideas about who and what we are supposed to be, how we are supposed to behave, and what we are supposed to be within the larger population.
>
> (p. 431)

Previous research indicates how AI/ANs accepted the notion that our children must attend public schools that teach AI/AN children imperialist ideas and colonialist practices (Lomawaima & McCarty, 2006). As generations pass, these ideals eventually replace traditional ideals and are often done without the explicit recognition of AI/ANs. The replacing of traditional ideals is found when we measure AI/AN success on test scores as opposed to engaging respective tribal values.

School turnaround efforts are problematic within AI/AN communities because they rely predominately on narrow measures of standardized academic achievement. Standardized testing can be biased and contrary to culturally sustaining pedagogies important to ethnic communities (Paris, 2012). Furthermore, standardized testing reinforces the idea of assimilation, wherein traditional Westernized education was used to replace AI/AN culture with mainstream White culture (Brayboy, 2006; Lomawaima & McCarty, 2006). Culturally sustaining/revitalizing pedagogies explicate the need to revitalize AI/AN culture that may incorporate language, ceremonies, stories, and other traditional activities into the curriculum. McCarty and Lee (2014) argue that Indigenous communities need an extension of culturally sustaining pedagogies that includes revitalization. Often, these cultural variables are not measurable by standardized testing and therefore are not emphasized by federal, state, and local education agencies. The problematic goal of assimilation is then further complicated by the notion that AI/AN students are being subjugated to educational policies that focus on AI/ANs living in a mainstream White society. The focus on test scores to measure academic success that have been proved ineffective (The Education Trust, 2013) are indicative of this reality.

With the relevant literature and TribalCrit theory, we sought to answer the following research question: How do tensions between AI/AN sociocultural perspectives and mainstream assimilationist perspectives shape school turnaround in Whiteriver?

We now turn to outlining the research methodology that was used to develop this case study prior to presenting the findings.

Methodology

The purpose of this study was to use case study methodology in order to gain a deeper understanding of how a leadership-focused school turnaround program influenced district administrator, principal, and teacher practices, policies, and attitudes uniquely in the Whiteriver Unified School District on the White Mountain Apache Indian Reservation. Additionally, we sought to understand the ways that school culture and student outcomes shifted throughout the school turnaround program experience with special attention to understanding the ways that specific school turnaround policies produced contradictions and tensions between local calls to more fully incorporate Apache culture in education and the imposition of assimilationist views of student achievement and school accountability. Prior to presenting the findings we provide a brief overview of the school turnaround literature, the case study methodology, and description of the district.

In this case study, we conducted semistructured interviews and focus groups with district-level administrators, school principals, instructional coaches, and teacher leaders. The research team also interviewed the PLE school turnaround program specialist who coached Whiteriver from 2011 to 2013. Furthermore, we triangulated data sources by also collecting key documents and teacher survey responses (Yin, 2003). The remainder of this section provides a detailed description of the participants and participant selection that the research team used to collect the data.

The Program

The WestEd West Comprehensive Center (WCC) in Arizona provides technical assistance to state and local education agencies in Arizona, Nevada, and Utah. In a joint effort to help the Whiteriver Unified School District (Whiteriver) address their school turnaround requirement, The WCC joined with the Partnership for Leaders in Education (PLE) program, a school turnaround leadership program, that is run as a partnership between the Curry School of Education and the Darden School of Business out of the University of Virginia (UVA). The mission of the PLE program is "to raise educational outcomes significantly by building on the capabilities of the Darden School of Business and the Curry School of Education to strengthen district and school leadership," (University of Virginia, 2016). The PLE program is an intensive leadership program that requires just over two years of training and monitoring with the ultimate goal of producing significant gains in student outcomes.

Whiteriver went through UVA's PLE school turnaround leadership development program between 2011 and 2013. Simultaneously, Whiteriver received a federal SIG to help fund their school district initiatives. It is important to note that Whiteriver initially entered federally mandated restructuring under NCLB in 2010. The NCLB restructuring plan Whiteriver elected, required them to fire all of their principals and hire new ones. Therefore, in 2011, Whiteriver entered the PLE program with completely new leadership teams that were put into place between 2010 and 2011.

The District

Whiteriver Unified School District (Whiteriver) is a K–12 school district located on the White Mountain Fort Apache Indian Reservation in northeastern Arizona. The majority of students who attend Whiteriver schools are members of the White Mountain Apache Tribe. The district oversees three elementary schools, one junior high, and one high school. Whiteriver participated in the PLE school turnaround program from 2011 to 2013. Due to the small size of the district, all five schools were able to participate in the PLE program, and we were able to gather data from 23 of the participants from all five schools.

The Participants

We purposefully selected Whiteriver for analysis. We selected the district based on their tenure in the PLE program (i.e. total completion of the PLE program), their geographic location (on the White Mountain Apache reservation), and the cultural composition of the community (i.e., high levels of AI students). The study participants included three district-level personnel, five principals, 15 lead teachers or instructional coaches, and 76 teachers who took an online survey. We refer to the lead teachers, instructional coaches, principals, and district personnel as leaders because the PLE requires the participation of district school leaders that included a combination of administrators, instructional coaches, and teachers.

At the administrative and the school principal level, we included all current principals and district administrators regardless of their position at the time Whiteriver went through the PLE program. At the time of the study, only the district superintendent remained in the district office from the among the original district-level administrators who worked for Whiteriver at the time the district entered school turnaround. The district superintendent had 19 years of experience in Whiteriver as a teacher, principal, and now superintendent for the last 5 years. We also interviewed the former district shepherd, who was in charge of overseeing the PLE school turnaround efforts. However, the district shepherd left the district the same year that Whiteriver completed the PLE program and his position was not replaced due to budgetary constraints (i.e., loss of grant funding for the position).

In terms of principal interviews, only one principal who started the first year of the PLE school turnaround program remained in his position. One principal joined the district at the start of the second year but came to the district with data-driven intervention experience from an urban district. Two principals were newly hired at the start of the 2014–2015 school year (the year after the district completed the PLE program) but were both promoted from other positions within the district. Specifically, one was an instructional coach during the PLE program years, and the other was working as a school counselor and basketball coach at that time. These two principals had close ties to the community, one being a tribal citizen and the other being married to a White Mountain Apache member. However, both of these principals were hired after those who were hired as the 'school turnaround' principals left their positions at diverse points throughout the PLE program. Finally, one principal assumed his position the year after Whiteriver completed PLE school turnaround program and had no prior experience in the district; however, this particular principal came to Whiteriver with prior training as a 'turnaround' principal in another nearby (nonreservation) rural area. Furthermore, we also interviewed the former high school principal who was present throughout the PLE school turnaround experience but had since moved on to a school turnaround consultant position in the area.

Fifteen instructional coaches and lead teachers were also interviewed as part of a focus group. The instructional coaches and teachers who participated in the focus group had various interactions with the tribal community being either tribal members, living in the tribal community as a nontribal member, or driving down from a predominately White neighboring town.

What Did We Learn?

In line with the research question, the results were categorized according to emergent themes on leadership, outcomes, sustainability. The next section describes the leadership in the school district that includes 15 lead teachers/instructional coaches, five school principals, a superintendent, a former school principal, and a former district administrator.

Leadership

One of the first notable findings in the study was tribal community leaders were not involved as stakeholders in the school turnaround process. The administrative leaders involved in the school turnaround process throughout the district were described by teachers as productive, innovative, and supportive in their respective positions. The majority of the principals felt that the PLE program helped their school leadership teams become more focused and thus allowed them to become more productive as a whole while maintaining the values of the community. Specifically, one of the values of the community is a coming of age ceremony. The junior high school principal had many students absent due to coming-of-age ceremonies because that is the age when the young tribal women have their 'coming of age' ceremonies—an important ceremony to the tribal culture for the White Mountain Apaches. This principal shared that

> those [ceremonies] happen in the spring and the fall, and at those times, we have a huge amount of absenteeism . . . but to me, that's more important than anything they're going to learn here . . . , because those activities need to be carried on. I'm a real strong proponent of that, these things have to continue."

The principals reported initially feeling very supported by the district office. However, as time went on the SIG grant that was funding the district-level school turnaround positions decreased to the point that Whiteriver lost these key district support positions. One principal put it this way:

> When I first got here, I felt tons of support from the district, we had a turnaround director . . . the curriculum director, and then they also had a secretary who did data analysis. [The district shepherd] would come and he would meet with me once a week. . . . Then my second year we lost the turnaround director, the data analysis position, and the curriculum director . . . so the support from the district I would say right now is lacking . . . [because] there's no one there to say 'this is our RTI plan district wide. . . . If we have questions on curriculum, there's no curriculum person to go to at the district level . . . so gosh I would love to see those three people back . . . not even those three people, but just those positions.

Due to lost funding, the Whiteriver district administration and school leadership teams began to engage in innovative hiring practices in the years following the PLE program. One former principal said, "this is a hard place to be, and it's hard for teachers to see kids experience the things they [do] . . . and so they leave." One way that some of the leaders are addressing this issue is by hiring qualified community members to fill key roles—an approach that was distinct from what occurred during the school turnaround period when all the principals were replaced with 'turnaround' principals and staff from other parts of the state (and who largely had little connection to the tribe and did not last long). The superintendent reported that he was actively looking to hire people "who are more vested in the community" as a strategy to decrease turnover in Whiteriver, especially at the principal and district level where they have struggled to retain leaders.

The majority of the principals' strategic goals and objectives focused on improving academic student outcomes, at the same time it was also clear that all of the principals and district administrators expressed personal motivations to help the community. Many of the school and district leaders discussed the importance of community goals like reducing the drugs, alcohol, and violence in the community through methods such as school discipline reinforcement. Furthermore, in partnership with the tribe, all the schools brought in behavioral health and social workers to work with students who dealt with these issues outside of school. The data indicate the leadership in Whiteriver considered cultural values and social-historical challenges as key to Whiteriver's success. However, these ideas did not always sync with school turnaround values which often gave precedence to academic measures when evaluating the district as a turnaround school. Out of the 76 teachers in the district, only 25% reported using culturally relevant pedagogy on a daily basis. Several administrators throughout the district discussed the importance of zeroing in on larger community goals rather than solely academic student outcomes, yet test scores remained the most important factor in school turnaround.

Outcomes

Instructional Improvement Practices

There were multiple strategies implemented that lead to changes in the curriculum and instructional practices in Whiteriver. Foremost data-driven instruction began to drive the changes. Data-driven instruction guided teacher professional development, observation, and feedback and was a key component to the strategic plans that lead to their student outcomes.

One of the principals reiterated to the research team that data-driven instruction "has always been that expectation." Across the schools, all the teachers in the study indicated that they used some level of data-driven instruction in their classrooms. However, the implementation of data-driven instructional practices varied across schools. Some of the schools had data binders that included information on student assessments, attendance, social and/or behavioral issues, discipline, and parent communications. In one school, these binders were inspected weekly. At other schools, data-driven instruction was viewed as an implied task of all teachers and not formally regulated. The schools without formal accountability for teachers on data-driven instruction practices felt that data-driven instruction had become embedded in their everyday practice. However, some of the participants in the focus group felt like there was over-testing:

> This process I think brought in a lot of new testing requirements and . . . I think for teachers they really feel that we are over testing now. The teachers don't feel like they have the time to teach now.

While the teachers/administrators engaged in the data-driven instructional practices as required by the school turnaround program, there was an underlying feeling that it was just another 'school improvement' program with a different name, much like the programs of the past that had been thrust on them as a "struggling school." The superintendent reiterated this point when he shared the following:

> You're wanting to take a system that was designed for White middle-class kids and force it on the kids that I work with. And, they don't want to be white middle class. It's not important to them. They are who they are. They are gonna be successful in their own way and in their own time. They're not going to do it because you said so. It's just not gonna happen.

School Achievement and Outcomes

From 2010 to 2014 in Whiteriver, there was a shift in student academic outcomes data. Measured by the Arizona Instrument to Measure Standards (AIMS) achievement data, there was an upward trend in reading and math scores from 2010 to 2014 (see Figure 5.1). However, there was a downward trend in writing and science. Writing scores across Arizona decreased, but it was more pronounced in Whiteriver's achievement data. Math and reading achievement improved across all the schools from 2010 to 2014.

Despite having a positive trend in reading and math AIMS scores, most of the leadership teams were more worried about developing the whole student over improving test scores alone. For example, the superintendent said, "I'm not as interested about the rating the government gives my kids or the school based on a test. I'm looking at what their future is going to be like. What do they see as possibilities for themselves?" This value was held throughout the district, when another principal stated,

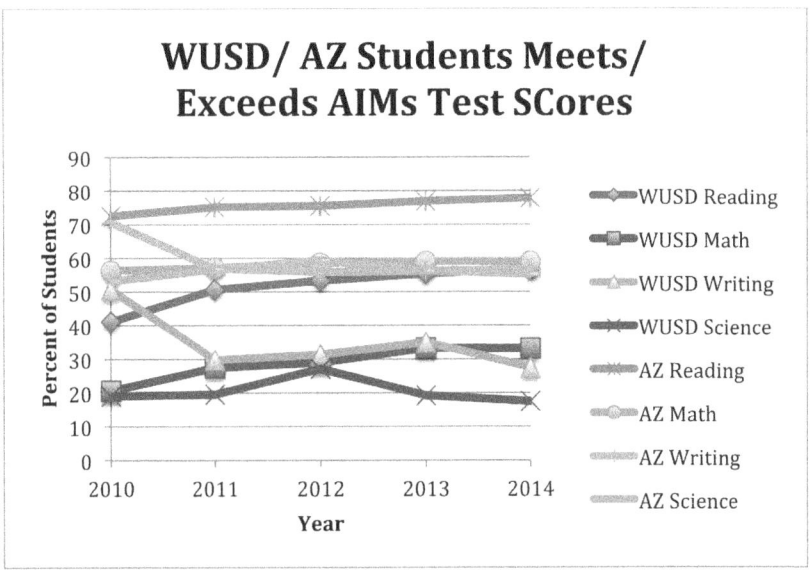

Figure 5.1 Whiteriver Meets and Exceeds District Averages in All Tested Subjects, 2010–2014.
Note: WUSD = Whiteriver Unified School District; AZ = Arizona.

"Those standardized tests don't reflect how hard those kids work every day in the classroom and how hard the teachers are working." But the emphasis on school district testing changed the student culture to focus on test scores, as one principal stated,

> we even have the student-led culture of data. The students know where they are on their Galileo, they know where they are in their grades any day.

The school leadership reiterated the need to maintain its culture; however, government policies on school turnaround continue to measure AI/AN academic achievement based on dominant measures of academic success. This became evident when all the academic measures used to gauge the success of the school's turnaround efforts did not include any references to the ways that cultural values were embedded in curricular innovations nor were the measures based on any tribal definitions of academic success.

School Culture

As indicated previously, school culture refers to the environment, attitudes, learning, classroom productivity, innovation, improvement, and habits of students, staff, and faculty. Two themes emerged related to school culture: discipline and community engagement. A discussion of the two school culture themes and a discussion on academic outcomes are outlined in the following. To begin, there is a description of the results from the discipline data.

Discipline was evidently a major issue before the PLE program and continues to be a major challenge throughout the school district. Teachers said that student discipline was a moderate to serious problem as opposed to not a problem or a minor problem within their schools. School leadership teams developed routines for dealing with discipline issues. For example, the high school principal shared that one of the key areas of focus at the secondary level was confronting their attendance issues. He said that "interventions ranged from phone calls to house visits to going and getting kids." Many of these efforts were accomplished through community engagement efforts.

Community engagement was also a major theme in the Whiteriver. In all the principal interviews and the teacher focus group session, the administrators and faculty indicated that community engagement was important to their work. Many of the schools did actively work to engage the parents. For example, during a principal's first year in Whiteriver, she found out that one of her first-grade students was missing over a week of school due to his sister's coming-of-age ceremony. The principal shared that despite being nervous about discussing the extended absences with the parent, the parent was receptive and told the principal, "[I'll] keep him home . . . for the more special parts of it . . . [but] when we're doing the cooking, you're right, maybe he could be in school." At the same time, there were still some who felt that as schools and a district, they could do much better in terms of engaging and collaborating with the families and the community. Our discussions incorporate the tribe's cultural values, which they felt would, in turn, help with the sustainability of school turnaround efforts.

Sustainability

At the time of this report, Whiteriver had completed the PLE program nearly two years prior. Some aspects of the PLE program were still being implemented in Whiteriver, but there was also evidence that the district abandoned some of the PLE school turnaround practices. The interviews, document analysis, survey, and focus group indicated that to sustain the PLE program at a higher level there needed to be a heavier emphasis on the community component, faculty and staff buy-in, and decreasing turnover.

Community involvement and collaboration with the tribe were frequently referenced as an area that needed greater attention in Whiteriver. In one instance, a principal said, "I think that it doesn't matter what we do on our level, you have to have that relationship with the tribe and you have to have that relationship with your surrounding community." The school leadership recognized the need to involve the community to continue to improve and sustain social and academic outcomes in their schools.

Another challenge that Whiteriver faced was an almost 30% turnover rate per year. As Figure 5.2 illustrates, there was an upward trend in turnover from 2010 to 2014. Administrator, faculty, and staff turnover was by far the most referenced challenge in the school district. Principals across the district emphasized how difficult it is to sustain school turnaround when faculty and staff continually need to be trained. The turnover in Whiteriver is due to a number of contextual factors that include, but are not limited to, its rural location and the difficulty that surrounds finding individuals willing and qualified to teach on the reservation. Due to the high turnover rates, the district superintendent started to put more of an emphasis on human resource development within the community.

Finally, the interviews showed that one of the biggest struggles in the school turnaround efforts was creating hope for the students. Although the schools showed improvement in student academic achievement and school culture, there was the underlying reality that when students graduated from the high school it would be hard for them to find employment in the Whiteriver area. One principal said that this was due to the reported 70% to 80% unemployment rate that the reservation faces. Several principals felt that this was a huge factor in the student achievement data. For this reason, the superintendent was excited to see a White Mountain Apache woman hired as his successor for the district's next

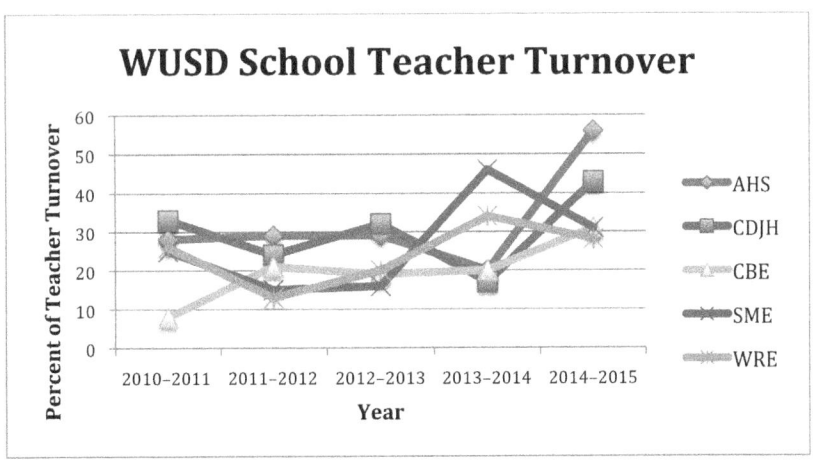

Figure 5.2 Whiteriver Teacher Turnover by School.

Note: AHS = Alchesay High School; CDJH = Canyon Day Junior High; CBE = Cradleboard Elementary; SME = Seven Mile Elementary; WRE = Whiteriver Elementary.

superintendent. The new superintendent joined one other current White Mountain Apache tribal member who was hired a year prior for a principal role in the district recently. The district superintendent said,

> I like having some of the administrators that have grown up here, because they get it. They know it. And they can help their teachers navigate some of the minefields that can be here. This is their home, they're not planning on leaving. . . . So hopefully through the stability, coupled with some training stuff, . . . we will start seeing some change.

The hope is that the incoming superintendent will bring increased stability to the Whiteriver leadership team and continue to grow the presence of White Mountain Apache members as teachers and administrators throughout the district, despite the fact that turnover and 'growing their own' has been an ongoing struggle in the past. Furthermore, the superintendent felt that the presence of a tribal member with a doctorate in a higher position of power might show some of the Whiteriver students what they could aspire to in their futures. The superintendent elaborated on this point by stating that despite the challenges that Whiteriver faces as a high-poverty rural reservation district, he hoped the new superintendent serves as a role model for students to see that there are successful Apache students who go on to achieve great things *in* and *for* the Whiteriver community. Furthermore, having a tribal member in school leadership presents a new opportunity to incorporate tribal cultural values into the curriculum and school policies and will also have the potential mitigate the assimilationist educational policies that have predominately focused on test scores and too often positioned the tribal community through a deficit lens.

Discussion

When thinking about educational policy and AI/AN students, it is fairly easy to criticize the historical injustices against tribal nations in the United States. The White Mountain Apache tribal students are still being measured by dominate measures of success placed on the tribe by non-Natives. This inherently is an act of colonization that privileges European American thought, knowledge, and power structures that dominate present-day society over indigenous ways of knowing (Brayboy, 2006). At the same time, these measures are forced on tribes and without resisting the terms of the dominant society, tribes are enacting the very definition of assimilation. If colonization is endemic and the governmental policies and educational policies toward Indigenous peoples have led to the problematic goal of assimilation, what does that mean for the slight improvements made in the academic outcomes of the Whiteriver students?

The results indicate the PLE school turnaround leadership development program did influence teacher and administrator practices, policies, attitudes, school culture, and, ultimately, the student outcomes in Whiteriver in some ways. The participants identified multiple contextual and cultural factors that affected the influence of school turnaround and reiterated how important the community is to the school turnaround process. Although most school turnaround policies overlook community engagement, the leaders in the school district recognized the need to work with the community and collaborated as much as possible. In the case of Whiteriver, only school leaders were brought to the table without engaging the tribal stakeholders. Trujillo and Renee (2015) emphasized the importance of schooling with diverse constituencies, and involving the community is imperative to this concept. The involvement of community is essential because without consultation of the tribe students' success will continue to be based on standardized state measures of academic achievement and will continue to contribute to the problematic goal of assimilation. Not to mention, tribal partnerships present opportunities for cost sharing on initiatives to sustain programs when federal funding subsidies.

Through the course of this study participants indicated that in order for school turnaround efforts to sustain themselves the community and school stakeholders need to be more involved in the process. Although the program focused on school achievement by way of data-driven instruction, the Whiteriver participants in the interviews attempted to focus more on school culture and community engagement as a means to address academic achievement and improved student outcomes. The process of focusing on cultural values may have been more dominant if standards for community engagement were embedded in the school turnaround policies and gave as much (or more) importance to the tribe's cultural values, as it did to test scores that help educators measure student progress. If including cultural values, new innovations in CSRP and community engagement are essential to student outcomes, Whiteriver sheds a ray of hope through their underlying resistance to complete assimilation

As was discussed in the findings, principals began reviewing their discipline policies, and one of the key drivers in the schools was to address the behavioral health of students that would contribute to a safe learning environment. The desire to create a safe learning environment drove the decision to hire school counselors, behavioral health workers, and social workers that were important to school culture according to many of the participants. Unfortunately, due to the loss of SIG funds, Whiteriver failed to keep several of the key positions in the district. Nonetheless, the district was able to keep some of the positions through partnerships with the tribe, specifically the behavioral health specialists. This goes back to collaborating with the tribe, or community in school turnaround efforts.

After firing and having turnover of 'top' principals from outside communities that school turnaround policies required, we found home-grown leaders were key to stability. The school district began to hire qualified White Mountain Apache tribal members to fill key school leadership roles. There are multiple reasons why this is beneficial, which includes tribal members understanding the community better because they were raised there, the community is more likely to trust and interact with educators who live in their community, and tribal members are not as apt to move away. Hiring practices are also important for developing tribal measures of academic success, for maintaining the identity of the tribe, and for developing culturally sustaining/revitalizing pedagogies (McCarty & Lee, 2014). Despite their current efforts, the participants in this study did recognize the need for stronger relationships with the community.

Another point to consider is the concept of colonization, particularly in spaces/places like Whiteriver where historically school–community engagement has been neglected and non-Natives have measured the academic success of AI/AN students for years. Brayboy (2006) talks about colonization being completed to the point that AI/ANs fail to recognize we are adopting dominant society's views. Meaning that AI/ANs see AI/AN students as failing because of how dominant society measures educational success. Implying that AI/ANs need to continually challenge dominant society's measures of success and create standards that are in unity with AI/AN measures of success. Tribal standards of success were not achieved in Whiteriver, and the measures used were still those of 'dominant' society. The need to create measures of success according to tribal standards is a similar recommendation found in the Meriam Report (1928) that reported AI/AN standards should not follow mainstream standards of success.

In addition, resisting dominant measures of success addresses the challenges with viewing students as test scores instead of taking asset-based, whole-child approaches to well-being (Peck & Reitzug, 2014). There is anticipation and optimism among some U.S. tribes about resisting the dominant standards of success and replacing them with alternative measures, such as the Navajo Nation's alternative accountability system. Going forward, it will be beneficial to observe how this accountability system outlined by the Navajo Nation will develop. Furthermore, it will be beneficial to observe how the new district superintendent, as a White Mountain Apache tribal member, will build on past school turnaround efforts to improve and (re)define student achievement.

Conclusion

Through a careful thematic analysis of the documents, interviews, focus group, and survey data, the present study sought to understand the influence that a turnaround leadership development program had on teacher, principal, and district practices, policies, attitudes, school culture, and student outcomes. In addition, the participants identified multiple contextual and cultural factors that affected the influence of the school turnaround program in each district. Probably most evident was the importance of customizing school turnaround efforts to the unique needs and environment of the schools and districts.

In Whiteriver, focusing on the socioemotional needs of the students in addition to academics was an important addition to the school turnaround program. It also meant understanding the cultural context of the reservation. The importance of family and community in school improvement was recognized by faculty and administrators; however, the execution of parental and tribal involvement could have been more effective. Some administrators and faculty in Whiteriver questioned the appropriateness of focusing on data-driven instruction as a panacea. This is evident even within the literature in CSRP that suggests curriculums need to become more centered on tribal-related education (McCarty & Lee, 2014).

Further research should consider and question the way success is defined for students beyond academic and career achievement (i.e., home, community, and service). The federal government, state government, and local education agencies should seriously examine the standards given to AI/ANs and consider giving individual tribes opportunities to define academic success among their tribal students. The recommendation for different educational standards according to the tribal beliefs is a recommendation from the Meriam Report in 1928 that is still relevant today.

The continued adoption of government education policies toward AI/AN students, without proper tribal nation government officials engaged in the stakeholder process, will continually ensure that AI/AN students remain in an assimilation process at the bottom of how the United States measures academic achievement. The problematic goal of assimilation demonstrates the failed policies throughout the past century, and although some improvement is shown here, it will likely be marginal until tribal communities are included in creating standards for their respective students. Nonetheless, the educators in Whiteriver demonstrated commendable levels of commitment to their school communities. It was clear that both districts' faculty and staff genuinely cared about the futures of the youth they taught and led.

Note

1. The work reported here was funded by the U.S. Department of Education grant number S283B120006 to WestEd. The findings and opinions expressed in this paper are those of the authors and do not necessarily reflect the views, positions, or policies of WestEd or the U.S. Department of Education.

References

Brayboy, B. M. (2006). Toward a tribal critical race theory in education. *The Urban Review*, 37(5), 425–446.

Buckrham, R. N. (2016). *Scapegoated, castaway, and forgotten: The dispensable principals of school turnaround* (Doctoral dissertation). The University of North Carolina, Greensboro.

Calkins, A., Guenther, W., Belfiore, G., & Lash, D. (2007). *The turnaround challenge: Why America's best opportunity to dramatically improve student achievement lies in our worst-performing schools: New research, recommendations, and a partnership framework for states and school districts.* Boston, MA: Mass Insight Education & Research Institute.

Cucchiara, M. B., Rooney, E., & Robertson-Kraft, C. (2015). "I've never seen people work so hard!" teachers' working conditions in the early stages of school turnaround. *Urban Education, 50*(3), 259–287.

The Education Trust. (2013). *The state of education for native students.* Retrieved February 17, 2017, from https://edtrust.org/resource/the-state-of-education-for-native-students/

Jacobson, S. L., Brooks, S., Giles, C., Johnson, L., & Ylimaki, R. (2007). Successful leadership in three high-poverty urban elementary schools. *Leadership and Policy in Schools, 6*(4), 291–317.

Lomawaima, K. T., & McCarty, T. L. (2006). *To remain an Indian: Lessons in democracy from a century of native American education.* New York, NY: Teachers College Press.

McCarty, T., & Lee, T. (2014). Critical culturally sustaining/revitalizing pedagogy and Indigenous education sovereignty. *Harvard Educational Review, 84*(1), 101–124.

Meriam, L. (1928). *The problem of Indian administration: Report of a survey made at the request of Hubert Work, Secretary of the Interior, and submitted to him, February 21, 1928.* Baltimore, MA: Johns Hopkins Press.

Mette, I. M., & Stanoch, J. (2016). School turnaround: A rural reflection of reform on the reservation and lessons for implementation. *The Rural Educator, 37*(2), 39–50.

Paris, D. (2012). Culturally sustaining pedagogy a needed change in stance, terminology, and practice. *Educational Researcher, 41*(3), 93–97.

Peck, C., & Reitzug, U. C. (2014). School turnaround fever: The paradoxes of a historical practice promoted as a new reform. *Urban Education, 49*(1), 8–38.

Reyhner, J., & Eder, J. (2015). *American Indian education: A history.* Norman, OK: University of Oklahoma Press.

Sharpes, D. (1979). Federal education for the American Indian. *Journal of American Indian Education, 19*(1), 19–22.

Trujillo, T., & Renee, M. (2015). Irrational exuberance for market-based reform: How federal turnaround policies thwart democratic schooling. *Teachers College Record, 117*(6), 1–34.

University of Virginia. (2016). *Darden curry PLE.* Retrieved from www.darden.virginia.edu/web/Darden-Curry-PLE/About/History/

U.S. Department of Education. (2001). *Part d: Native American education improvement.* Washington, DC: U.S. Department of Education.

Von der Embse, N. P., Pendergast, L. L., Segool, N., Saeki, E., & Ryan, S. (2016). The influence of test-based accountability policies on school climate and teacher stress across four states. *Teaching and Teacher Education, 59*, 492–502.

Willis, P. S. (2014). *Turnaround leadership: Examining the practices of successful turnaround high school principals* (Order No. 3635766). Available from ProQuest Dissertations & Theses Global. (1615100648). Retrieved from http://login.ezproxy1.lib.asu.edu/login?url=http://search.proquest.com.ezproxy1.lib.asu.edu/docview/1615100648?accountid=4485

Yin, R. K. (2003). *Case study research: Design and methods* (3rd ed.). Thousand Oaks, CA: Sage Publications.

Part II
Technical Solutions for Justice Issues

6 (Dis)Connected

Youth Peer Culture During a School Racial/Ethnic Integration Reform[1]

Ana Lilia Campos-Manzo, Grace Hall, Luis Enrique Ramos, and Christina Ignatiadis

President Barack Obama added *Stronger Together* to the 2017 federal budget of the U.S., which included $120 million for district schools and $115 million for magnet schools to develop and implement income-based integration programs (U.S. White House, 2016). And on January 26, 2017, President Donald Trump proclaimed that "expanding school choice," a market approach that both President George W. Bush and President Obama supported, "can help make sure that every child has an equal shot at achieving the American Dream" (U.S. White House, 2017). Pushing school choice forward, Secretary of Education Betsy DeVos argues that "people want . . . choices for their kids . . . [and] the only thing standing in the way is the teachers' unions" (Klein, 2019). Today, racial/ethnic integration reform occurs in a 'school choice' environment where families 'shop' for quality education.

Education research in this area has focused on integration programs' academic outcomes, neglecting to explore youth peer cultures (Brunn-Bevel & Byrd, 2015; Liu, 2012; Tyson, 2011). Likewise, sociology of childhood has focused on White-gendered youth peer cultures (Thorne, 1993; Pascoe, 2011); only recently exploring how race/ethnicity and racism (Campos-Holland, 2017; Scott, 2003) and academics (Campos-Holland, Hall, & Pol, 2016) shape youth peer culture (hereafter peer culture). Thus, an exploration of how youth of color experience school-based peer culture in suburban and magnet integration programs is timely.

Using a socio-spatial qualitative approach (Campos-Holland et al., 2016), we interviewed 74 adolescent boys and girls, between 13 and 17 years of age, of African American, Latinx/a/o, Jamaican American, Nigerian/Saint Lucian, and multiracial/-ethnic descent. Participants were enrolled (or had been enrolled) in one (or both) integration programs: youth of color being bused from a predominantly minority city to community schools in predominantly white suburbs (hereafter suburban schools), and/or youth of all racial/ethnic backgrounds being bused to integrated magnet schools in suburban and urban areas (hereafter magnet schools), both embedded in a racially/ethnically and socioeconomically segregated U.S. northeastern metropolitan area with a dominant 'school choice' culture (see Table 6.1).

Conceptually, we draw from the 'new' sociology of childhood and critical race theory (Campos-Holland, 2017; Corsaro, 2017; Delgado & Stefancic, 2013) to analyze youth's narratives. The findings suggest that white peer cultures use racial/ethnic micro-aggressions to police racial boundaries, but such practices vary in intensity and character across suburban and magnet schools. Before discussing the results in detail, it is important to root this analysis within the relevant literature.

Background

This study emerges from the field of education and the sociology of childhood. Specifically, it aims to contribute to the racial/ethnic integration and peer culture literature.

Racial/Ethnic Integration During the School Choice Era

President Barack Obama's *Stronger Together* (2017) is rooted in a long history of racial/ethnic integration reforms. *Brown v. Board of Education* (1954) declared separate schools for White, African American, and Mexican American children unconstitutional (Chapman, 2014; Nieto, 2004). *Milliken vs. Bradley* (1974), however, declared racial/ethnic segregation constitutional until districts are found to have deliberately promoted segregation (Pettigrew, 2004). In response, some suburban districts came to voluntarily host busing programs for youth of color to avoid legal scrutiny, enhance school funds, and limit the number of students of color (Chapman, 2014; Pettigrew, 2004). However, *Parents Involved in Community Schools v. Seattle School District* (2007) declared race/ethnicity-based integration unconstitutional.

Consequently, the U.S. has come to replace racial/ethnic integration with income-based integration, which does not guarantee racial/ethnic integration, and instead interacts with school choice policies, including magnet, charter, private, and interdistrict school programs (Renzulli, 2006). This market approach to education commodifies learning, where school administrators and teachers sell education, standardized state testing evaluates the product, and parents and students 'shop' for quality education across a 'school choice' system, all indicative of the reciprocal relationship between "individual freedom, capitalism, and inequality" (Aggarwal, 2014, p. 93; Campos-Holland et al., 2016).

Parents of different racial/ethnic and socioeconomic status, however, have differential access to social networks, social capital, and information that shapes their ability to navigate the 'school choice' system (Aggarwal, 2014). This variation in resources produces a racialized 'shopping' experience for quality education. Black/African American and Latinx/a/o

Table 6.1 Evergreen's Socioeconomic and Educational Characteristics, Percentages and Dollars

	U.S.	State[a]	W-Greenville	D-Greenville	E-Greenville	Suburbs[u]
Race/Ethnicity (Population)	311,536,594	–	63,340	125,130	51,241	365,796
Latina/o	16.6%	13.9%	09.5%	43.4%	27.0%	13.7%
Black/African American	12.2%	09.4%	06.4%	35.0%	23.2%	11.2%
White/Caucasian	63.3%	70.5%	75.4%	16.7%	39.8%	68.6%
Earnings (Population)[o]	35,644	–	52,823	26,819	36,117	46,027
<high school graduate	$19,652	$22,270	$31,625	$17,405	$22,827	$25,764
high school graduate[i]	$27,528	$33,524	$29,540	$25,021	$33,604	$33,869
some coll. or assoc. degree	$33,702	$40,152	$39,502	$28,261	$34,941	$39,461
bachelor's degree	$50,254	$59,515	$53,179	$43,936	$55,754	$55,745
graduate or prof. degree	$66,493	$77,705	$81,148	$55,927	$58,654	$70,995
Edu. Attainment (Population)[e]	206,587,852	–	44,355	73,443	35,618	254,614
<high school graduate	13.9%	10.9%	06.1%	30.4%	16.4%	10.0%
high school graduate[i]	28.1%	27.8%	17.5%	29.8%	34.5%	28.5%
some coll. or assoc. degree	29.0%	25.0%	17.7%	24.5%	30.2%	26.2%
bachelor's degree	18.0%	20.4%	26.6%	08.8%	12.4%	19.9%
graduate or prof. degree	10.8%	16.1%	32.2%	06.4%	06.4%	15.3%

Note. U.S. Census (2014), 2013 Estimates, *American Fact Finder*, retrieved November 30, 2015 and January 13, 2016 from http://factfinder.census.gov/; [a]to maintain the research site confidential, the state population and the name of the state is omitted; [e]for the population of 25 years and over; [i]includes equivalency; [o]earnings median during the past 12 months, inflation-adjusted dollars, for the population of 25 years and over with earnings; [u]participants also attended schools in 12 surrounding suburbs.

families aim to access a quality of education, including the resources more readily accessible in predominantly white schools, but poor and working-class families of color struggle to navigate the school choice system, and 'choice' schools engage in exclusionary practices (Aggarwal, 2014; Fiel, 2015; Nieto, 2004; Pattillo, 2015; Sikkink & Emerson, 2008). Moreover, white families respond with 'white flight' at the slightest increase of students of color (Nieto, 2004). White families, however, are more likely to gentrify neighborhoods of color when school choice programs are accessible (Pearman & Swain, 2017). Overall, the salience of racial/ethnic boundaries, scarcity of valued resources, and school choice systems "heighten competition for schools and promote segregation" (Fiel, 2015, p. 150).

The few students of color who access integration programs in a school choice system experience positive academic outcomes, including higher test scores, lower dropout and truancy rates, and greater access to college preparation courses, and later in life, they earn higher degrees and more money and live integrated lives (Campos-Holland et al., 2016; Chapman, 2014; Liu, 2012). Racial/ethnic integration programs, however, do not guarantee the quality of education (Chapman, 2014; Eder, 1995; Tyson, 2011).

Predominantly white schools expose students of color to racial/ethnic micro-aggressions—"brief verbal, behavioral, or environmental indignities that communicate hostile, derogatory, denigrating, and hurtful messages"—in contexts that heighten stress, depression, and anxiety and "denigrate the experiences of African American and Hispanic students" (Allen, Scott, & Lewis, 2013, pp. 117–119; Huber, 2011; Tyson, 2011). Specifically, adults and peers assume white youth are 'intellectually gifted' and Black/African American and Latinx/a/o youth are 'academically deficient,' keeping students of color from enrolling in advanced courses or acting surprised at their high grades (Chapman, 2014; Tyson, 2011). Thus, youth of color face disrespect, low academic expectations, instant suspicion, and heightened punishment (Allen et al., 2013; Chapman, 2014; Huber, 2011). Furthermore, Latinx/a/o and Asian American youth experience racist nativism, including the continuous questioning of their citizenship status and enforcement of English-only hegemonic practices (Huber, 2011; Huynh, 2012).

Magnet schools, the most prevalent school modality in the school choice system, has been promoting racial/ethnic integration since the 1960s (Wang & Herman, 2017). No longer able to use race/ethnicity in their admission process, magnet schools attract a diverse student body through specialized curriculum (Wang & Herman, 2017). As a result, magnet schools are heterogeneous and perform higher on standardized tests than their community–public school counterparts (Bifulco, Cobb, & Bell, 2009; Campos-Holland et al., 2016). Critics, however, suggest that advanced courses in magnet schools continue to be segregated. For instance, Davis

(2014) found that advanced courses in magnet schools have white and Latinx/a/o integration but continue to neglect African American students.

Racism and School-Based Peer Cultures

U.S. schools involve segregation by age and race/ethnicity, fostering the development of racialized peer cultures (Bernal, 2002; Campos-Holland, 2017). According to Corsaro (2017), a sociologist of childhood and adolescence, children and youth produce, participate in, and maintain peer cultures, a "stable set of . . . routines, artifacts, values, and concerns" to meet the needs of their peer groups (p. 19). Schools then serve as hubs of an "interlocking network of peer localities" and simultaneously "devalue, misinterpret, or omit" the histories, experiences, and languages of youth of color (Bernal, 2002, p. 106; Chapman, 2013; Corsaro, 2017, p. 152; Holloway & Valentine, 2005). Thus, racialized peer cultures are a dominant experience in U.S. schools. For instance, hierarchies of popularity during adolescence are highly gendered and involve a racial-exclusionary process, with youth of color being "ranked lower" and excluded from the popular cliques (Adler & Adler, 1998, p. 200). Racial/ethnic segregation dominates, with peers policing social boundaries between racial/ethnic groups, such as white versus Black peer cultures, and within racial/ethnic groups, such as "Mexican preppy" girls versus hardcore "chola" girls (Lewis, 2003; Proweller, 1998).

Moreover, racism intersects with class and gender to produce racial/ethnic micro-aggressions that maintain a stratified peer culture (Campos-Holland, 2017; Modica, 2015). For instance, as racism intersects with classism, youth label white working-class youth as 'bad kids'; lower income Black youth as 'hood-raised,' 'thugs', or 'ghetto kids'; and academically struggling Latinx/a/o and Black/African American youth as 'bad,' 'loud,' and 'careless' (Eder, 1995; Rosenbloom, 2010; Waldron, 2005). Moreover, low-income Mexican American girls face criminalization in rural peer cultures, all while white girls enjoy white privilege in predominantly White peer cultures (Bettie, 2014). Similarly, racism intersects with gender to shape school-based peer cultures. Pascoe (2011) highlights how white boys use homophobia to reinforce their hegemonic masculinity, all while imposing hyper-surveillance and control over boys of color on the rare occasions they use homophobia or interact with white girls. Regardless of the offender, racial and ethnic micro-aggressions require youth of color to skillfully cope by diffusing racist messages while aiming to "maintain group acceptance" (Eder, 1995, p. 48).

These racialized peer cultures have an impact on students' academic outcomes. For instance, feeling respected by their classmates and having a best friend who values academics increases youth's academic well-being (Jones, Audley-Piotrowski, & Kiefer, 2012; Nelson & DeBacker, 2008). Furthermore, peer heterogeneity increasing African Americans and Latinx/a/o students' grade point average (Goza & Ryabov, 2009), and higher peer socioeconomic status increases youth's academic well-being for all racial/ethnic groups (Goza & Ryabov, 2009; Riegle-Crumb & Callahan, 2009).

Since school connectedness and academic well-being are strongly tied together (Jones et al., 2012), and peer culture is a significant part of student life in both White suburban schools and magnet schools' integration programs (Campos-Holland et al., 2016; Eder, 1995), it is important to consider whether integration programs provide the peer environment to enable all students (Carter, 2001). Specifically, how do youth of color experience youth peer culture in magnet and suburban integration programs?

Theoretical Framework

To engage in this exploration, we conceptually draw from the 'new' sociology of childhood, including the racialized adult–youth binary and the racialized interpretive reproduction (Campos-Holland, 2017; Corsaro, 2017; Valentine, 1997). First, adult-dominated society grants adults greater power, pressing youth to search for personhood (Coleman, Catan, & Dennison, 2004; Valentine, 1997). Aiming to control youth's resistance, adults engage in 'adultism'—the misuse of their greater power over youth (Flasher, 1978). Adultism, then, intersects with racism, with adults ascribing racialized meaning onto youth's bodies (Pini, 2004; Rios, 2011). Moreover, adults with institutionalized roles impose a web of racialized hyper-surveillance and controls over youth of color across institutions (Rios, 2011). Thus, "youth of color navigate a racialized adult-youth binary that is complicated by a gendered racialization in an adult, white, and male-dominated society" (Campos-Holland, 2017, p. 229).

In such societal context, youth appropriate information from adult cultures to meet peer needs and ultimately create and maintain a series of peer cultures embedded in various institutional locales, including schools (Corsaro, 2017). In a white-dominated society, race is firmly rooted in sociopolitical and economic systems that justify pervasive, collective, systemic, and institutionalized racist practices that misrepresent, exploit, silence, and take for granted the lives of youth of color (Bernal, 2002; Delgado & Stefancic, 2013; Ladson-Billings, 2009; Milner, 2007). Then, the racialized interpretive reproduction involves youth's "creative appropriation of racism as it intersects with sexism and classism to meet the needs of their peer groups within racialized institutional contexts across their life courses" (Campos-Holland, 2017, p. 229).

Methodology

Methodologically, we also used a critical approach, centering the experiences of youth of color in an adult and white-dominated society.

Critical Approach

In 2013, we combined the "doing research with children" (Greig, Taylor, & Mackay, 2012) and "children's geographies" (Bartos, 2012) critical methodologies, both approaches that acknowledge and address the impact adultism can have in the data collection process and prioritize the youth participants' over the adult researcher's line of inquiry. Doing so, we engaged boys and girls of color in a youth-centered and participant-driven exploration of their socio-spatial environments, including a virtual neighborhood tour on Google Maps (Campos-Holland et al., 2016). The participants listed the places where they spent time and used Google Maps' street and satellite views to visit each site, openly discussing their lived experiences within, across, and in-between locations. This is when Maria, 16, a Puerto Rican girl, introduced us to the local racial/ethnic integration reform.[2] She lived in a socioeconomically marginalized and predominantly Black and Latinx/a/o city we call Downtown Greenville[3] (hereafter D-Greenville) but enrolled in one of the predominantly white community schools in the suburbs through an integration program. This decision was costly: "A girl thought it'd be funny for her friends to throw me off the monkey bars. 'She's from [D-Greenville]. She's a thug.' I was like, 'Why would I keep going to this school?'" Like Maria, others shared similar narratives. It was then that we began to explore Maria's metropolitan area we call 'Evergreen' and the relevant local policy.

Research Setting

Located in the Northeast region of the U.S., Evergreen is a racially/ethnically and socioeconomically segregated metropolitan area composed of three cities and the surrounding suburbs. In addition to D-Greenville, this metropolitan area includes the predominantly white 'West Greenville' City (hereafter W-Greenville), which has high socioeconomic indicators; the more racially/ethnically and socioeconomically diverse 'East Greenville' City (hereafter E-Greenville); and the surrounding suburbs with high socioeconomic indicators and predominantly white populations (see Table 6.1).

In 2013, the interview protocol did not include questions about the racial/ethnic integration reform. Instead, the topic emerged in participants' socio-spatial explorations. While on Google Maps, participants navigated from home(s) to park(s), school(s), religious space(s), shops, community organization(s), and all the in-between spaces. The interviewer asked, "What do you think about this place?" "What have been your experiences with peers?" and "What about adults?" The 'racial/ethnic integration reform' emerged in response to the questions about school(s) in relation to home(s). Most important, each youth discussed their friendships across schools, youth centers, and their residential neighborhoods, continuously comparing and contrasting their multiple peer cultures.

When we returned in 2015, in contrast, the interview protocol did include questions about the racial/ethnic integration reform, with a focus on participants' peer experiences in magnet and suburban schools, for instance, "What schools have you attended?" "What is your opinion of magnet schools?" "What do you think of suburban schools?" and (if youth attended a magnet [or a suburban] school) "What was your experience with peers in that school?"

Data Management and Analysis

Post data collection, we transcribed each interview and conducted a grounded thematic analysis. The 74 participants discussed peers in relation to the racial/ethnic integration reform 567 times. These instances were then coded by the first and third author using a collaborative approach, sitting side by side to thematically explore participants' experiences and perspectives (see Auerbach & Silverstein, 2003). As coding became more refined, we separated participants' experiences in magnet schools from those in suburban schools, explored the different types of microaggressions youth experienced, and memoing began to reveal participants' very gendered experiences. Thus, the first author conducted a comparative analysis across gender and race/ethnicity to capture variation, the results of which are discussed in the following section.

Results

White peer cultures use racial/ethnic micro-aggressions to police racial boundaries. However, such practices vary in intensity and character across integration programs—suburban schools and magnet schools.

Racial/Ethnic Micro-Aggressions in the Suburbs

Youth of color enrolled in suburban schools' integration program faced an intolerant white adult culture and an aggressive white-peer culture.

White Adult Culture

Suburban schools were embedded in predominantly white communities that stigmatized D-Greenville as poor and crime-ridden. Accordingly, the white adult culture was struggling with the integration reform and some youth of color faced racial/ethnic micro-aggressions from adults in school. Maria recalled her time in a suburban school during elementary school:

> Parents would tell their child, "You're not allowed to play with [D-Greenville] kids." Once I was doing an art project with a boy and

they took a picture of us laughing. The mom saw the picture [on the school website] and told my teacher, "I don't want my kid associating with street rats who are going nowhere." There were PTA [parent–teacher association] meetings about how to get rid of us.

This also involved white teachers using racial/ethnic micro-aggressions in the classroom. Tey, 13, a multiracial/-ethnic girl, and her sister attended a suburban school. She recalled:

My sister's teacher pulled her out of class and said, "We're going to be talking about gangs and I don't want to offend you." My sister said, "Just because I'm from [D-Greenville] doesn't mean I'm in a gang." My dad was so mad.

Beyond parents and teachers, Maria recalled the adult power dynamics in school: "If the superintendent came, the teachers would tell the kids, 'Please play with [Maria] until the superintendent leaves.' I was like, 'I rather be on the swings by myself than sit around kids who are gonna insult me all day!'" Youth of color connected White adult culture with the White peer culture in their suburban schools. Flower, 16, a Jamaican American girl, stated, "Obviously their parents are not raising them well enough."

Aggressive White Peer Cultures

White children and youth in suburban schools created, participated in, and maintained white peer cultures that stigmatized youth of color from D-Greenville. While navigating such hostile peer dynamics, youth of color noted the significance of arrival time to school and assimilation into white suburban culture. Caridad, 17, a Latina, moved from a D-Greenville magnet school to a suburban school during middle school. She explained, "My transition was really difficult. The kids in [the suburb] are not prejudice, but there's difference if you're from [D-Greenville]. They think I'm different." In contrast, Mariana, 17, a Latina who had attended suburban schools since elementary school, had easily assimilated. She stated, "Some kids from [D-Greenville] go during high school, but they're already drawn to the [D-Greenville] lifestyle by then. So, they'll be like, 'Oh I hate [the suburb].' I guess they're real 'hood' and left [back to D-Greenville]."

Black girls of Puerto Rican, African American, and Jamaican American descent faced *gendered* racial/ethnic micro-aggressions, including continuous scrutiny over their hair. Maria recalled her time in suburban school:

I'm Puerto Rican. My hair is kinky, dark, thick, and curly. In elementary school, I didn't have the beautiful beach waves of flat fine hair other girls had, but I had long hair. So, I had it blown out to fit in.

> Then I had to pull it back for art class and these kids would always say, "We're gonna cut your hair! Cut your hair! Cut your hair!" Then this boy took my ponytail, cut it, let it drop to the floor, and ran away. I cried and cried. I had been growing my hair out since I was an infant!

White peer culture continuously questioned Black girls' bodies. Flower had faced micro-aggressions at suburban schools since elementary. She explained:

> People in [my suburban school] are like, "You wear a weave! I don't like that. Why are you so dark?" Makes me be like, "Okay, why are you so pale?! Why doesn't your hair curl when it gets wet?!" "That's racist." "You sure?! 'Cuz the way you're saying it seems equally as such." But in [D-Greenville], girls be like, "Oooh, where'd you get your hair from? I love your skin complexion."

The racial/ethnic micro-aggressions against Black girls in white peer cultures were gendered and continuously focused on their physical appearances.

Also, white peer cultures used *nativist* racial/ethnic micro-aggressions that questioned the citizenship status of Black, white, and Brown Latinas. Allie, 17, a Latina, was born and raised in D-Greenville and attended school in a suburb only a few miles away. Yet, her White peers expressed a continuous desire to identify her nationality:

> They judged me a lot 'cuz of 'my accent' they said I had. I look White [very light skin and short blond hair], but I'm Puerto Rican. So, when I started talking, people would look at me. I'm like, "What?!" They're like, "Where are you from?" Those kids are so stuck up.

Allie's Puerto Rican accent triggered an immediate othering that took her by surprise. Although Maria similarly self-described as light skin, the white peer culture at her suburban school attacked both her Black features and linguistic characteristics. She explained, "When it rained, the water made my hair curl. I got tanner as summer got on. I spoke Spanish! They're like, 'Where are you from?' I'm like, 'I was born in [D-Greenville] and I've lived there my whole life.'" Unlike Allie and Maria, Caridad is a Brown Latina who faced her peers' continuous assumptions about her Latinidad. She explained, "They assume I'm very Hispanic and that I speak Spanish. They be askin' me, 'Are you from Puerto Rico?' I'll be like, 'No, I'm from [D-Greenville].' My English is better than my Spanish." White peer cultures imposed nativist racial/ethnic micro-aggression to enforce Latinas' outsider status across race.

Beyond gender and nativism, girls of color faced continuous *socioeconomic* racial/ethnic micro-aggressions. Maria explained, "There's richer people in the suburbs, which means more money goes to schools. As a Latina from [D-Greenville], nobody wanted me there. Kids would openly say, 'Why the [f***] would you put these ghetto thuglings hood rats in this school?!'" These micro-aggressions were occurring in a context where White peers assumed youth of color from D-Greenville were poor. Flower illustrated: "My mom [a registered nurse] drives an Acura and my father [a police officer] drives a Benz. Kids in [my suburban school] are like, 'Why does your father drive a Benz?!'" A similar practice drove Allie out of her suburban school:

> If you wear the same shoes, they'll say, "You can't afford no shoes?!" When the iPhone came out, I still had an Android and some dude was like, "Do you want my phone? You need it more than I do. I'll give it to you for free." That was an [a**hole] thing to say. I really hated it. After two months I was like, "I gotta go."

Although Flower and Allie varied in their socioeconomic status, they were both subjected to the same racialized socioeconomic assumptions white peer cultures made about youth of color from D-Greenville.

Also, the *socio-spatial stigmatization* of D-Greenville was a prominent element in white peer cultures. Although Caridad attended school only nine miles away from D-Greenville, she faced her white peer's continuous stereotypes. She explained, "[My suburban school] is different and racist. They ask really weird questions. 'Are there a lot of shootings in [D-Greenville]? Does it snow there?'" These ongoing micro-aggressions produced a dichotomous peer dynamic in which white peer culture was pitted against D-Greenville kids. Ricky, 15, a multiracial/-ethnic boy, had attended suburban schools since kindergarten. He illustrated:

> In 8th grade, I'd hide so my [suburban white] friends wouldn't see me get off the [D-Greenville] bus. They were nice to me, had my back, and nothing could tear us apart, but things changed in 10th grade. The [D-Greenville] kids said they didn't like me 'cuz I'd talk to them on the bus and be a whole another person in school when I hung out with [suburban] kids. So, I started hanging out with my [D-Greenville] friends and my [suburban] friends didn't like it. I lost them. I was sad. [Suburban] kids dislike [D-Greenville] kids 'cuz they get into arguments, and [D-Greenville] kids get expelled or suspended.

Like Ricky, Caridad self-identified as 'friendly' and struggled with this peer dichotomy. She explained:

> A group of [D-Greenville] girls... don't think [suburban] kids respect them; so, they're really rude to [suburban] kids and [suburban] kids can't be nice to us. When I'm friendly to [suburban] kids, the girls be

like, "Oh you're friends with her?! She's probably making fun of you right now." I'll be like, "Nah [no], I don't think so." They hate each other. This makes some kids go back to [D-Greenville] schools.

Although it took Ricky a while to choose a side, he ultimately chose the D-Greenville kids, while Caridad was in the middle of wanting to belong and being rejected. Both, however, involved the stigmatization of D-Greenville.

As some youth of color reacted to racial/ethnic micro-aggressions, the white peer cultures stigmatized D-Greenville youth as 'bad' and adult authorities punished Black boys and girls. Flower recalled being a 'shy girl' prior to suburban school, where she was intensely subjected to micro-aggressions from second to fourth grade. In search of an accepting peer culture, Flower returned to D-Greenville schools to find that she no longer fit there either. Thus, she returned to suburban school, this time unwilling to accept racial/ethnic micro-aggressions:

> I wasn't gonna take their [sh**] anymore. So, all my anger came out 5–10th grade. I tormented and bullied everybody who used to bully me. I thought I was so hood, but hood is not cute. I was in IS [in-school suspension] at least once a week. So, I came around 11th grade, but I'm still not socially accepted. I just give up. They still think what they think, but they're more cautious of what they say around me.

This dichotomous peer dynamic ultimately involved adult control over Black girls and boys through school punishment.

This dichotomous peer dynamic also shaped how D-Greenville youth navigated off-campus life in both the suburbs and D-Greenville. In 11th grade, Flower decided to become more outgoing. This, however, involved her peer group navigating the racial stigmatization of D-Greenville and the performative expectations of white peer culture. She explained:

> [Jay], [Lisa], and I went [from D-Greenville] to river front in [the suburb]. We all took the bus; and mind you, it was a blazing hot Saturday. In Jesus name I pray, Amen. [Ash] really wanted to go, but she felt that taking the bus was too informal 'cuz people in [the suburb] are stuck up. But everyone else went and we saw fireworks! Then [Ash] and her sister get there a half hour after the fireworks and wanted to go home right away. Then they don't want to go do things in [D-Greenville] either 'cuz: "Its ghetto" or "It's so bad."

Wanting to socialize with her school and neighborhood peer cultures, Flower was constantly reminded of the racial boundary. She continued to explain:

> My friend [Gina] had this party in the south of [D-Greenville]. So, the suburban [school] kids found out and my friend [Denai] didn't want to be affiliated with them in front of the kids from [D-Greenville]. And then [San], who is originally from [the suburb], had never driven in the city before and it was nighttime. So, she didn't wanna go.

Navigating this racial boundary, youth of color found it difficult to integrate into both their school and neighborhood peer cultures.

Although most youth of color experienced racial/ethnic micro-aggressions in the suburbs, a few 'cool' boys of color and assimilated Latinas enjoyed a gendered sense of belonging within white peer cultures. Jack, 16, an African American boy, felt accepted: "In [my suburban school], the kids thought I was cool. They were outgoing and I was friends with everybody, especially people in the same sports teams." Similarly, Kevin, 14, a Latino, found a place of belonging in his suburban school. He recalled his transition: "It took me a couple of months to make new friends 'cuz I was scared. But since the first day, everybody was trying to talk to me and make me feel like I was part of the school." Similarly, assimilated Latinas rejected D-Greenville kids and prioritized their relationships within suburban white peer cultures. Mariana explained: "I've been going to [suburban] schools since elementary school. It's small there, but everyone is nicer than [D-Greenville] kids. We talk on the phone, text, chat, and do all that."

Searching for a Place to Belong

For youth of color facing racial/ethnic micro-aggressions in the suburbs, however, the 'school choice' system afforded them a search for quality education and an accepting peer culture elsewhere. Maria explained:

> My sister has a [brown] complexion and silky wavy hair, but she's from [D-Greenville]. In kindergarten [at our suburban school], she did not expect kids to not want to play with her and she would get really sad. Once she took a pencil and tried to cut herself! So, we all moved to [D-Greenville] schools and felt finally accepted!

Maria's sense of belonging, however, was short-lived. The expectations of self-presentation she had been subjected to in white peer culture were not acceptable in D-Greenville schools. She illustrated: "I was picked on for being the 'white' girl. I was pale, had freckles, spoke differently than [D-Greenville] kids, wore a pristine Girl Scout style, and was very keen on fixing people's grammar. So, I got picked on." Youth of color returning to D-Greenville schools brought white peer culture to a Black/Latinx peer culture, ultimately producing another peer dichotomy, the 'returning youth' from the suburbs versus 'D-Greenville youth' who had been attending their community schools throughout their schooling.

In response to their white practices, D-Greenville youth imposed an 'acting-white' rhetoric onto the returning youth. Allie explained, "They're like, 'You talk white!' I'm like, 'No I'm not. I'm Puerto Rican.' 'You don't talk Puerto Rican.' 'What?!' No one ever said that to me when I was in [my suburban schools]!" Flower illustrated further as she recalled the six months in fifth grade when she attended school in D-Greenville: "I had never been around so many Black kids in my life! 'Wait, how do I act?!' They were like, 'Oh yeah, you're bougie.' I was like, 'Not really. I just don't like y'all.'" Although Flower stood out as a 'D-Greenville kid' in the suburbs, she became the 'bougie' girl in D-Greenville schools.

Beyond D-Greenville school-peer cultures, the suburbs transformed youth of color, both through micro-aggressions and assimilation and made it difficult for them to fit into their neighborhood peer cultures. Flower illustrated: "Kids in [my neighborhood] say, '[Flower], you dress so white.' You can say that I conformed into white culture, but I kind of haven't and kind of have. I'm trying to throw everything in it and then create myself." This othering made youth of color ambivalent about their belonging. Mariana illustrated further: "I'm more polite and I don't use slang. Like, they'll say, 'Yo' what up?!' and I'm more like, 'Hi, how are you?' Like I can't talk like them. I feel weird." While white peer cultures had embraced Mariana and overtly rejected Flower, they both struggled to be accepted in their neighborhood peer cultures in D-Greenville. In contrast, Caridad, who began to attend suburban school in high school and was struggling with rejection in suburban schools, enjoyed after-school and summer activities with her neighborhood peer culture. Also, Tey, who had been bused to suburban schools since first grade, enjoyed both peer cultures. She explained: "My [D-Greenville] friends are Puerto Rican, Black, and Jamaican, but my school friends are Jewish. I feel normal in [D-Greenville], but my school friends invited me to a bar mitzvah. My [D-Greenville] friends said, 'Ooooh, you go to a White school!'"

Those who managed to connect with their neighborhood peer cultures in D-Greenville and had suffered micro-aggressions in suburban schools shared their pain with their neighborhood peers. Ralph, 15, a Haitian/Nigerian boy, who attended community schools in D-Greenville throughout his schoolings, stated, "My friend goes to a [suburban] school and he told me that most people there are racist because of his skin color." Tony, 17, a Latino who attended an E-Greenville magnet school, illustrated further: "My friend [Justin] goes to [a suburban school] now, and it took him two months for people in the grade to start to recognize him and realize that he was a student there." The racial/ethnic micro-aggressions youth of color faced within white peer cultures in the suburbs was a well-known fact among youth in D-Greenville.

Back in the suburbs, those who returned or had stayed found ways to cope with white peer culture's continuous racial/ethnic micro-aggressions. Flower illustrated, "I grew up with the kids on the bus. We all came from [D-Greenville] to a whole new environment, slowly adapting but still not accepted. So, we supported each other." Also, Flower continued, "I come from a strong family. I'm 6-foot tall, and trust and believe, I'll be the next Victoria's Secret angel. So, I'm not wasting energy on somebody's ignorance." Moreover, the racial/ethnic micro-aggressions had a significant impact on how youth of color approached life. Allie explained, "Before I went to [suburban school], I thought people were always gonna be nice, but they were really stuck up. So, now I appreciate the people around me a lot more." Youth of color responded to racial/ethnic micro-aggressions with peer support, self-confidence, and an ongoing reflection about life.

Integrative Peer Cultures in Magnet Schools

Unlike the suburban schools, magnet schools were located in D-Greenville, E-Greenville, and the more diverse suburbs. Peter, 16, a Jamaican American boy, had attended a D-Greenville magnet school and a suburban school and compared the two programs. He stated, "In [my suburban school], there's kids who don't care about you and don't know how to control their mouth. But [my magnet school] had more kids who cared about each other." Racial/ethnic micro-aggressions were rare in the integrated peer cultures embedded in magnet schools.

Adult Teacher Culture Promoting Integration

Although there is variation across schools, the goal of magnet schools in Evergreen is to provide youth of diverse backgrounds with quality education. To make this possible, the adult teacher culture promoted an appreciation for diversity through curriculum and the school's social environment. Jeremiah, 17, an African American/Puerto Rican boy from D-Greenville who attended an E-Greenville magnet school, stated, "Our teachers cultivate acknowledgment of our difference. The diversity made me realize I'm Black and Puerto Rican. Knowing my history has definitely defined who I am and made me more racially conscious." This awareness was combined with racial/ethnic pride.

Fernando, 16, a Latino from D-Greenville, attended an E-Greenville magnet school. The main school entrance was decorated with over 30 flags that represented students' identities. "I signed the Puerto Rican and American flags," said Fernando. The school environment promoted peer integration through extracurricular activities. Fernando recalled, "You have 30 minutes for lunch and 30 minutes for a club. Everyone does a club.... There's boating, fishing, basketball, and other clubs. Once I went fishing." In addition to clubs, Fernando explained, "I watch the morning announcements with the same 10–12 kids all four years.... Afterwards, we just talk to each other and we're really close." Fernando then shared his school's promotional video, in which youth's voices continuously emphasized pride in their integrated peer culture, to which he responded, "Oh yeah, they all come to you like they know you. It's true."

According, youth rarely experienced adult-driven racial/ethnic micro-aggressions. Smith, 15, an African American boy from D-Greenville who attended an E-Greenville magnet school, was the only participant to report such an incident. "This math teacher is horrible! She said to our substitute, 'Thank you for watching these monkeys.' We were just looking at each other like, 'What?!'" This, however, was extremely rare. Instead, the adult teacher culture in magnet schools promoted an appreciation for diversity and encouraged integrated peer cultures, ultimately minimizing racial/ethnic micro-aggression.

Racially/Ethnically Integrated Peer Cultures

In magnet schools, youth experienced integrated peer cultures that explored and appreciated differences in their everyday lives. King, 14, an African American boy from a suburb, attended magnet schools in D-Greenville. He stated, "A lot of white kids in magnet schools get a good education with Puerto Rican and Black kids! Like, I have a whole bunch of Bosnian friends and we teach each other our languages." Fernando illustrated further:

> No matter who you are, everyone is friendly and will accept you. There are kids from a variety of cultures, races, religions, and classes. If a kid comes with just one shirt all year, or if a rich kid is upset 'cuz the teacher said no, no one makes fun of them. It's like, who cares!

Rather than stigmatizing difference, youth of color in magnet schools engaged in racially/ethnically integrated peer cultures that welcomed diversity.

Within the socioeconomically and racially/ethnically segregated Evergreen, youth of color also enjoyed interacting with peers who resided across cities and suburbs. Amy, a 13-year-old African American girl who resided in E-Greenville and attended a D-Greenville magnet school, stated, "At [my magnet school], everybody is coming from a different place. [Amy] lives in [a suburb]. [Lisa] lives in [a different suburb]. [Fe, Ida, and Jenai] live in [D-Greenville]. Meeting people beyond my own town is cool." Shane, 14, a Latina who lived in D-Greenville attended a magnet school in the suburbs, explained further: "Kids start talking about things that happen in [the suburb]. I never knew about the festival to honor the town. So, we went and it was fun." Although 50% of the student body resided in town, the appreciation for difference dominated the integrated peer cultures in magnet schools.

Hidden Racial/Ethnic Micro-Aggressions

Within the integrated peer cultures in magnet schools, however, it was youth with academic or white privilege who witnessed and experienced racial/ethnic micro-aggressions by white peers against youth of color. Rosie, 17, a white girl who lived in and attended magnet school in D-Greenville, explained: "Usually kids start [magnet school] when they're young, but [Nancy] came in 5th grade and would say really offensive things about [D-Greenville] kids 'cuz she was from [the suburbs]. One time she said she was scared of [D-Greenville] people, [mostly people of color]." Such racial/ethnic micro-aggressions emerged as white youth struggled to transition from white peer culture in suburban schools to an integrated peer culture in magnet schools.

Similar to youth with white privilege, youth of color who gained access to academically exclusive peer groups that were predominantly white reported racial/ethnic micro-aggressions. Jeremiah's E-Greenville magnet school was one of the best schools in the state and included an academically competitive peer dynamic. He explained, "I hung out with a mostly-white group that thought, 'You have to be [academically] competitive in order to hang with us.' But there was just the racial undertones to how they thought." With access, Jeremiah witnessed and experienced racial/ethnic micro-aggressions:

> I've been friends with two white-female students for 3 years and there were a few instances of racism: [1] two Black-female students got into [the largest state university], but my white friends didn't and they blamed it on affirmative action; [2] we were reading a drama about South African apartheid, *Master Herald and the Boys*, and one of them said, "Well, I'm Master Herald [the White teen] and you're one of the boys [middle-age Black men]." So, I didn't talk to them and they became pestered.

White privilege extended to the classroom, where Jeremiah's white peers could not relate to his racial consciousness:

> Talking about race in competitive academic circles was not their idea of an intellectual conversation. When we talked about the [C]onfederate flag in class, their first thought was not racism or slavery. It was state rights. I've been to Florida and it just means racism.

These cumulative micro-aggressions pressed Jeremiah to disengage from his academically exclusive peer group. Since it was only the academically and racially privileged youth who witnessed or experienced racial/ethnic micro-aggression, it is possible that more instances were covertly occurring and were inaccessible to most youth of color in magnet schools.

Discussion

While academic well-being is strongly tied to connectedness (Chapman, 2014) and school-based youth peer cultures involve racial power dynamics (Scott, 2003), the education and sociology of childhood literature had, respectively, neglected school-based peer culture and racism. Contributing to this literature, this study illustrates how youth weave their peer cultures within racialized school contexts and consequently engage in differentially racialized peer cultures.

At the frontlines of income-based integration reform, youth of color experienced a racialized youth–adult binary and a racialized youth peer culture. In suburban schools, white parents aggressively held onto their families' white privilege while teachers stood inactive or supported white-dominance in schools, which prompted youth to collectively produce, participate in, and maintain white-dominated peer culture that engaged in overt racial/ethnic micro-aggressions against youth of color. In contrast, teachers in magnet schools encouraged an appreciation for diversity and celebrated students' racial/ethnic identities, which encouraged a racially integrated peer culture and pushed white dominance to the margins involving white youth's covert use of racial/ethnic micro-aggressions against youth of color. Therefore, it is important to consider the varied dynamics youth of color navigate with both youth and adult cultures, involving a racialized interpretive reproduction process that produces racially stratified youth peer cultures. There is much more to explore in the study of contemporary school racial/ethnic integration. First, future research should explore how youth of color experience peer culture within racial/ethnic integration reform in different racial/ethnic contexts, such as different metropolitan areas with different racial/ethnic dynamics. Also, it will be important to decipher the intersection between gender and race/ethnicity that produce such different experiences for youth of color in the same integration program. Last, the assimilation and resistance of youth of color to aggressive white-dominated peer cultures in integration programs shaped their experiences, but the impact of their response needs be explored at both the individual and community levels.

President Obama aimed to increase and support integration programs in community and magnet schools with *Stronger Together* (2017). As policy makers and educators create, evaluate, and implement integration programs, it is important to take school-based peer culture, white privilege, and the local racial dynamics into account. In doing so, predominantly white schools must address white privilege, and integrated schools must consider how to improve peer integration. To do so, it will be important to model successful programs or develop new programs that prioritize the well-being of youth of color and encourage white adults and children to acknowledge and resist their white privilege during the integration process.

Notes

1. Funded by the Woodrow Wilson Foundation's Career Enhancement Fellowship, the Mellon Mays Undergraduate Fellowship, Posse Foundation's Summer Leadership Award, and Connecticut College's Career and Professional Program, Center for the Critical Study of Race and Ethnicity, R.F. Johnson Faculty Development Fund, Margaret Sheridan '67 Research Initiative Fund, and the Research Matters Faculty Grant.
2. To protect participants, all legal names have been replaced with pseudonyms. The first time a participant appears, we provide their pseudonym, age, gender, race/ethnicity, and integration program(s). Thereafter, we only provide their name and relevant characteristics.
3. The youth centers, cities, suburbs, metropolitan area, and state will remain confidential to protect the participants.

References

Adler, P., & Adler, P. (1998). *Peer power: Preadolescent culture and identity*. New Brunswick, NJ: Rutgers University Press.

Aggarwal, U. (2014). The politics of choice and the structuring of citizenship post-Brown v. Board of Education. *Transforming Anthropology*, 22(2), 92–104. doi:10.1111/traa.12030

Allen, A., Scott, L. M., & Lewis, C. W. (2013). Racial micro-aggressions and African American and Hispanic students in urban schools: A call for culturally affirming education. *Interdisciplinary Journal of Teaching and Learning*, 3(2), 117–129. doi:EJ1063228

Auerbach, C., & Silverstein, L. B. (2003). *Qualitative data: An introduction to coding and analysis*. New York, NY: New York University Press.

Bartos, A. E. (2012). Children caring for their worlds: The politics of care and childhood. *Political Geography*, 31(3), 157–166. doi:10.1016/j.polgeo.2011.12.003

Bernal, D. D. (2002). Critical race theory, Latino critical theory, and critical raced-gendered epistemologies: Recognizing students of color as holders and creators of knowledge. *Qualitative Inquiry*, 8(1), 105–126. doi:10.1177/107780040200800107

Bettie, J. (2014). *Women without class: Girls, race, and identity*. Los Angeles, CA: University of California Press.

Bifulco, R., Cobb, C. D., & Bell, C. (2009). Can interdistrict choice boost student achievement? The case of Connecticut's interdistrict magnet school program. *Educational Evaluation and Policy Analysis*, 31(4), 323–345. doi:10.3102/0162373709340917

Brunn-Bevel, R. J., & Byrd, W. C. (2015). The foundation of racial disparities in the standardized testing era the impact of school segregation and the assault on public education in Virginia. *Humanity & Society*, 39(4), 419–448. doi:10.1177/0160597615603750

Campos-Holland, A. (2017). Sharpening theory and methodology to explore racialized youth peer cultures. *Sociological Studies of Children and Youth*, 22, 223–247. doi:10.1108/S1537-466120180000022011

Campos-Holland, A., Dinsmore, B., & Kelekay, J. (2016). Virtual tours: Enhancing qualitative methodology to holistically capture youth peer cultures. *Studies in Media and Communications*, 11, 225–260. doi:10.1108/S2050-206020160000011020

Campos-Holland, A., Hall, G., & Pol, G. (2016). Over-tested generation: Youth and standardized-state testing in a racialized educational context. *Sociological Studies of Children and Youth, 21*, 189–251. doi:10.1108/S1537-46612016 0000020008

Carter, P. L. (2001). Between a "soft" and a "hard" place: Gender identity in the schooling and job behaviors of low-income minority youth. *Sociological Studies of Children and Youth, 8*, 211–233. doi:10.1016/S1537-4661%2801% 2980010-6

Chapman, T. K. (2013). You can't erase race! Using CRT to explain the presence of race and racism in majority white suburban schools. *Discourse: Studies in the Cultural Politics of Education, 34*(4), 611–627. doi:10.1080/01596306.20 13.822619

Chapman, T. K. (2014). Is desegregation a dream deferred? Students of color in majority white suburban schools. *The Journal of Negro Education, 83*(3), 311–326. doi:10.7709/jnegroeducation.83.3.0311

Coleman, J., Catan, L., & Dennison, C. (2004). You're the last person I'd talk to. In J. Roche, S. Tucker, R. Flynn, & R. Thomson (Eds.), *Youth in society* (pp. 227–234). Thousand Oaks, CA: Sage Publications.

Corsaro, W. A. (2017). *The sociology of childhood*. Thousand Oaks, CA: Sage Publications.

Davis, T. M. (2014). School choice and segregation: "Tracking" racial equity in magnet schools. *Education and Urban Society, 46*(4), 399–433. doi:10.1177/ 0013124512448672

Delgado, R., & Stefancic, J. (2013). *Critical race theory: The cutting edge*. Philadelphia, PA: Temple University Press.

Eder, D. (1995). *School talk: Gender and adolescent culture*. New Brunswick, NJ: Rutgers University Press.

Fiel, J. (2015). Closing ranks: Closure, status competition, and school segregation. *American Journal of Sociology, 121*(1), 126–170. doi:10.1086/682027

Flasher, J. (1978). Adultism. *Adolescence, 13*(51), 517–523.

Goza, F., & Ryabov, I. (2009). Adolescents' educational outcomes: Racial and ethnic variations in peer network importance. *Journal of Youth & Adolescence, 38*(9), 1264–1279. doi:10.1007/s10964-009-9418-8

Greig, A. D., Taylor, J., & MacKay, T. (2012). *Doing research with children: A practical guide*. Thousand Oaks, CA: Sage Publications.

Holloway, S. L., & Valentine, G. (2005). Children's geographies and the new social studies of childhood. In C. Jenks (Ed.), *Childhood: Critical concepts in sociology* (pp. 163–188). London, UK: Routledge.

Huber, L. P. (2011). Discourses of racist nativism in California public education: English dominance as racist nativist micro-aggressions. *Educational Studies, 47*(4), 379–401. doi:10.1080/00131946.2011.589301

Huynh, V. W. (2012). Ethnic micro-aggressions and the depressive and somatic symptoms of Latino and Asian American adolescents. *Journal of Youth and Adolescence, 41*(7), 831–846. doi:10.1007/s10964-012-9756-9

Jones, M. H., Audley-Piotrowski, S. R., & Kiefer, S. M. (2012). Relationships among adolescents' perceptions of friends' behaviors, academic self-concept, and math performance. *Journal of Educational Psychology, 104*(1), 19–31. doi:10.1037/a0025596

Klein, A. (2019, January 23). DeVos: "Teachers' unions are the only thing standing in the way" of school choice. *Education Week*. Retrieved from https://blogs.

edweek.org/edweek/campaign-k-12/2019/01/DeVos-voucher-Heritage-D.C.-choice-conservative.html

Ladson-Billings, G. (2009). Just what is critical race theory and what's it doing in a nice field like education? In E. Taylor, D. Gillborn, & G. Ladson-Billings (Eds.), *Foundations of critical race theory in education* (pp. 17–36). Abingdon: Routledge.

Lewis, A. E. (2003). *Race in the schoolyard: Negotiating the color line in classrooms and communities.* New Brunswick, NJ: Rutgers University Press.

Liu, S. Y. (2012). Decreased births among Black female adolescents following school desegregation. *Social Science & Medicine*, 74(7), 982–988. doi:10.1016/j.socscimed.2011.12.029

Milner, H. R. (2007). Race, culture, and researcher positionality: Working through dangers seen, unseen, and unforeseen. *Educational Researcher*, 36(7), 388–400. doi:10.3102/0013189X07309471

Modica, M. (2015). *Race among friends: Exploring race at a suburban school.* New Brunswick, NJ: Rutgers University Press.

Nelson, R. M., & DeBacker, T. K. (2008). Achievement motivation in adolescents: The role of peer climate and best friends. *The Journal of Experimental Education*, 76(2), 170–189. doi:10.3200/JEXE.76.2.170-190

Nieto, S. (2004). Black, white, and us: The meaning of "Brown v. Board of Education" for Latinos. *Multicultural Perspectives*, 6(4), 22–25. doi:10.1207/s15327892mcp0604_7

Pascoe, C. J. (2011). *Dude, you're a fag: Masculinity and sexuality in high school.* Oakland, CA: University of California Press.

Pattillo, M. (2015). Everyday politics of school choice in the Black community. *Du Bois Review: Social Science Research on Race*, 12(1), 41–71. doi:10.1017/S1742058X15000016

Pearman, F. A., & Swain, W. A. (2017). School choice, gentrification, and the variable significance of racial stratification in urban neighborhoods. *Sociology of Education*, 90(3), 213–235. doi:10.1177/0038040717710494

Pettigrew, T. F. (2004). Justice deferred: A half century after Brown v. Board of Education. *American Psychologist*, 59(6), 521–529. doi:10.1037/0003-066X.59.6.521

Pini, M. (2004). Technologies of the self. In J. Roche, S. Tucker, R. Flynn, & R. Thomson (Eds.), *Youth in society* (pp. 160–167). Thousand Oaks, CA: Sage Publications.

Proweller, A. (1998). *Constructing female identities: Meaning making in an upper middle class youth culture.* Albany, NY: State University of New York Press.

Renzulli, L. A. (2006). District segregation, race legislation, and black enrollment in charter schools. *Social Science Quarterly*, 87(3), 618–637. doi:10.1111/j.1540-6237.2006.00400.x

Riegle-Crumb, C., & Callahan, R. M. (2009). Exploring the academic benefits of friendship ties for Latino boys and girls. *Social Science Quarterly*, 90(3), 611–631. doi:10.1111/j.1540-6237.2009.00634.x

Rios, V. (2011). *Punished: Policing the lives of black and Latino boys.* New York, NY: New York University Press.

Rosenbloom, S. R. (2010). "They don't wanna get their education": Peers and collective dis-identity in a multiracial urban high school. *Children and Youth Speak for Themselves*, 13, 3–31. doi:10.1108/S1537-4661%282010%290000013005

Scott, K. A. (2003). In girls, out girls, and always black: African-American girls' friendships. *Sociological Studies of Children and Youth*, 9, 179–208. doi:10.1016/S1537-4661%2803%2909010-X

Sikkink, D., & Emerson, M. (2008). School choice and racial segregation in US schools: The role of parents' education. *Ethnic and Racial Studies, 31*(2), 267–293. doi:10.1080/01419870701337650

Thorne, B. (1993). *Gender play: Girls and boys in school.* New Brunswick, NJ: Rutgers University Press.

Tyson, K. (2011). *Desegregation interrupted: Tracking, Black students, and acting white after Brown.* Oxford, UK: Oxford University Press.

U.S. Census. (2014). American Fact Finder. *Community Facts.* Retrieved March 5, 2016, from http://factfinder.census.gov/faces/nav/jsf/pages/index.xhtml

U.S. White House. (2016). Meeting our greatest challenges: Opportunity for all. *The Budget for Fiscal Year 2017.* Retrieved March 28, 2016, from www.Whitehouse.gov/sites/default/files/omb/budget/fy2017/assets/opportunity.pdf

U.S. White House. (2017). *National school choice week 2017 proclamation.* Retrieved October 14, 2017, from www.whitehouse.gov/the-press-office/2017/01/26/president-trump-releases-national-school-choice-week-proclamation

Valentine, G. (1997). "Oh yes I can": "Oh no you can't": Children and parents' understandings of kids' competence to negotiate public space safely. *Antipode, 29*(1), 65–89. doi:10.1111/1467-8330.00035

Waldron, L. M. (2005). The messy nature of discipline and zero tolerance policies: Negotiating safe school environments among inconsistencies, structural constraints and the complex lives of youth. *Sociological Studies of Children and Youth, 11,* 81–114. doi:10.1016/S1537-4661(05)11004-6

Wang, J., & Herman, J. (2017). Magnet schools: History, descriptions, and effects. In R. A. Fox & N. K. Buchanan (Eds.), *The Wiley handbook of school choice.* Hoboken, NJ: John Wiley & Sons.

7 Unfinished Bridges Over the Digital Divide

Engagement and Equity in 1:1 Technology[1]

Stacy Gherardi

Toward an Equity-Oriented Analysis of Educational Technology

Little occurs in schools without implications for equity. Despite this, the real yet subtle ways in which inequity manifests often allow for the perpetuation of inequitable policies. In some areas, acknowledgment has brought about change. While more remains to be done (Sleeter, 2012), research into culturally responsive teaching and curriculum has helped to raise the consciousness of some educators and administrators in regards to the equity implications of what is taught and how (Griner & Stewart, 2013). However, the tendency to reify rather than disrupt the implicit values and assumptions of policy has dominated rhetoric and research on educational technology.

Although the decision to adopt new technology can hold significant implications for equity, technology has largely been claimed as a neutral or valueless resource (Amiel & Reeves, 2008). When the intersection between equity and technology has been explored, it has generally been framed within the context of a "digital divide" in access. This concept is easy to understand but misses other key connections between technology and equity (Burbules, Callister, & Taaffe, 2006). With the advent of increasing access to technology, especially through the proliferation of smartphones, many advocate that concerns about *how* technology is used should anchor dialogue about the relationship between technology and social justice (Warschauer, 2004; Warschauer & Matuchniak, 2010).

As technology becomes increasingly critical to social inclusion (Warschauer, 2004), some schools, especially those serving historically excluded groups, have begun to view technology in increasingly social terms. In these spaces, discourse around technology goes beyond resource use and decisions about technology use center on opportunities for addressing the achievement gap and creating a *level playing field* for students (Darling-Hammond, Zielezinski, & Goldman, 2014; Duncan, 2012). Even as the *potential* for technology to impact educational equity is being considered in these situations, the specific ways in which technology policies interact with culture and socioeconomic background are poorly understood and tend to be overlooked.

What follows is an exploration of the ways in which factors such as culture, language, socioeconomics, and school–family relationships interacted with technology policy in Southwest School District (SSD), a midsized suburban school district in the Midwest. This predominantly low-income, predominantly Latino school district implemented a 1:1 laptop program in an effort to *level the playing field* for its students. External recognition seemed to suggest that this district was a model of 1:1 implementation; it was annually designated an "Apple Distinguished Program" due to its innovative and pervasive implementation of Apple 1:1 technology (Apple Distinguished Program, 2017) and was a host to visitors from across the country seeking to experience schools transformed by technology. Beyond this, the district was home to one school recognized as a "Title I" model school as a result of the lack of notable gaps in achievement between white students and students of color. By internal measures which assessed teacher practices, time spent using devices, and curricular changes, the program was successful in changing instruction, engaging students, and providing new opportunities for diverse learners. Yet, a closer look at the way the policy impacted parent and community engagement tells a different story, one in which many families appeared to be less engaged or even actively excluded from meaningful participation in educational opportunities, one in which the clash between policy and the socioeconomic realities of struggling families was largely disregarded by administrators. This chapter highlights how contradictions between perspectives were navigated and whose perspectives drove decision-making and implementation in the 1:1 program, suggesting that the interaction between technology, families, and communities is a critical avenue for consideration when similar policies are created and implemented. Through the analysis of contradictions and centering the perspectives of those impacted by the policy, the chapter presents a three-dimensional conception of equity that goes beyond redistribution of resources as a prerequisite for the critical implementation of technology policy.

Technology and Equity in the Literature

With the increased prevalence of internet access in the mid- to late 1990s came much attention to the gaps in access that inevitably emerged. As a result, discussions around the relationship between technology and equity were largely centered around the notion of a *digital divide* that sought to describe the problematic racial and socioeconomic gap between those with access to internet technology and those without (Hoffman & Novak, 1998; Rogers, 2001). Because these gaps in access were evident in educational technology, this notion was readily applied to education. And although the digital divide paradigm is still evident in discussions about technology and equity, evidence suggests that this divide is shrinking. A recent Pew survey of middle and high school teachers found that 81% agreed that "all or most" students had access to the technology they needed to learn at school and that 72% agreed that "all or most" had this access at home, with teachers of low-income students being the most likely to suggest insufficient access at both school and home (Purcell, Heaps, Buchanan, & Friedrich, 2013). As of 2006, the number of students per internet connected computer was 36.5% higher in high-minority schools than in low-minority schools. While this is a significant discrepancy, it was 40% higher in 1998. Even more interesting, the gap between low-poverty and high-poverty schools in terms of student-to-computer ratio was only 5.6%. This evidence suggests that while an access gap remains, it is shrinking.

Evidence regarding the relationship among technology access, use, and achievement is more complicated. Some data support the notion that differences in student performance can be attributable to differences in access to technology, especially for poor and minority students (Chan, 2011). Other evidence suggests that the provision of free computers to minority students contributes to their performing higher than minority peers who did not receive computers (Fairlie, 2012). Whereas some teachers describe the use of mobile devices as an equalizer for low-income students (Restrauri, 2013), data also support the idea that increased access to technology actually serves to exacerbate existing achievement gaps. Vigdor, Ladd, and Martinez (2014) found that introduction of home computers resulted in small but significant and lasting negative impacts on math and reading scores for students of color and poor students, while another study found that a home computer access program supported student engagement and independent learning, mildly increased parent engagement, and had small positive effects on economic and social benefits at home (Jewitt & Parashar, 2011). Lim, Zhao, Tondeur, Chai, and Chin-Chung (2013) found that while there remains a gap in technology usage in-school, there is also evidence for a gap in outcomes among students with similar technology use/access. As with the evidence for computer-supported learning as a whole (Kulik, 2003; Bebell & O'Dwyer, 2010), evidence on the relationship between technology and racial or socioeconomic disparities is mixed at best.

"Our Students Need More"

Given the complexity of evidence around the equity implications of technology, the stories of schools that deploy technology as a potential lever for addressing inequity are important sources of data; the story of SSD provides one such opportunity for exploration. SSD was part of a mixed-methods case study in 2014–2015 examining the relationship between inclusive education and the 1:1 program. The study utilized document analysis, teacher surveys, site visits, and administrator and teacher interviews, as well as available public achievement data, to explore the ways in which the 1:1 program did, or did not, drive a paradigm shift toward inclusive education. These data uncovered a story of the contradiction between the stated equity goals of the 1:1 program and the ways in which subsequent policy decisions and implementation effectively undermined those goals. Carter and Welner (2013), describe the ways in which efforts at achieving equity through looking at achievement alone fail to recognize the fundamental opportunity gaps which perpetuate inequity. The story of SSD illustrates the reality that even opportunity-oriented policies (such as 1:1 programs) can undermine efforts at increasing equity when they are implemented without concerted attention to the lived realities of students, families, and staff.

Serving students who were 80% low-income, 80% Latino, and 25% English Language Learners, SSD was well aware of the social and digital disparities in their community. Prior to the introduction of the 1:1 program, one district school had earned accolades for the lack of an achievement gap between either White and Hispanic students or between low-income students and their peers. And yet, overall achievement in the district was average or below average despite efforts at reform that included new models for special education, a strong push to implement Positive Behavior Interventions and Supports, the introduction of full-day kindergarten, the expansion of Early Childhood programming, and efforts at reforming the literacy curriculum. The stubborn persistence of low-achievement inspired teachers and administrators to look elsewhere for solutions, with 1:1 technology emerging as the central focus of these efforts.

One key player in the decision to adopt the 1:1 program was a teacher who had piloted such a program in their classroom. Ultimately, this individual became an outspoken advocate for 1:1, gaining the attention of school and district administrations who saw the success of this pilot as an opportunity to bring *21st-century learning opportunities* to their students. In explaining the impetus behind the move to 1:1, the founder (later director) of the 1:1 program suggested, "Our students need more. They are coming in with all these challenges and 9–3 just isn't enough for them." Thus, the decision to move toward a districtwide 1:1 program, one that included students bringing laptops home, appears to have been highly driven by perceptions about the relationship between technology and equity. By allowing their students *21st-century* learning opportunities at school and home, the administrators in the district largely saw the 1:1 program as enabling access to poor or previously disconnected students and families.

The rest of this chapter describes the ways in which the 1:1 program did and did not deliver on that promise. Whereas many positive outcomes can be attributed to the 1:1 program, several contradictory consequences emerged. Student engagement and differentiation for diverse learners increased, yet test scores decreased. A test-score gap between White students and students of color emerged and then receded. Teachers reported that while some parents were highly connected and engaged, others had been largely cut off. As the story of this district demonstrates, the social implications of educational technology go beyond questions of redistributing access.

Methods

Data described here were collected as part of a comprehensive case study of the target district that explored how the implementation of the 1:1 program influenced teacher attitudes/responses to inclusive education. Documentary analysis of district publications, websites, and historical meeting minutes provided background information on the 1:1 program, as well as data regarding how the policy was messaged and implemented. Interviews with the 1:1 program director and administrators at each of the district's eight schools provided additional qualitative data regarding the 1:1 program's purpose, implementation, and administrative perceptions of outcomes. Nineteen teachers representing all eight district schools, all grade levels, and varied teaching positions (general education, special education, bilingual, and the arts) were interviewed to better understand their opinions about the 1:1 program. The ways in which teachers made sense of the program, its impact on their instruction, its role in changing student outcomes, and issues of implementation were all addressed in these interviews. Qualitative data were inductively coded and grouped by source (documents, administrators, or teachers). Following coding, themes applied to documents, teacher interviews and administrator interviews were compared in order to assess similarities and differences in identified themes between data sources. One final source of data was a districtwide teacher survey reflecting opinions about the 1:1 program, its impact on various aspect of teaching and learning, and its impact on student outcomes. These data were analyzed for frequency and descriptive statistics and triangulated with qualitative findings.

The study employed a definition of inclusive education described by Artiles, Kozleski, Dorn, and Christensen (2006):

> Inclusive Education is an ambitious and far-reaching notion that is, theoretically, concerned with all students. The concept focuses on the transformation of school cultures to (1) increase access (or presence) of all students (not only marginalized or vulnerable groups), (2) enhance the school personnel's and students' acceptance of all students, (3) maximize student participation in various domains of activity, and (4) increase the achievement of all students.
>
> (p. 67)

The study ultimately sought to understand the ways in which the 1:1 program impacted efforts toward redistribution of opportunity to learn, recognition of all domains of student/family diversity, and representation of student/family voice (Waitoller & Artiles, 2013). Although the original study relied on the language of inclusive education to explore this phenomenon, the redistribution, recognition, representation framework was drawn from Fraser's (1997) work describing dimensions of social justice. For the purposes of this chapter, examples of shifts away from inclusive education were also interpreted as evidence of the ways in which policy implementation can occur in ways that perpetuate injustice and contradict stated goals of increasing equity.

A Model Program

Some of the most conclusive data regarding the use of educational technology relate to characteristics of effective implementation. Evidence suggests that the existence of technology itself is not likely to bring about significant changes in classroom instruction (Penuel, 2006; Dunleavy, Dexter, & Heinecke, 2007). Teachers need ongoing training and technical support, and they need to be challenged to use technology in ways that reshape (rather than replace) traditional learning activities (Puentedura, 2010).

Using these principles as guidelines, SSD did everything right. The program began as a voluntary pilot which expanded every semester. As excitement around the pilot classrooms grew, so did the program until the decision to have a fully 1:1 district was made in 2012. The district immediately went about creating a structure to support this program, creating roles for "i-coaches" (teachers themselves) who would help to train and collaborate with other teachers to plan innovative programming (Cooley, 2001). Instead of mandating the way technology was used, administrators largely employed a strategy of highlighting risk-taking and success with the devices. Despite some annoyance with this strategy on the part of teachers, "[n]o one gets recognized for anything they do that isn't related to technology," the strategy appeared to be effective in building the desire for computer-centered instruction among teachers.

It is, perhaps, due to the contrast between the sleek, new technology and the social realities of SSD that it immediately began earning attention and accolades. Although one teacher reflected skepticism about the widespread publicity—"I think the administration wants to be able to point to the program and say 'look what our little brown kids are doing'"— administrators saw this as a way to share their success in making 1:1 programs work in challenging places. Their motto, "If we can do it here . . ." reflected the deep connection administrators saw between the social realities of the district and the 1:1 program. In seeking to share their success, the district regularly hosted "site visits" for educators or administrators to observe the program in action and ask questions of SSD staff. The program also earned "Distinguished Program" status from Apple computers; this award is based on strong evidence that 1:1 programs (using Apple devices) demonstrate visionary leadership, innovative learning and teaching, ongoing professional learning, compelling evidence of success, and flexible learning environments (Apple Distinguished Schools, 2017). Whether or not the external recognition helped to support continued educational improvement, the recognition that the 1:1 program at SSD was a "model program" was critical to sustaining it and imparted a sense of purpose to many educators and administrators.

Beyond the emotional impact of this recognition, there is strong evidence that the 1:1 program brought about change and improvement in a number of areas relating to teaching and learning. Based on survey data, 71.8% of teachers agreed or strongly agreed that the 1:1 program had increased student engagement, and 69% agreed or strongly agreed that they differentiated instruction more often and that it supported their ability to differentiate effectively. Teacher interviews also reflected this change, with almost all teachers remarking on the shift they had made from large-group to small-group or individualized instruction. This effect was supported by a shift toward formative assessment reflected in surveys and interviews; teachers were using technology to collect up-to-date data on student performance and tailoring instruction accordingly. If data-based and student-centered instruction support student learning, the 1:1 program in SSD had managed to make some major strides toward solidifying the use of these approaches across all eight schools and nine grade levels.

Despite these positive findings, general opinions of the program were mixed. Broadly, teachers reflected mildly positive opinions of the program; 60% agreed or strongly agreed that they had a positive opinion of the program with 29% reflecting a neutral opinion. However, many could identify both positive and negative outcomes resulting from the introduction of 1:1 technology. Only 56% felt that it had contributed to student academic growth in students. More significantly, only 21.9% felt that it had supported parent engagement with student learning and 37.1% reporting that they felt it had decreased parent engagement in this area.

Student data add to the complex story of how this "model program" impacted student performance. Over the time in which the 1:1 program was implemented, test scores decreased overall and what appeared to be a gap in achievement between White and Hispanic students and between students receiving free and reduced-priced lunch versus those who did not increased. What follows is an exploration of how the interaction of culture, socioeconomics, and unaddressed dimensions of equity serve as a potential explanation for the unfulfilled potential of what was, by all other measures, a successful program.

Policy Details and the Socioeconomic and Cultural Implications of 1:1

The oft-repeated observation that the "devil is in the details" is an apt description of how small policy decisions within the large decision to implement a 1:1 program ultimately influenced outcomes at SSD. In addition to big decisions about how to implement and message the program, many small decisions about how exactly to make it work were necessary. Decisions regarding whether and how to assess technology fees to families, whether and how to support internet access, whether and how to use devices for homework, whether and how to use technology to communicate with families, and even decisions about how much paper would be utilized and sent home were made largely at the level of district administration in consultation with school-level administration. While teacher leadership was encouraged, teacher voice on a large-scale was largely absent, and student/parent/community voice was limited to those few families who attended district board meetings or initiated contact with the administration. Whereas the broad features of policy initiation and implementation were supported by research and had their intended effect, decisions about the issues described earlier may not have; one potential explanation is the strong lack of representation of staff/faculty, students, and families in making these decisions.

In exploring the unintended consequences of 1:1 technology on historically disadvantaged student groups, in this instance, Hispanic and low-income students specifically, perhaps the best place to start is the beginning. Funding for the purchase of devices and infrastructure drew down district savings and represented a huge initial investment with additional expenditures over the years. This investment alone reflected the depth of the SSD's commitment to this program as a potential lever for improving achievement. While this money covered the devices themselves, in order to allow them to be brought home an insurance system was devised. A fee of $60 for the first student and then $25 for each additional student in the family was assessed to those who chose to have their students bring devices home. Students who did not purchase this insurance left their devices at school for 2012–2013 and 2013–2014. Naturally, this reality made many uncomfortable. In some ways, it seemed to reinforce the very digital divide the program was seeking to address. Beyond this, it was limiting the degree to which teachers could provide what the district saw as the benefits of computer-based learning to students once they left school. Many teachers felt that because all their students did not have the computers at home, they could not realistically assign technology-based homework; students also could not gain the benefit of independent learning from their device unless they were at school.

In response, the policy changed. In 2014–2015 and 2015–2016, all families were assessed the technology fee at the time of student registration.

Unlike other registration fees that were waived for students receiving free and reduced-priced lunch, this fee was not. Individuals were instructed to not mark families as "registered" fully until the fee was paid. Those who expressed concerns about their ability to pay were to be directed to school administrators to discuss a payment plan on a case-by-case basis. Concerns were expressed by some staff about the impact this had on the registration process itself, with some families registering late because they did not have $60 on the first day. Because of issues of overcrowding of some schools in the district, students who registered late were more likely to be "force transferred" to another district school, whichever school had space in that grade level. This phenomenon of lower-income students being likely to register late and, thus, more likely to be force transferred was not new. However, many teachers questioned the impact of the technology fee on reinforcing or exacerbating this problem. Despite their concerns, administration tended to disregard this as an issue over which they had little control, failing to recognize the reality that a policy they had implemented in order to provide additional opportunities to socioeconomically disadvantaged students had served to effectively dislocate a number of students.

Outside of this issue, sentiments regarding the mandatory technology fee were mixed. Administrators shared that they had only one or two families in most cases who "never" paid; in most cases, those students did not take home their devices as a result although some administrators demonstrated more flexibility. Principals indicated that the rest worked out payment plans. They felt that overall this approach had served to reduce inequity in allowing all students to bring devices home. Teachers, however, expressed more concern. They indicated that it was often they who were the most in tune with families' realities and that this was a larger burden on families than many understood. Teachers also indicated that at least one or two students in every class did not have internet access at home. Knowing this, teachers still struggled to require web-based homework. On this issue, administrators were more likely to see "one or two students" as an outlier whereas teachers were more likely to express concern for the impact on those few students.

The issue of technology fees and home internet access highlights critical considerations in the interaction between 1:1 policy decisions and the socioeconomic status of students and families. The decision to allow students to bring laptops home itself sent a message that this device is essential to student learning. What did that mean for families who had to sacrifice to pay for these devices? Teachers reported that they heard mixed sentiments from families regarding the program. On one hand, the program and devices themselves were impressive and served to support the message that the district had "21st Century Schools." For many parents, this was a point of pride and they were eager for their children to access devices they may not have been able to purchase themselves.

However, teachers also reported a number of parents who were frustrated by the fees and the constant need to monitor devices to ensure that they were safe and charged. For these families, the new device was more trouble than it was worth. Ultimately, the voices of teachers and families were largely disregarded in this area as administration saw universal access as a necessary step in its move toward equity. Again, the contradiction between explicit efforts toward providing equal opportunity and the realities of how these policies differentially impacted students were not addressed.

Another critical consideration is whether the introduction of the 1:1 program and/or mandatory fees/ home access, had an impact on gaps in performance between low-income students and their peers. Data from 2011 to 2016 tell an interesting story. In the years leading up to 1:1 implementation, the district had achievement that was at about the 50th percentile statewide. Perhaps more interesting was the relative lack of gaps in achievement between Hispanic students and White students and between students identified as low income (eligible for free and reduced-priced lunch) and their peers. This trend actually led to the recognition of one district school as a Title 1 School of Excellence due to the positive performance of these historically underperforming student groups. However, over the course of 1:1 implementation, the district experienced a steady decline in test scores—likely attributable to changes in state testing requirements—as well as a rapid increase and then a decrease in achievement gaps between White and Hispanic students and low-income students and their peers. This gap was especially pronounced in math.

It is important to understand factors other than technology that likely influenced these data. Perhaps most important is the change in the state test used to assess academic progress. From 2011 to 2014, the ISAT (Illinois State Achievement Test) was used to assess progress although the cut score used to determine proficiency was raised in 2012–2013, and then Common Core content was added the following year. Subsequently, the Common Core–based PARCC (Partnership for Assessment of Readiness for College and Careers) was used from 2014 to 2016. It is also critical to note that the overall percentage of students meeting or exceeding in the district dropped dramatically (approximately 60%) with the introduction of PARCC. Thus, year to year comparisons of performance provide little useful data in measuring actual achievement.

Perhaps the best way to explore the potential impact of the 1:1 program on academic performance is to use a longitudinal model. Figures 7.1 and 7.2 depict the scores of a cohort of students who were in third grade in 2010–2011 and eighth grade in 2015–2016. Recall that the 1:1 program was introduced in 2012–2013 and the mandatory tech fee introduced in 2014–2015. While analysis of actual changes in achievement is impossible as a result of the changes in tests, analysis of changes in the relative performance of student groups is interesting. Over that period—which includes two years prior to 1:1 implementation and four years of

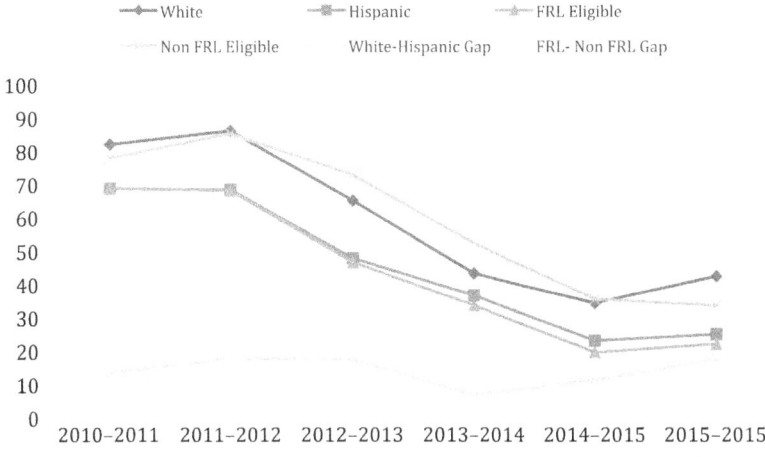

Figure 7.1 Percentage of Students Meeting/Exceeding Standards in English Language Arts and Between-Group Gaps

Note: FRL = free and reduced-price lunch.

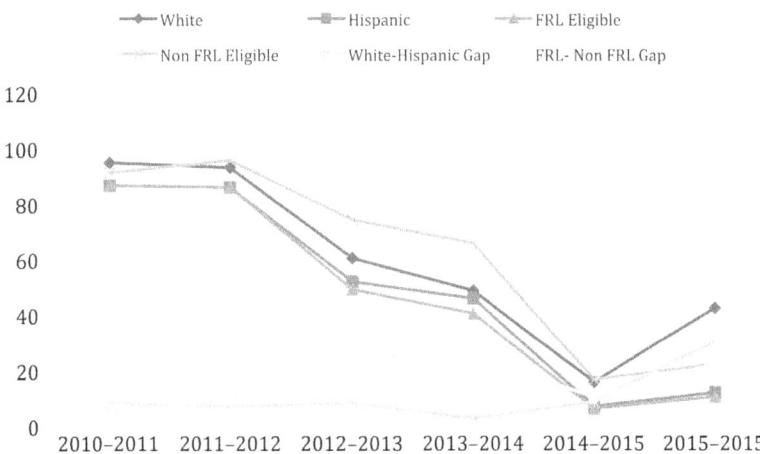

Figure 7.2 Percentage of Students Meeting/Exceeding Standards in Math and Between-Group Gaps

Note: FRL = free and reduced-price lunch.

implementation—gaps between White and Hispanic students went from 13.4% to 17.5% in English language arts and from 8.3% to 30.3% in math. The gap between students qualifying for free and reduced-priced lunch and those not qualifying went from 9.1% to 11.5% in English language arts and from 4.5% to 32.8% in math. Gaps in achievement increased even between years in which the same state test was utilized, suggesting that other factors had an impact.

While the rising and falling gaps cannot be attributed directly to 1:1 policy or decisions to require devices to go home, one reality remains. If the intention of the program was specifically to support and address students who "needed more," test scores did not support the effectiveness of the policy. In short, laptops were likely not the cause—at least not the sole cause—of decreasing achievement and increasing gaps, but they also did not prevent or remedy these realities. Whereas years with lower gaps often reflected lower overall performance, the last year of data suggests that White students are "rebounding" from the decrease in achievement while other students are not. Data in the coming years will be critical to a better telling of the story of the potential impact of this program on Hispanic and low-income students.

What does all this mean for 1:1 technology and equity in achievement? Teachers in the district frequently voiced the sentiment that "technology can't fix everything." They grappled with the daily realities many of their students faced, in which they could not afford basic necessities like adequate food, housing, transportation, or medical care. This caused a number of teachers to question the decision to prioritize technology when these basic concerns remained. Their concerns provide one potential explanation for the unintended relationship between the 1:1 program and achievement for poor students. One teacher described her feelings about the relationship between technology and student needs in terms of Maslow's Hierarchy: "It's like we're ignoring all that stuff at the bottom while we say 'here, here's a computer!'"

Policy always involves trade-offs: whose perspectives dominate the conversation and push policy forward in particular directions, whose voices are silent, and whose gains and losses are of key concern. Perhaps, it is the case that in this situation the resources and attention necessary to create a model 1:1 program required the diversion of resources and attention from other areas. Despite the intentions of the policy makers to harness the power of digital access to promote social inclusion for their students, it seems possible that this effort was not as successful at meeting the desired aim as initiatives that seek to address social inequity more directly.

Engagement for All?

The fact also remains that the outcomes described earlier echo some previous research citing a growth in racial achievement gaps with the introduction of home computers. In SSD, too, gaps in performance between Hispanic and White students grew over the course of implementation. This speaks to the need to consider culture in this analysis. While an entire book could be written about the cultural dimensions of technology, for the purposes of this chapter, we focus on an issue that stood out in qualitative and quantitative data: parent engagement. This area appeared to be both an unintended consequence of the 1:1 program and a potential explanation for the decrease in performance between traditionally well-connected and well-resourced student groups and their peers.

Teacher surveys reflected that only 25% to 30% of teachers disagreed or strongly disagreed that 1:1 technology had increased parent engagement, parent connections with academics, or facilitated teacher–parent communication. This was the most negatively discussed aspect of the 1:1 program in teacher interviews, with many feeling that parents either did not know how to interact with the technology effectively or they disengaged because they no longer needed to, for example, help with homework. In terms of school–parent communication, the use of apps to facilitate more frequent communication were lauded by administrators. However, teachers saw these efforts as generally having the effect of increasing communication and engagement for already-well-connected families while decreasing it for those who previously were less engaged. In this way, they saw technology contributing to a parent-engagement gap.

In some ways, this phenomenon was not entirely unintended. Some administrators described the 1:1 program as a sort of "workaround" for parent engagement among student groups where it had traditionally been low. One principal suggested that parents not understanding homework or not having sufficient English to help students had been an excuse in the past but was no longer valid, going so far as to say that "they really don't need their parents anymore with all the tools we can provide." For this administrator, parents were ancillary (at best) or potential barriers to student learning and laptops had provided an adequate replacement for the benefits of parents and children learning together. Such statements clearly illustrate the deficit view of parents and families permeated some administrators' concepts of equity in which the school held a position of power over parents and families. One teacher found themselves frustrated by this very removal of parents from at-home learning, explaining how computer-based homework seemed to discourage parents from asking students what they were working on or even from checking student work. They felt this was most pronounced for less-connected parents but saw it happening across the board. They felt that the more engaging the devices were for students, the less they encouraged parent engagement with student academics.

Outside of parent connections to student learning, the issue of how technology was used to communicate with parents was critical. Administrators saw increased outgoing communication from themselves and teachers through Facebook, Twitter, and apps like Remind which sent parents regular text messages as increased engagement. "If we tweet 5 times per week that is five times more connection we have with parents," suggested one principal. While teachers agreed that they used technology to communicate more, the reciprocity in parent–school communication appeared to suffer. One teacher felt that parents were able to "avoid" real dialogue about their students because everything happened electronically. Others, especially teachers of students with disabilities, expressed the struggle they had with schools no longer sending home paper reminders and paper homework. Parents were used to "checking the backpack" to stay informed; effectively using the digital tools provided required a new mind-set and skills that parents had not yet adopted.

The disagreement between administration and teachers about whether the 1:1 program had supported or hindered engagement largely depends on the definition of engagement and whether it is transactional or relational. Whereas principals noted increased transactions occurring, teachers reflected a loss of both the teacher–parent and student–parent relationship. This disparity speaks to a larger issue around the use of technology like the 1:1 program in isolation to address concerns about educational equity and suggests a framework through which we might understand the unfulfilled potential of the 1:1 program described here.

From Redistribution to Recognition and Representation

Equity is a concept with many names. It is often used interchangeably with social justice and, in educational literature, the notion of inclusive education. Waitoller and Artiles (2013) describe a three-dimensional model of inclusive education based on work by Fraser (1997). In this model, the three dimensions identified are redistribution (to meaningful educational opportunities), recognition (of diversity in all its dimensions), and representation (of students, families, and communities to express experiences of exclusion and voice their own solutions). While each dimension is critical, they also exist in tension with one another, with efforts at increasing one dimension sometimes undermining another.

In applying this model to the efforts SSD took to address what they saw as inequity, it appears that this policy reflected a fairly one-dimensional approach to addressing these concerns. While the 1:1 program effectively redistributed opportunities to learn using technology and evidence-based instruction, the program largely overlooked dimensions of recognition and representation. Deep inquiry into the ways in which various elements of student and family diversity would interact with technology and related policy decisions was not a priority. Similarly, engagement with students and families around how they understood (1) the initial problem of "inequity," (2) potential solutions to this problem, and (3) the interaction between the 1:1 program and these organic articulations of problems and solutions did not take place. The incorporation of the 1:1 program into a larger, community-based agenda aimed broadly at including those student groups they saw as "needing more" could have served to address teachers concerns that "computers can't fix everything," supported parent engagement and would have likely led to the identification of novel problems and solutions that, once addressed, could have increased the potential reach of the district administration's efforts at redistribution.

It is also important to consider the ways in which a redistribution-only approach serves to exacerbate existing power differentials in schools. In SSD, equity was seen as something that could be achieved *in spite* of the realities families and the community presented. The focus on giving devices rather than equipping students and families often served to highlight or even exacerbate existing deficit perspectives around family and community factors. While some specific goals may have been achieved through providing laptops, the story of SSD suggests the needs for policies and approaches to implementation which emphasize the ways that technology could connect and empower, rather than replace, families.

Conclusion

The story of this district should not be interpreted as reflecting an adverse effect for technology on educational equity, nor should it be interpreted as highlighting an inherent limitation in the use of educational technology to address educational equity. Positive results in areas of student engagement and the redistribution of meaningful opportunities to learn (through technology access, differentiated and student-centered instruction) suggest that 1:1 programs do hold potential in addressing inequity that stems from a lack of access to these opportunities. And yet, this case study suggests that this is not enough to fundamentally change educational experiences or outcomes for many students. The use of technology as a lever to address equity must be supported by a commitment to go beyond redistribution to digital resources.

Just as inequity stems from multiple, intersecting sources, solutions must address multiple dimensions. It is not enough, as teachers themselves reflected, just to give kids or families a computer. Deeper assessment aimed at understanding the complexity of students and the community in which they are able to voice their own concerns and solutions is necessary to prevent a situation in which implementation of efforts at redistribution reinforce existing divisions. Beyond this, the implicit assumptions of administrators (and the policies they craft) must be examined. For some, the very idea of a level playing field may be equated with the provision of resources or through circumventing parents and families; such exclusively redistributive and deficit-oriented thinking serves to undermine the broader equity intentions and potential of increasing technology access. Interestingly, SSD itself seems to have begun to embrace this reality as they continue to work to improve their programming. At the writing of the paper, the district was hosting a "Twitter chat" about equity in schools. While this may seem a small step, the willingness of current administrators to speak openly about issues of equity, to encourage their staff to explore what they have referred to this "elephant in the room," and (hopefully) their willingness to take meaningful steps toward recognition and representation may support a more positive return on their 1:1 investment.

As schools across the country grapple with the how and why of educational technology, they cannot ignore the ways in which these questions directly interact with socioeconomics and culture at a deep level. The increasing reliance on technology in society coupled with the persistence of gaps in access to, use of, and outcomes from technology demand that we pay close attention to the role of technology in schools serving historically marginalized students (Warschauer & Matuchniak, 2010). In places seeking to address equity through the redistribution of access to technology, a renewed focus on the recognition of student diversity and the representation of student and community voice present key opportunities to build on the promise of bridging the digital divide.

Note

1. Portions of the title and data utilized for this chapter are taken from Gherardi, S. A. (2016). *Unfinished bridges over the social divide: A case study in technology and inclusive education* (Doctoral dissertation under embargo). University of Illinois at Chicago, Chicago, IL.

References

Amiel, T., & Reeves, T. C. (2008). Design-based research and educational technology: Rethinking technology and the research agenda. *Educational Technology & Society*, 11(4), 29–40.

Apple Distinguished Schools. (2017). Retrieved from www.apple.com/education/apple-distinguished-schools/

Artiles, A. J., Kozleski, E. B., Dorn, S., & Christensen, C. (2006). Learning in Inclusive Education research: Re-mediating theory and methods with a transformative agenda. *Review of Research in Education*, 65–108.

Bebell, D., & O'Dwyer, L. M. (2010). Educational outcomes and research from 1:1 computing settings. *Journal of Technology, Learning, and Assessment*, 9(1), n1.

Burbules, N. C., Callister, T. A., & Taaffe, C. (2006). Beyond the digital divide. In *Technology and education: Issues in administration, policy, and applications in K12 schools* (pp. 85–99). Bingley, United Kingdom: Emerald Group Publishing Limited.

Carter, P. L., & Welner, K. G. (Eds.). (2013). *Closing the opportunity gap: What America must do to give every child an even chance*. New York: Oxford University Press.

Chan, T. C. (2011). How do technology application and equity impact student achievement? *International Journal of Cyber Ethics in Education*, 1(2), 1–14.

Cooley, V. E. (2001). Implementing technology using the teachers as trainers staff development model. *Journal of Technology and Teacher Education*, 9(2), 269–284.

Darling-Hammond, L., Zielezinski, M. B., & Goldman, S. (2014). Using technology to support at-risk students' learning. *Stanford Center for Opportunity*

Policy in Education. Retrieved from https://edpolicy.stanford.edu/publications/pubs/1241.

Duncan, A. (2012, March 8). *The new platform for learning*. Retrieved from www.ed.gov/news/speeches/new-platform-learning

Dunleavy, M., Dexter, S., & Heinecke, W. F. (2007). What added values does a 1:1 student to laptop ratio Bring to technology-supported teaching and learning? *Journal of Computer Assisted Learning, 1*(1). Retrieved from http://pkp.sfu.ca/ojs/demo/present/index.php/jce/article/view/171/56.

Fairlie, R. W. (2012). Academic achievement, technology and race: Experimental evidence. *Economics of Education Review, 31*(5), 663–679.

Fraser, N. (1997). *Justice interruptus: Critical reflections on the "postsocialist" condition*. New York: Routledge.

Griner, A. C., & Stewart, M. L. (2013). Addressing the achievement gap and disproportionality through the use of culturally responsive teaching practices. *Urban Education, 48*(4), 585–621.

Hoffman, D. L., & Novak, T. P. (1998). *Bridging the racial divide on the Internet*. Retrieved from www.researchgate.net/profile/Thomas_Novak2/publication/240313230_The_Growing_Digital_Divide_Implications_for_an_Open_Research_Agenda/links/545fabb10cf2c1a63bfdb95b.pdf

Jewitt, C., & Parashar, U. (2011). Technology and learning at home: Findings from the evaluation of the Home Access Programme pilot. *Journal of Computer Assisted Learning, 27*(4), 303–313.

Kulik, J. A. (2003). *Effects of using instructional technology in elementary and secondary schools: What controlled evaluation studies say*. Arlington, VA: SRI International. Retrieved from https://downloads.kennisnet.nl/mediawijzer/Onderzoeken/Kulik_ITinK-12_Main_Report.pdf

Lim, C. P., Zhao, Y., Tondeur, J., Chai, C. S., & Chin-Chung, T. (2013). Bridging the gap: Technology trends and use of technology in schools. *Journal of Educational Technology & Society, 16*(2), 59–68.

Penuel, W. R. (2006). Implementation and effects of one-to-one computing initiatives: A research synthesis. *Journal of Research on Technology in Education, 38*(3), 329–348.

Puentedura, R. (2010). *SAMR and TPCK: Intro to advanced practice*. Retrieved from http://hippasus.com/resources/sweden2010/SAMR_TPCK_IntroToAdvancedPractice.pdf

Purcell, K., Heaps, A., Buchanan, J., & Friedrich, L. (2013). *How teachers are using technology at homes and in their classrooms*. Retrieved from www.pewinternet.org/2013/02/28/ how-teachers-are-using-technology-at-home-and-in-their-classrooms/

Restrauri, D. (2013). Teachers must let students use their mobile phones in class. *Forbes*. Retrieved from www.forbes.com/sites/deniserestauri/2013/08/19/teachers-must-let-students-use-their-mobile-phones-in-classrooms-2/#1c4f1fe03e1d

Rogers, E. M. (2001). The digital divide. *Convergence, 7*(4), 96–111.

Sleeter, C. E. (2012). Confronting the marginalization of culturally responsive pedagogy. *Urban Education, 47*(3), 562–584.

Vigdor, J. L., Ladd, H. F., & Martinez, E. (2014). Scaling the digital divide: Home computer technology and student achievement. *Economic Inquiry, 52*(3), 1103–1119.

Waitoller, F. R., & Artiles, A. J. (2013). A decade of professional development research for inclusive education: A critical review and notes for a research program. *Review of Educational Research, 83*(3), 319–356.

Warschauer, M. (2004). *Technology and social inclusion: Rethinking the digital divide*. Cambridge, MA: MIT Press.

Warschauer, M., & Matuchniak, T. (2010). New technology and digital worlds: Analyzing evidence of equity in access, use, and outcomes. *Review of Research in Education, 34*(1), 179–225.

8 How the Free-Market Approach to Charter Schools Has Failed the Minoritized Students Who Were Intended to Benefit the Most

Brittany Larkin and Carlee Escue Simon

The Charter School Promise

The concept of "charter schools" has evolved throughout the years. The initial inspiration was formed by the morphing of two separate ideas by two distinct and opposing idealists. The initial catalyst was Milton Friedman's (1962) *Capitalism and Freedom* in which he describes decentralizing the government's role in public education through the use of vouchers to create a "market" for education. Friedman idealized the role of the government as the manager of standards and provider of the funds required to maintain what he termed a *neighborhood effect*, defined as the common knowledge and degree of literacy required for general citizenship to participate in a democratic society. Friedman's vision established the private sector as the provider of educational services. This allows parents the freedom to spend their government-vouchered funding at the school of their choice, thus creating a private market of competition to drive the profession of teaching and satisfy the needs of the consumer while supporting the mission of establishing a *neighborhood effect* (Friedman, 1962).

The second concept was one of Ray Budde's (1988) theories to reorganize the public school system with specific roles for administrators, teachers, and students. It reflected teachers at the top of the paradigm with the expertise to make instructional decisions and the autonomy to carry out those decisions. The role of administrators was to create a culture of positive support for teachers and the learning process while managing the logistics of operating a safe school. The students' roles were to be responsible for their own learning and behavior.

The ideas of Friedman and Budde began to merge when Al Shanker, president of the American Federation of Teachers at the time, pushed to establish a new approach to education and the structures of governance (Figure 8.1). Shanker (1988) picked up Budde's ideation and gave him public credit for appropriately naming the idea *charter schools*. Shanker then expounded on Budde's idea by designing a nesting concept allowing for new subschools within an existing school building to serve as

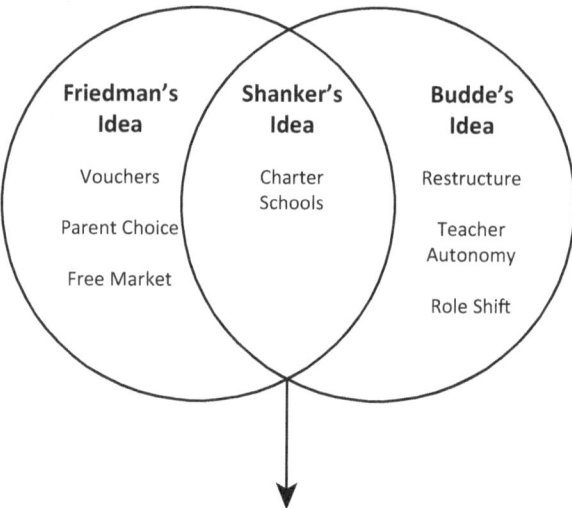

Figure 8.1 The Merging and Morphing of Ideas

innovative hubs for teachers to make autonomous curricular decisions outside of the constraints of the traditional school policies (Kolderie, 2005). These *charter schools* would serve as laboratories where teachers could experiment with teaching and learning techniques to meet the needs of particular student groups. The successful results of the *charter school* labs would then be implemented in the larger traditional school system (Kahlenberg & Potter, 2014).

Minnesota was the first state to adopt Shanker's idea of a *charter school*. In 1991 Minnesota expanded its policy to allow charter schools to be authorized by local boards of education and the state department of education. Since then, states have adopted charter school laws into their legislation with individualized state-specific contributions, thus making charter school law comparison among and across states challenging and complicated. Examples of state-modified charter school legislation include nondistrict authorizers, state-level appeal options and processes, school district charter options, and third-party private for-profit management companies. While the initial ideals of Friedman and Budde were merged together into one concept of "charters and choice," the concept and usage of charter schools have now morphed into a multibillion-dollar free-market privatization movement that lacks stability, accountability, and transparency. Time has not served the charter school movement well. Many states are experiencing negative outcomes associated with the lack of meaningful and effective charter school regulation. However, those that are profiting and benefiting from the charter school movement are powerful, vocal, and aggressively ensuring that the movement stays intact despite indicators that identify serious concern for quality education. The remaining sections of this chapter use Florida as a case study to illustrate how this policy has gone wrong.

Case in Point: Florida

In 1994, Jeb Bush challenged incumbent Lawton Chiles in a tight race for governor of Florida, with Chiles narrowly securing his second term over Bush. After his defeat and amid rampant speculation of political jockeying, Bush focused on a campaign to improve Florida public schools through the novel idea beginning to unfold in other states: charter schools. First, he solicited the support of Willard Fair, a well-known civil rights leader in Miami, to gain his support for charter school legislation and to partner in opening the first charter school in one of the poorest urban cities in Florida (McGrory, 2015). During this time, Bush also founded a nonprofit organization named the Foundation for Florida's Future. According the organization's website, their mission is "to make Florida's education system a model for the nation" through the implementation of a formula with six necessary components: rigorous academic standards, standardized measurement, data-based accountability, effective teaching, outcome-based funding, and school choice (Foundation for Florida's Future, n.d.). However, the *St. Petersburg Times* reported that the major contributors to Bush's nonprofit included the largest companies and special interest groups in the state and an extensive list of national Republican Party benefactors (Nickens, 1998). Shortly after the establishment of the Foundation for Florida's Future, initial charter school policy was introduced into Florida legislation in 1996.

In 1998, Bush ran for governor of Florida again. He won and remained governor until 2007. After his terms as governor, Bush instituted the Foundation for Excellence in Education in 2009. According to the foundation's website, the Foundation for Excellence in Education was created in response to the outcry for help from state legislators in helping them implement Florida's Formula for Student Achievement outlined in Bush's inaugural foundation (Foundation for Excellence in Education, 2017). The Foundation for Excellence in Education, with the ironic acronym FEE, has lived up to its touts of being the national leader in education reform through its strong presence and campaign contributions in states that are drafting charter school laws. The charter school policy watchdog Cashing in on Kids, produced by In the Public Interest and The American Federation of Teachers, uncovered some scandalous and seemingly unethical activities surrounding the FEE. For example, the watchdog group uncovered evidence of how the FEE was helping legislators draft charter school policy that would financially benefit the corporate funders of FEE, which, in turn, make substantial campaign donations to the legislators (Cashing in on Kids, n.d.b). Sadly, the charter school ideation continues to erode as the allure of profit outweighs the focus of quality education necessary in order to produce the "good neighborhood effect."

Charter Schools: The Great Equalizer or the Great Divider?

Charter School Advocates Say

The National Alliance for Public Charter Schools (NAPCS) is the leading national nonprofit organization committed to advancing the public charter school movement, according to its website. The NAPCS focuses on shaping federal and state policy, increasing public funding to grow charter schools, and improving "the overall health and perception of the movement in order to increase our influence with policymakers" (NAPCS, n.d.). NAPCS declares that charter schools are the best educational option for all students, because, as they claim, charter schools produce higher achieving students, close the achievement gap, and send more students to college than traditional schools. It is not entirely clear what evidence is used to make this declaration; however, it is a sentiment commonly made by many in the pro-charter movement. It is important to note that charter school performance varies greatly by state and the policies that regulate it.

The Florida Department of Education's (FLDOE) Office of Independent Education and Parental Choice published a report indicating many of their charter schools operate under innovative missions and themes focusing on the arts, sciences, and technologies, and many others provide services to students with disabilities and to students at risk of failure (FLDOE, 2015). In a 2014 report by the FLDOE on student achievement in charter schools, there is ample evidence that charter school students are outperforming traditional school students on assessments. This report shows a higher percentage of students passing the state standardized assessment in each subgroup: white students, African American students, Hispanic students, students receiving free or reduced-price lunches (FRPL), students with disabilities, and English language learning (ELL) students (FLDOE, 2014). The report also has data to support that charter schools have a smaller achievement gap than the traditional schools in gaps between white students and African American students and between White students and Hispanic students in each subject area except algebra. Finally, the report stated that 46% of all charter schools in Florida received an overall school performance grade of A from the FLDOE, as opposed to only 34% of the traditional schools receiving an A. These achievement scores paint a glorious picture of charter school success for the state of Florida, especially if these are the only data examined to measure success.

Yet, the Florida Education Association paints more details onto the picture. If the measure of success is student achievement scores, charter schools have the autonomy to manipulate the participants. A statewide study found evidence indicating that charters are resegregating schools and had selective admissions and dismissals. In particular, the study found that in one county with nine of its charters receiving a school grade of A by the state, eight of those schools' student demographics did not match the demographics of the school district at large (Florida Education Association, n.d.). Furthermore, there were three charters with overwhelmingly more wealthy white students making up their student body, with no plans to increase their diversity; additionally, they had policy for dismissing students for low grades, poor standardized test scores, or retention at grade level (Florida Education Association, n.d.). With the autonomy to manipulate which students are assessed, thus reflecting the success of the school, it is no wonder the charters are achieving better on this measure.

Another measure of success is evident in the level of satisfaction and turnover rates of the teachers in a school. Not surprisingly, salaries and benefits play a huge factor in teacher satisfaction and retention. The Florida Education Association's statewide study found that 25% of charter school teachers earned less than the starting salary for the district's beginning teachers (Florida Education Association, n.d.). In addition to the lower salaries, charter school law in Florida allows charter schools the option to participate in the Florida Retirement System or not, and the autonomy to not participate in the school district's collective bargaining agreements (FL K–20 Education Code XLVIII). Therefore, most charter schools' teachers received no health coverage or retirement benefits (Florida Education Association, n.d.). The Florida Education Association (n.d.) also found that nearly 40% of the charter schools in one county had at least 60% new faculty and staff, and half of those were 100% teacher turnover. Because the charters in Florida are not paying beginning teachers at least what they would make in the district schools, and not participating in the retirement system, they are not able to recruit highly qualified veteran teachers away from the district, and the rookie teachers only stay in the charters until a position opens in the district schools. This turnover rate makes it nearly impossible for the school to develop a strong culture and positive learning environment that all educators know to be critical to the success of a school, most specifically high poverty and/or at-risk student populations. Furthermore, recruitment wastes human resources costs—budgets that could be spent on instruction.

Arguably the ultimate measure of school failure is the closure of the school. In the 18 years that charter school laws have been in place in Florida, 965 charter schools have opened, and 33% of those have closed (FLDOE, 2016). That is, 313 school closings and 652 schools in operation, of which only 183 or 28% were classified as high-performing schools by the FLDOE (2016). Charter school law specifies the purpose of charter schools in Florida is to "meet high standards of student achievement" and to "promote enhanced academic success"; it is unacceptable that only 28% of the charters meet this requirement (fewer than 20% if those schools that have closed are taken into account; Florida K–12 Education Code XLVIII). Even with the assumption that the remaining 72% of operating charters are performing at least as well as traditional schools, this indicates that the families that have chosen to send their children to charter schools would be just as satisfied with public education. But what about the families in those 313 schools that closed? And what about the taxpayers who fund them?

Evidence in Charter School Closures

The NAPSC claims school closure is a positive indication that the accountability component of the charter schools' market system is working well (NAPSC, 2016). That is an easy piece of bait to swallow from a detached business-minded perspective, but the hook that makes it real can be seen in the news reports headlines: "Students, Teachers Left Scrambling After School Suddenly Closes" (WESH-TV, 2015) and "Children Attending Tapestry Park Charter School Will Have to Find a New Place to Go to School Starting Next Monday" (WJHG-News, 2005). Researchers criticize Florida charter schools in publications such as "Florida's Charter Schools Unsupervised: Taxpayers, Students Lose When School Operators Exploit Weak Laws" (Yi & Shipley, 2014) and "A local charter school decides to close its doors Friday, giving staff only four days to pack up and find another job. Nearly 80 children will have to be placed somewhere else" (Lanee', 2014).

For this case study, evidence was collected from 211 of the 313 closed schools from the websites of both the NAPSC and the FLDOE to discover who the children are that this policy has failed. Of the 211 schools, 102 served students within preK through fifth grades, 90 served students within sixth to eighth grades, and 70 served students within 9th to 12th grades. Because each school served various grade levels, for example, some were K–12 schools while others were K–8 or 6–8 schools, and so on, the reported numbers included schools that served students within any of the grade ranges indicated. None of the 211 charter schools participated in a union for educators. The average number of years these 211 schools held an active charter was 3.9 years (ranging from 2 months to 17 years). Yet, the average number of years the now-closed charter schools had actual students enrolled was only 2.7 years. This is a troubling comparison of averages and leaves many questions unanswered.

Over a 10-year period (2005–2015) when the 211 charter schools closed, 27,330 students were dispersed and required to find a new educational institution. Table 8.1 outlines the demographic breakdown of students displaced by the 211 charter school closures from 2005 to 2015, including the comparative state averages of students.

This is staggering and concerning data as it demonstrates that the most at-risk students were left without a school and lacking educational stability.

Even more troubling evidence of the state's policy failure is that 22 of the 211 charter school closures occurred during the school year, leaving students literally days to enroll in another school and countless teachers unemployed. Additionally, this put an undue financial burden on the receiving schools. In Florida, schools submit a student count in October and in February each year to determine the amount of state funding they will receive; each of those 22 schools closed their doors between October and February (FLDOE, 2016). That totaled 2,538 students who

Table 8.1 Demographic Breakdown of Students Displaced by Charter School Closures from 2005 to 2015

Demographic	Count	%	State Average (%)*
White	7,327	27	45
Minorities	20,737	76	55
African American	14,275	52	23
Hispanic	5,833	21	23–31
Asian	193	0.7	2–3
other	243	1	3–4
FRPL	15,964	58	46–59
ELL	915	3	8–10
ESE	2,175	8	19
Total	27,330		

Source: FLDOE (2016).

Note: FRPL = free or reduced-price lunch; ELL = English-language learner; ESE = exceptional student education.

* Ranges show increases over the 10-year period.

earned state and local money for the charter school at $10,000 per pupil revenue (average revenue from 2006–2013) or $25,380,000 paid to the charter school that, in turn, closed their doors, sending the students to either another charter or a traditional school with no funding to educate them or the ability to be paid back (*Governing*, 2016). In other words, because the charter school had collected the state and local money for the students, when those students went to another school, the receiving school had to accept them with no funding to educate them. Who were these students that inevitably fell behind their peers during this midyear closure and scramble? Table 8.2 offers the demographic analysis of those 2,538 students.

The claim from the NAPCS that charter school closures are evidence that the market system is working begs the question: working for whom? In fact, the claim that charter school closures are beneficial in any way is entirely nonsensical and lacks any ethical or fiduciary responsibility for the constitutionally mandated education of Florida's children and the commitment to taxpayers. The preamble of the Florida Constitution's Education Article IX indicates:

> The education of children is a fundamental value of the people of the State of Florida. It is, therefore, a paramount duty of the state to make adequate provision for the education of all children residing within its borders. Adequate provision shall be made by law for a uniform, efficient, safe, secure, and high quality system of free public schools that allows students to obtain a high quality education.
> (Florida Legislature, 2002)

This mandate has no obligations to choice or free-market values. The Education clause guarantees uniform, efficient, safe, secure, and high-quality

Table 8.2 Demographic Breakdown of Students Displaced by Mid-School-Year Charter Closures from 2005 to 2015

Demographic	Count	%
White	772	30
African American	1,166	46
Hispanic	545	21
Asian	9	0.3
other	43	2
FRPL	1,390	55
ELL	162	6
ESE	189	7
Total	2,538	

Source: FLDOE (2016).

Note: FRPL = free or reduced-price lunch; ELL = English-language learner; ESE = exceptional student education.

Free-Market Approach to Charter Schools 147

education in free public schools. Closing charter schools jeopardizes all these guarantees and certainly can be argued as violating a constitutional mandate.

Evidence in Litigation

Charter school litigation is an underresearched area that deserves consideration when evaluating the effectiveness of a public policy or law. Along with the Florida charter school closing data, we examined the lawsuits affiliated with charter schools. Using the West Law Next database, all litigation ruled on in Florida state courts involving charter schools from 1996 until 2015 was examined. The investigation revealed 16 legal cases. As represented in Figure 8.2, of those 16 cases, seven were appealing the Charter School Commission's (CSC) decision to reverse a school district's (SD) decision to terminate or not renew a charter agreement (four of those resulted in reversals), and two were appeals of the CSC's decision to uphold a school district's decision (all were upheld). There were also four cases in which a charter school filed a suit (one case of a charter denial, two funding issues, and one liability issue), but the ruling fell against the charter in each of these cases. The final category, which held two cases, is operations, and in each of these cases, a specific charter school was not named as these were cases filed by a district against the state.

Further investigation was conducted to learn more about the charter schools named in these cases and where they are now. Two of the 16 cases did not name a charter school, leaving 14 named charter school cases for investigation. Only four of those charter schools operated independently (i.e., without a hired for-profit management company). Those four include Trinity School for Children, an operational lawsuit which sought and won to consolidate two charter schools into one (School

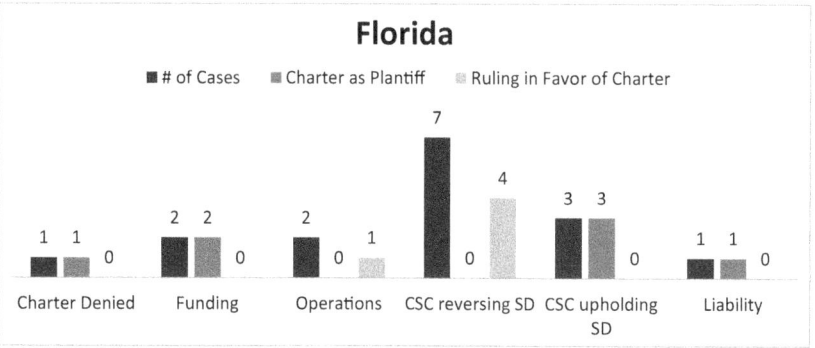

Figure 8.2 Florida Court Cases by Type, Plaintiff, and Ruling.
Note: CSC = Charter School Commission; SD = school district.

Board of Hillsborough County *v.* Tampa School Development Corporation, 2013). This charter school was still open in 2015 and identified as successful according to the consistent letter grade of A given by the FLDOE from 2010 to 2014 (FLDOE, 2016). The other three independent charters were closed after they lost the appeal to either terminate or not renew their charter contracts.

Seventy-one percent ($n = 10$) of the charter school cases ruled on in Florida included charter school management companies. Two of those cases involved authorizers that manage multiple charter schools but under very specific circumstances. United Cerebral Palsy of Central Florida was denied a charter agreement from the School Board of Osceola County, which was reversed by the CSC and affirmed in the court (School Board of Osceola County *v.* UCP of Central Florida, 2005). This organization now manages seven other charter campuses in Florida (UCP of Central Florida, 2016). The other organization is a charter school system managed by the city of Pembroke Pines. This city within Broward County has converted all of their schools into charter in order for the district to share capital outlay funds (City of Pembroke Pines *v.* School Board of Broward County, 2013). Pembroke Pines is still operating this charter system and has consistently received an A rating from the FLDOE (2016).

Four cases involved charter school management companies that are no longer in business. The Academies of Excellence, Inc. were denied a charter in Osceola County and again in Volusia County; then the CSC reversed the decisions, and the courts affirmed that decision (School Board of Osceola County *v.* Academies of Excellence, Inc., 2005; School Board of Volusia County *v.* Academies of Excellence, Inc., 2008). Yet, while the courts found the school districts did not have good cause to deny the charters, Academies of Excellence, Inc. operated schools are no longer open and there is no evidence this company remained operational. Similarly, the Universal Education Services, Inc. was denied a charter in Osceola County, which was overturned by the state and affirmed in the courts, yet there is no evidence this company is still in operation (School Board of Osceola County *v.* Universal Education Services, Inc., 2008). Finally, there is Successful Enterprises, Inc., which operated Spiral Tech Elementary Charter whose charter agreement was terminated by the School Board of Miami-Dade County (Spiral Tech Elementary Charter School *v.* School Board of Miami-Dade County, 2008). In this case, the CSC agreed with the school district's decision as did the court, thus closing Spiral Tech; there is no evidence that Successful Enterprises, Inc. remains operational.

The remaining four cases were all associated with the same for-profit management company, Charter Schools USA. In the first case, while a specific charter was not named, Charter Schools USA moved to dissolve writs of garnishment issued to a student and the motion was denied (Charter Schools USA, Inc. *v.* John Doe, 2015). In another case, PM Wells Charter School, managed by Charter Schools USA, sought exemption from special assessment fees and liens by foreclosure; however, the courts found public schools to not be exempt, and legislation does not allow exemption for charter schools (Remington Community Development District *v.* Education Foundation of Osceola, etc., 2006). While this charter is still in operation, its rating from the state department has been inconsistent, with a rating of B in 2011 and 2012, C in 2013, and A in 2014 (FLDOE, 2016). Finally, Charter Schools USA attempted to open charter schools in both Seminole and Polk Counties under the name Renaissance Charter School. In both of these cases, the school districts appealed the CSC's decision to overturn their verdict to deny a charter to Renaissance Charter School. In both cases, the court reversed the CSC's decision citing the "applicant failed to demonstrate by clear and convincing evidence that its proposed educational program met the statutory requirement that it substantially replicated that of an existing high-performance school" (School Board of Seminole County *v.* Renaissance Charter School, Inc., 2013; School Board of Polk County Florida *v.* Renaissance Charter School, Inc., 2014). Interestingly, while Charter Schools USA's application for a charter did not meet the statutory requirements in two counties, apparently it did meet those requirements in seven other counties. Charter Schools USA currently manages five charter schools in Broward County, three in Miami-Dade County, three in Orange County (although they did reject one in 2011 for unrealistic budgeting and too much control by the management company), two in Osceola County, six in Palm Beach County, and two in St. Lucie County (FLDOE, 2016). Charter Schools USA has one charter school that was closed in Polk County (FLDOE, 2016).

Complications With Charter Schools and Management Companies

There are a few major barriers and complications with charter schools and management companies for researchers, regulators, and taxpayers. One of the major benefits of public education is transparency that may have flaws in the system, but there is a legal requirement for transparency. Individuals who have questions about funding or education decisions have all rights and abilities to request information from public school districts. Two main concerns for this study that have an impact on transparency were name changes of charter schools and the private aspect of management companies.

Individuals that research charter school data are continually overburdened with chasing down names. Charter schools have the ability to change names and can essentially "rebrand" when needed. Although in this study the name changes of charter schools were minimal, the ability and ease with which a school can change its name at any point in time create issues when tracking data. Management companies add to this issue. Many management companies have affiliate corporations, supporting branch companies that provide services and/or facilities, and proprietary privacy allowed to for-profit corporations not afforded or granted to public institutions. These private corporations are able to use funding in ways that no public school would ever be able.

For example, as previously discussed, Charter Schools USA is a for-profit management company headquartered in Florida with additional charter schools in Georgia, Illinois, Louisiana, South Carolina, and North Carolina. A branch corporation, Red Apple Development, manages its facilities. This company has well-established relationships with Foundation for Florida's Future, Governor Rick Scott's education transition team, and Florida's Education Commission. These relationships have familial connections as well as financial (Cashing in on Kids, n.d.a):

> According to the *Tampa Bay Times*, Charter Schools USA paid out over $200,000 in political contributions during the 2012 election cycle. The company also contributed $50,000 to a Georgia PAC to expand charter schools in the state. . . . A 2002 *St. Petersburg Times* investigation claimed Hage and other Charter School USA employees established non-profits that went on to apply to oversee schools run by the company. At the time, at least one school board indicated there was no community support for the school, and a school board attorney noted, "We understand how this game is played, and how they're opening cookie-cutter schools all over the state."
>
> (Cashing in on Kids, n.d.a)

The ability to use funds to support political campaigns, super political action committee, and associated nonprofits not only removes instructional dollars from students, but it also creates ethical concerns associated with transparency. In essence, the management company is using taxpayer-provided instructional funding as transfer funds for private campaign support and financing. Public money is becoming private. This transfer removes transparency and leaves the taxpayer with no recourse for accountability.

Where Did We Go Wrong?

In theory, charter schools began in a reasonable and arguably good place with good intentions for public education. Ideas of autonomy, innovation, creativity, ownership, and improvement are ones every institution of learning yearns to be a part of. Closing achievement gaps and spurring rigor are goals of public education. So, where did this policy go wrong? Evidence from this case study indicates it went wrong when public money was made private. As soon as the policy provided opportunities for private companies to manage and oversee public institutions of learning funded with enormous amounts of public taxpayer money, the initial ideation of high-quality education began to dissolve. As soon as people in power discovered they could legally use taxpayer dollars for personal profit and gain at the expense of a public service, things went wrong.

How can we get back on track? Expanding accountability and reporting expectations is necessary immediately. The rate of teacher turnover must be minimized and reported. High rates of teacher turnover are inexcusable and have long-term deficits to high-quality education. Student selectivity and inequitable disciplinary procedures are detrimental as well. Preventing admission and/or student removal creates environments that can be artificial and capriciously established. All schools should be accountable to their admission pool and their student expulsion or mobility rates. Like that of teacher turnover, reporting these data and answering to these data are minimal expectations that charter schools should be held accountable to.

We must stop allowing individuals to profit from public education. Education management companies need to be severely restricted and regulated if not completely abolished. We need to prevent "rebranding" of charter schools in order to track data appropriately. The current mechanism allows for failing charter school businesses to close and open repeatedly without the ability to track their history efficiently and effectively. And we must stop putting schools in competition with each other. Our nation does not do this with any other public service. The very notion of competition means someone fails. We cannot, as a society, fail our children! The argument that school closing is a sign of a working market minimizes the actual impact on individual children and their families. Within this study, 22 charter schools closed during the academic school years from 2005 to 2015. That left 2,538 children impacted by the proclamation of a "working market." It is fair to say that this did not feel like "working" to those children or their families. This level of obtuse thinking is detrimental to society and absolutely counter to the guarantee stipulated within the Florida constitution. Establishing policy and systems that depend on failure and drain resources is nonsensical.

References

Budde, R. (1988). *Education by Charter: Restructuring school districts: Key to long-term continuing improvement in American education.* Andover, MA: The Regional Laboratory for Educational Improvements of the Northeast 7 Islands.

Cashing in on Kids. (n.d.a). *Charter schools USA*. Retrieved from http://cashinginonkids.org/corporate-profiles/charter-schools-usa/

Cashing in on Kids. (n.d.b). *Jeb Bush's friends are cashing in on kids.* Retrieved from http://cashinginonkids.com/jeb-bush-cashing-in-on-kids/

Charter Schools USA, Inc. *v.* John Doe, No 93, 152 So. 3d 657 (Fla. Dist. Ct. App. 2014), reh'g denied (Dec. 30, 2014), review dismissed, No. SC12–163, 2015 WL 3819931 (Fla. June 17, 2015).

City of Pembroke Pines *v.* School Board of Broward County, 125 So. 3d 157 (Fla. Dist. Ct. App., 2013).

Florida Department of Education. (2014). *Student achievement in Florida's charter schools: A comparison of the performance of charter school students with traditional public school students.* Retrieved from www.fldoe.org/core/fileparse.php/7778/urlt/Charter_Student_Achievement_Report_1314.pdf

Florida Department of Education. (2015). *Florida's charter schools: Fact sheet.* Retrieved from www.fldoe.org/core/fileparse.php/7696/urlt/Charter_Oct_2015_11-20-15.pdf

Florida Department of Education. (2016). *Florida charter school by district.* Retrieved from www.floridaschoolchoice.org/information/charter_schools/directory/default.aspx

Florida Education Association. (n.d.). *Statewide charter school study.* Retrieved from https://feaweb.org/statewide-charter-school-study

Florida K-12 Education Code XLVIII. (1996). Charter Schools, §1002.33.

Florida Legislature. (2002). *Constitution of the state of Florida: Article IX education.* Retrieved from www.leg.state.fl.us/statutes/index.cfm?submenu=3#A9

Foundation for Excellence in Education. (2017). *About us.* Retrieved from www.excelined.org/about-us/

Foundation for Florida's Future. (n.d.). *Florida formula for student achievement.* Retrieved from http://afloridapromise.org/pages/Florida_Formula.aspx

Friedman, M. (1962). The role of government in education. *Capitalism and Freedom.* Retrieved from www.edchoice.org/who-we-are/our-founders/the-friedmans-on-school-choice/article/the-role-of-government-in-education/

Governing. (2016). Education spending per student by state. Retrieved from www.governing.com/gov-data/education-data/state-education-spending-per-pupil-data.html

Kahlenberg, R. D., & Potter, H. (2014). Restoring Shanker's vision for charter schools. *American Educator, 38*(4), 4.

Kolderie, T. (2005). Ray Budde and the origins of the "charter concept". *Education/Evolving.* Retrieved from www.educationevolving.org/pdf/Ray-Budde-Origins-Of-Chartering.pdf

Lanee', J. (2014, December 16). Transition Elementary Charter School closing Friday claiming financial issues. *WPTC.* Retrieved from www.wptv.com/news/region-c-palm-beach-county/west-palm-beach/transition-elementary-charter-school-closing-friday-claiming-financial-issues

McGrory, K. (2015, March 6). Birth of a charter school and Jeb Bush's vision for education. *Tampa Bay Times.* Retrieved from www.tampabay.com/news/politics/stateroundup/birth-of-a-charter-school-and-jeb-bushs-vision-for-education/2220403

National Alliance for Public Charter Schools. (2016). *A closer look at the charter school movement.* Retrieved from www.publiccharters.org/wp-content/uploads/2016/02/New-Closed-2016.pdf

National Alliance for Public Charter Schools. (n.d.). *About the national alliance.* Retrieved from www.publiccharters.org/get-the-facts/about-us/

Nickens, T. (1998, September 13). Policy group proved shrewd for Bush. *St. Petersburg Times.* Retrieved from www.campaignfinance.org/statehtml/policy_group_proved.html

Remington Community Development District *v.* Education Foundation of Osceola, etc., 941 So. 2d 15 (Fla. Dist. Ct. App. 2006).

School Board of Hillsborough County *v.* Tampa School Development Corporation, 113 So. 3d 919 (Fla Dist. Ct. App. 2013).

School Board of Osceola County *v.* Academies of Excellence, Inc., 914 So. 2d 981, (Mem)-982 (Fla. Dist. Ct. App. 2005).

School Board of Osceola County *v.* UCP of Central Florida, 905 So. 2d 909 (Fla. Dist. Ct. App. 2005).

School Board of Osceola County *v.* Universal Education Services, Inc., 990 So. 2d 1210 (Fla. Dist. Ct. App. 2008).

School Board of Polk County Florida *v.* Renaissance Charter School, Inc., 147 So. 3d 1026 (Fla. Dist. Ct. App. 2014).

School Board of Seminole County *v.* Renaissance Charter School, Inc., 113 So. 3d 72 (Fla, Dist. App. 2013) reh'g denied (May 28, 2013).

School Board of Volusia County *v.* Academies of Excellence, Inc., 974 So. 2d 1186 (Fla Dist. Ct. App. 2008).

Shanker, A. (1988, July 10). Convention plots new course: A charter for change. *Where We Stand, New York Times.* Retrieved from http://locals.nysut.org/shanker

Spiral Tech Elementary Charter School *v.* School Board of Miami-Dade County, 994 So. 2d 455 (Fla. Dist. Ct. App. 2008).

UCP of Central Florida. (2016). *Campuses.* Retrieved from www.ucpcfl.org/

WESH-TV. (2015, May 8). *Students, teachers left scrambling after school suddenly closes: Acclaim Academy charter school closes without warning Wednesday.* Retrieved from www.wesh.com/news/students-teachers-left-scrambling-after-school-suddenly-closes/32865880

WJHG-News. (2005, October 12). *Charter school closing.* Retrieved from www.wjhg.com/community/schools/headlines/1904597.html

Yi, K., & Shipley, A. (2014, June 18). Florida's charter schools unsupervised: Taxpayers, students lose when school operators exploit weak laws. *Sun Sentinel.* Retrieved from http://interactive.sun-sentinel.com/charter-schools-unsupervised/investigation.html

9 When Achievement Gaps Are Acceptable

School-Level Data Practices and Subgroup Accountability Pressure in Economically and Racially Segregated Schools

Rachel Garver

Subgroup accountability policy aims to balance the pursuit of excellence with attention to equity. It has been the central lever of federal education policy to promote equity while raising academic standards since the 2001 reauthorization of the Elementary and Secondary Education Act (ESEA), also known as No Child Left Behind (NCLB). Subgroup accountability is the requirement that student subgroups delineated by gender, race, disability, and language status make adequate yearly progress (AYP) in addition to the student body overall. Tasked with implementing the accountability requirements of ESEA, states determine which schools fail to make AYP and establish a graduated series of sanctions (e.g., increased monitoring, state takeover) for cited schools.

Prior to NCLB, certain states had accountability policies that held schools responsible for the academic performance of their entire student body. Research revealed that under these conditions schools sometimes sought more favorable ratings by focusing their efforts on the students who were most likely to improve and by disregarding low-performing students, who were disproportionately Black, Latinx, and students with disabilities (Booher-Jennings, 2005; Vasquez Heilig & Darling-Hammond, 2008). In response, lawmakers showed widespread support for including subgroup accountability in NCLB (Center on Education Policy, 2003), and it remains in the most recent reauthorization of ESEA, the Every Student Succeeds Act, although with more discretion for states in setting the benchmarks for AYP. The success of federal policies that require states to monitor and address educational inequality is vital to counteract regional variation in the public's and policymakers' will to promote equity. Embedded within congressional legislation, subgroup accountability is one of few remaining sources of federal pressure for equity, as the justice and education departments under Trump no longer perceive it as part of their role to address educational access and discrimination like they did under the Obama administration.

The evidence is mixed as to whether a citation under subgroup accountability fulfills its intention to focus schools on the student subgroups identified by the state as failing to make AYP. Weinbaum, Weiss, and Beaver (2012) found that instructional practices do not differ between cited and uncited schools, nor do they vary depending on the subgroup(s) identified. Some research has suggested that student subgroups do make progress the year following their identification, although the growth in achievement varied by subgroup (Lauen & Gaddis, 2012). Schools are more likely to make progress the year following a citation when they have a "focused failure"—when they fail to make AYP for one subgroup as opposed to failing to make AYP for multiple subgroups or school-wide student performance (Hemelt, 2011; Lauen & Gaddis, 2012). On the other hand, Krieg (2011) found that when a school is cited for the performance of one racial subgroup, other racial subgroups see a decline in achievement the following year, suggesting that efforts are directed toward some students to the detriment of others. Studies that explore the mechanisms of implementation behind subgroup accountability's variable success in improving the performance of identified subgroups are lacking.

In this chapter, I draw on an ethnographic study of Germaine Middle School (GMS)[1] to demonstrate how school-level data practices mediate a school's response to a citation under subgroup accountability policy. Subgroup accountability's regulatory power can be amplified, reduced, or vary by subgroup, depending on the ways that teachers and school administrators make sense of student achievement data. In the case of GMS, an economically and racially segregated school, the staff invoked the intensive needs of the student body in a way that normalized the lagging achievement of certain subgroups and lessened the pressure that subgroup accountability exerted. My findings suggest school demographics influence teachers' and administrators' data practices such that subgroup accountability policy is less likely to promote equity in schools where the student body is primarily high-poverty students of color with large populations of English learners (ELs) and students with disabilities (SWDs).

School-Based Data Practices and Subgroup Accountability Policy

Accountability policies are responsible for the rapid expansion of student achievement data and for encouraging data-driven decision making (DDDM) over the last two decades (Coburn & Turner, 2012; Datnow, Park, & Kennedy-Lewis, 2012; Henig, 2012; Jennings, 2012; Roderick, 2012). Data use under accountability policy is guided by a techno-rational logic that assumes a linear relationship between the availability of data and the efficiency of responses that effectively improve student performance (Datnow et al., 2012; Ingram, Louis, & Schroeder, 2004). However, the notion that more data leads to improved student outcomes overlooks the intervening mechanisms that are necessary for transforming data into practice. Individuals bring meaning to data; data do not speak independently or contain a singular message waiting to be uncovered (Horn, Kane, & Wilson, 2015; Ingram et al., 2004; Marsh, 2012; Spillane, 2012).

Teachers and administrators at all levels of governance interpret data, and it is this process that introduces variability into the transformation of data into practice. Accordingly, the potential of policies that rely on DDDM to improve student outcomes depends on their alignment with practitioners' data use (Ingram et al., 2004). Subgroup accountability is especially sensitive to school-based data practices because it relies singularly on responsiveness to student growth on standardized test scores, as opposed to, for instance, subgroup entitlement policies that seek greater equity by mandating particular services for ELs or SWDs. Teachers' and administrators' perceptions of state standardized tests, the state's calculations, and the value of data use in identifying student needs more generally all potentially shape their response to subgroup accountability pressure (Garver, 2017).

Researchers have begun to foreground the role of individual and collaborative meaning-making, balancing top-down and bottom-up notions of policy implementation and providing evidence for an alternative to the techno-rational theory of data use (Datnow et al., 2012). Individuals' experiences, beliefs, and training influence their orientations to data, their approach to analysis, and the conclusions they draw (Datnow & Hubbard, 2015; Datnow & Park, 2018). Meaning is also co-constructed through social interactions, which has brought sites of teacher collaboration to the center of scholarship on data practices (Coburn & Turner, 2011, 2012; Daly, 2012; Datnow & Park, 2018; Farley-Ripple & Buttram, 2015; Horn, 2007; Jimerson, 2014). Practitioners who work together are likely to have shared interpretations of data (Coburn & Talbert, 2006; Daly, 2012; Datnow & Park, 2018; Datnow, Park, & Kennedy-Lewis, 2013), and the character, norms, and power dynamics of social relationships shape data practices (Daly, 2012).

Individual and collaborative uses of data are impacted by the organizational, policy, and cultural contexts in which they are situated (Coburn & Turner, 2011, 2012). School leaders create the day-to-day structures surrounding data use, delineating professional learning teams, establishing routines, and enforcing protocols or norms of interaction around data. Federal, state, and district policies influence which data teachers and administrators utilize and how they are organized, imposing systems of meaning built on particular categories and classification systems (Coburn & Turner, 2011, 2012; Datnow & Hubbard, 2015; Henig,

2012). Moreover, data use varies between schools depending on their relationship to the accountability regime (Datnow & Hubbard, 2015; Jennings, 2012). Schools with a citation or at risk of sanctions will interact with performance data differently than schools in good standing. Diamond and Cooper (2007) found that cited schools in Chicago targeted their energies toward students just below the proficiency cutoff, while noncited schools were more likely to engage in comprehensive instructional and curricular changes that benefited all students.

Prior research has provided evidence for a framework that casts accountability policy as a context for school-level data use. In this chapter, I am setting forth the case of GMS to emphasize that this relationship is bidirectional. How teachers and school administrators respond to subgroup accountability pressure is influenced by, for example, their perception of the validity of standardized test scores and their trust in the state department of education that identifies lagging subgroups. Coburn and Talbert (2006) explain: "how individuals and groups respond to . . . accountability pressures is likely to be shaped by their preexisting beliefs related to evidence and research" (p. 491). I consider how teachers' and administrators' data practices—influenced by multiple factors beyond the policy context (e.g., school composition)—condition the potential of subgroup accountability.

Theoretical Framework

My attention to school-based data practices is derived from neo-institutional organizational theories that emphasize the agency of teachers and administrators in policy implementation. School actors have discretion in how they interpret and enact policies, which is necessary to apply uniform mandates to diverse local contexts (Ball, Maguire, Braun, & Hoskins, 2011; Lipsky, 1980). The translation of policy to practice depends in large part on how teachers and administrators marry policy demands, personal beliefs, and local capacity (Hallett & Ventresca, 2006; Lipsky, 1980; Spillane, 2006). Sensemaking theory, which assumes that understandings precede and inform practice, closely examines this cognitive process, identifying which factors are most significant to teachers' and administrators' reasoning (Coburn, 2004). In this chapter, I consider the importance of school demographics or, more specifically, economic and racial segregation, in teachers' and administrators' understanding of student performance data and, thereby, in their response to subgroup accountability pressure.

Methodology

This study is derived from a larger project about how policies designed to promote equity have an impact on how staff at economically and racially segregated schools such as GMS deliberate and make decisions about comparative student need. In accordance with neo-institutional organizational theory, I used ethnographic methods to document how teachers and administrators negotiated policy mandates, including subgroup accountability. I captured beliefs and behaviors that influenced the translation of policy to practice with participant observation and interviewing.

GMS is a public middle school (grades 6–8) in a large urban school district. I purposefully selected a high-poverty school without a student subgroup in the majority to highlight the dilemmas that staff faced in assessing and responding to student needs. GMS's student body is diverse for an economically and racially segregated school, with Black, Latinx, and Asian students each accounting for more than 20% but less than 50% of the student body. ELs and SWDs each constituted about 15% of the student body.

I was embedded within GMS for the 2014–2015 academic school year. I observed in classrooms and common school spaces (e.g., the cafeteria, hallways) for 122 days, and I conducted 73 semistructured interviews with students, teachers, parents, and school and district administrators. I also collected documents from the field, such as handouts with student performance data or meeting agendas. In this chapter, I draw primarily on participant observation of more than 100 staff meetings where student data or accountability policies were typically discussed and on 47 interviews with school and district staff. Interview protocols included questions that sought participants' perceptions about which students are most in need and which students thrive at GMS and about how they came to these conclusions.

I began analyzing field notes and interview transcripts with themes entailed by my research questions and theoretical framework (e.g., subgroup accountability policy, policy sensemaking, local resources, and capacity) and by open coding the data to generate an extensive list of emergent themes (e.g., data practices, standardized testing, concerns for compliance; Glaser & Strauss, 1967; Miles, Huberman, & Saldaña, 2014). I developed a codebook with the inductive and deductive themes and then recoded the entire data set with MAXQDA, a qualitative analysis software program.

Findings

Data Practices, Handed-Down and Homegrown

The state cited GMS for failing to meet AYP for SWDs, Asian students, and multiracial students. Despite the prospect of intensified sanctions from the state and a poor rating made public, the teachers and administrators at GMS did not demonstrate special concern for the state-identified subgroups. I argue elsewhere that the state's citation was delegitimized by a lack of transparency in the state's calculations, a concern about the validity of state standardized test scores, and a hesitation to make instructional changes in response to state accountability data (Garver, 2017). Here, I shift attention from the state's to GMS's data practices. With a commitment to equity but reservations about the state's data practices, the staff at GMS independently analyzed standardized test and classroom-based interim assessment data to come to their own conclusions about their achievement gaps. Subgroup accountability policy shaped GMS's data practices concretely and conceptually nonetheless, promoting some interpretations of data over others (Coburn & Turner, 2011; 2012; Datnow & Hubbard, 2015; Henig, 2012). GMS utilized state test data that was produced to comply with NCLB, and they relied on the same official subgroup categories monitored at the federal and state levels. Although the staff began the year analyzing the previous Spring's state test scores in isolation, they soon progressed to examining disparities in subgroup growth over time, in line with subgroup accountability. The policy's concrete and conceptual tools filtered down to GMS, where teachers and administrators used them to uniquely construct understandings about comparative student need.

Under the principal's guidance, administrators and teachers examined student performance data at staff meetings with the goals of identifying GMS's achievement gaps, assessing which gaps were most troubling, and developing corresponding responses. I employ the term *achievement gaps* throughout my findings as the teachers and administrators at GMS did—to refer to disparities in academic performance between student subgroups. While the staff framed its focus on achievement gaps as a concern for educational equity, some educational scholars have problematized how the term decontextualizes the academic performance of students in a school system that has afforded vastly unequal opportunities to students based on race and ethnicity (Ladson-Billings, 2006). Achievement gaps, a concept that emerged with the accountability movement at the end of the 20th century (Superfine, 2013), emphasizes outcomes and minimizes attention to inputs in analyzing disparities between student subgroups. Cognizant of the epistemological biases internal to the concept, I use the term *achievement gaps* for several reasons. First, the teachers and administrators at GMS repeatedly utilized the term in making sense of data. Neo-institutional theories of policy implementation, which emphasize practitioners' sensemaking in understanding how policies are put into practice, require consideration of emic understandings of subgroup accountability. Second, my focus in this chapter is the potential for subgroup accountability pressure to promote equity, and achievement gaps is a term that belongs to the lexicon of the accountability policy regime (Superfine, 2013). Subgroup accountability relies on achievement gaps to identify schools that are inequitable, and schools must eliminate achievement gaps to improve their accountability status. There may be reasons, such as those I suggest later, to question the promise of subgroup accountability; however, while it is active, *achievement gaps* is a term that remains relevant to the policy landscape and, thereby, to the practitioners tasked with interpreting and implementing federal and state mandates. Last, all the students at GMS lived in a high-poverty community, and fewer than 1% of the students were White. The academic year before my study, less than 30% of students tested proficient on the state math exam and less than 25% of students tested proficient on the state English language arts (ELA) exam. Most students at GMS had intensive needs and suffered from what Ladson-Billings (2006) refers to as the education debt. When teachers and administrators at GMS discussed their achievement gaps, they were referring to disparities among low-income, students of color. They used data as a tool to confront the murky problem of determining who was most in need in a school where all students had intensive needs. Attention to these within-school inequalities instead of the intra- and interdistrict disparities that research have shown are far more relevant to students' academic opportunities and achievement (Berliner, 2009; Downey & Condron, 2016; Owens, Reardon, & Jencks, 2016) is itself an artifact of subgroup accountability pressure and the logic of federal education policies.

Below, I highlight how teachers and administrators invoked GMS's demographic context and their perceptions of the student body to imbue their student performance data with meaning. I consider how these school-based data practices created conditions that potentially increased, decreased, or varied the pressure that subgroup accountability exerted. In the case of GMS, teachers' and administrators' data use both decreased the pressure of subgroup accountability and varied it by subgroup, which helps explain why the citation was insignificant to daily practice. GMS's racial and economic segregation contributed to making subgroup accountability less effective in promoting equity.

"We Could Have an Awesome Gap": Contextualizing Data With School Demographics

Teachers and administrators at GMS contextualized the achievement gaps they identified in their data within GMS's student demographics. They deliberated about the best way to organize and analyze the data considering the intensive needs across GMS's low-income student body and the fact that many students belonged to multiple low-performing subgroups. The organization of a data set encourages some understandings and discourages others (Simmons, 2012; Spillane, 2012). Through seemingly technical discussions about the appropriate units of comparison and the degree of disaggregation needed, teachers and administrators co-constructed understandings about the severity of their achievement gaps. By affecting the urgency around the achievement gaps identified in the data, GMS's data practices, in turn, conditioned the response to subgroup accountability pressure.

Units of Comparison and a High-Needs Student Body

Staff members at GMS played with different comparisons to identify achievement gaps in their data. In a staff meeting, the principal led the teachers in comparing subgroups' performances to schoolwide averages. At other times, staff members compared subgroups to subgroups, such as the Latinx to the Black average performance. At one bilingual education department meeting, an assistant principal congratulated the teachers that there was no significant gap between the state test scores of GMS's two largest EL populations—native Spanish speakers and native Bangla speakers. Depending on the comparison used, GMS's achievement gaps could appear more or less severe or could even disappear completely. For example, Spanish-speaking ELs did not appear to be lagging in comparison to Bangla-speaking ELs, but they did fall far behind the schoolwide average performance level.

Particular to schools such as GMS, where the student body is low-performing, within-school comparisons (e.g., subgroup-to-schoolwide and subgroup-to-subgroup) prioritized equity over excellence. More than 70% of students in math and more than 75% of students in ELA failed to test proficient on the state exam the year prior to my study.

Some teachers and administrators sought to contextualize the gaps at GMS through comparisons to student performance in other schools. One ELA teacher suggested that each subgroup should be compared to that subgroup's average performance in the district: "It would be good to look at how they did relative to other students in the city." This teacher was not ready to conclude that a subgroup at GMS was struggling without establishing that their performance was unusually low for the district. An assistant principal proposed that GMS's gaps might not be so bad when juxtaposed to performance data from schools with similar demographics:

> Do they break this data down, do they compare it to other schools, similar schools? . . . Are we equivalent, below, about the same? . . . Is it something specific to here? . . . The problem is we are not looking at other schools . . . we could have an awesome gap.

The oxymoronic notion of an "awesome gap" only became possible in comparing GMS to a cohort of similar schools with high-need student bodies. In this way, the assistant principal insinuated that GMS's economic and racial segregation not only contributed to the school's overall low performance but also helped explain disparities among subgroups. Teachers' and administrators' efforts to compare GMS to other schools in the district diminished the gravity of the school's achievement gaps.

The intensive needs of GMS's student body were invoked by staff members to temper the urgency around equity work and, thereby, created conditions that lessened the intensity of subgroup accountability pressure.

Disaggregation and Students Who Belong to Multiple Low-Performing Subgroups

The prevalence of students at GMS who belonged to multiple low-performing subgroups complicated teachers' and administrators' efforts to understand the achievement gaps in their data. The large number of low-performing Black male students in special education led staff members to question which subgroup should be of most concern. Staff members were uncertain whether Black boys' data looked poor because they were overrepresented among low-performing SWDs or whether GMS had a racial and/or gender gap. Analyzing the state data at an administrative meeting, the principal expressed a desire to better pinpoint the students in need:

> If a high concentration of low-performing SWDs are Black students it would influence the numbers significantly, and the same thing with males. . . . What I'd like to look at is how much of the gap remains when you take out the males or SWDs.

The principal was hopeful that their data analyses could help them understand whether GMS primarily had a weakness in working with boys, Black students, or students with disabilities.

Racial and gender disproportionality in special and bilingual education complicated GMS's efforts to isolate subgroup categories that accounted for the most variance in performance, absent more advanced statistical techniques. (See Lachat and Smith, 2005, on how schools' technological capacities to disaggregate data impact their data use.) While SWDs tended to be Black and male, ELs tended to be Latinx and Asian at GMS. The lack of clarity about which subgroup should be of most concern meant that doubt surrounded the identification of any achievement gap in GMS's data. In this way, the prevalence of students in multiple low-performing subgroups created conditions that lessened the pressure exerted by a citation under subgroup accountability policy.

"An Acceptable Gap": Interpreting Data Through Subgroup-Specific Perceptions

Teachers' and administrators' subgroup-specific perceptions of students also shaped how data were interpreted (Datnow & Park, 2018). Most notable was the distinction between the lagging performance of SWDs and ELs versus racial and gender subgroups. While SWDs and ELs had characteristics that justified their inferior performance, Latinx, Black, and male students did not, according to the logic expressed in conversations surrounding GMS's achievement gaps. In turn, disparities related to disability or language status garnered less anxiety than those related to race and gender. These differences in subgroup-specific perceptions may mediate how a citation is received, suggesting that subgroup accountability pressure is not uniform, but rather differentiated by the subgroup identified.

After examining the state test data for disparities between subgroups in an administrative meeting, the principal asked the assistant principals (APs) to develop goals for each gap—a reasonable gap GMS can "be OK with" for each lagging subgroup. The notion that some gaps were "acceptable" emerged from the distinctions made between ELs/SWDs and gender/racial subgroups, as the following field notes demonstrate:

> The principal draws attention to the achievement gap between ELs and non-ELs: "It is a 15 point gap. Do we want that gap to be zero? . . . Five points or less?" AP 1 responds, "yeah, you want to set a realistic goal." AP 2 suggests they need more information in order to set a goal, but then adds: "Off the top of my head, three to five percent." "So you want to reduce this here 15% gap to a five percent gap?" the principal clarifies. AP 2 responds: "Yep, I think that's realistic." "How about students with disabilities?" the principal asks. AP 3 notes, "that's a big gap." The principal asks them again: "What would be acceptable? What wouldn't look so abhorrent?" AP 1 resolves that "it should be zero then." AP 3: "Gut reaction is five." "Why five?" AP 1 questions. The principal jumps in: "They have learning disabilities." AP 1 inquires why one group should achieve less than any other group. The principal continues to explain: "We are looking at people with cognitive impairments." AP 1 concedes that a gap makes sense for students with disabilities. The principal returns to finding an achievement gap to aim for: "What number would feel like more in the ballpark?" AP 2: "Fifteen to 20 percent."

Although AP 1 suggested that they should aim for no gaps, the administrators came to a consensus that disparities were reasonable in comparing ELs to non-ELs and SWDs to non-SWDs. According to their reasoning, SWDs' impairments justified a gap at least three times as large as a gap appropriate for ELs. Their beliefs align with prior research that has shown that state and school administrators find AYP requirements for ELs and SWDs unreasonable because of the constant arrival of ELs to the US and of SWDs' learning difficulties (Center on Education Policy, 2003; DeSimone, 2009). At GMS, what constituted a reasonable disparity (if any disparity at all was reasonable) varied by subgroup and, thereby, conditioned how gaps identified in the data were received. Revealing a disability gap in the data was far less likely to cause alarm than an EL gap, and both were less urgent than gender or race gaps.

The administrators were wary of communicating these differential expectations to their staff, demonstrating awareness of their power as 'sense givers' for teachers (Coburn, 2005; Weick, Sutcliffe, & Obstfeld, 2005). They worried that such beliefs would encourage teachers to generate excuses for the lagging performance of some subgroups and undermine their sense of ownership for their students' performance. In front of the teachers, the principal and the APs presented unwavering disapproval of any achievement gaps. In fact, the principal anticipated the exceptional status that ELs and SWDs had in the minds of many educators when addressing teachers at a staff meeting: "We should not just be taking it for granted that IEP [Individualized Education Plan] students will do worse . . . there's something wrong about that . . . we can't take that for granted."

Despite these efforts, teachers expressed beliefs similar to those that the administrators discussed in private. At an ELA department meeting, the literacy coach communicated the principal's focus on achievement gaps to her team, but she was met with some resistance:

LITERACY COACH: We've got to close this achievement gap . . . especially with IEP students and ELs . . .
TEACHER: I can't see closing the gap with special education and ELs with the general population. . . . You can't in the same amount of time, do the same thing with ELs or with SWDs. They need more time!

According to this teacher, SWDs and ELs faced particular challenges that made the expectation they would achieve at the same rate as general education students unrealistic. She reasoned that the amount of instructional time that ELs and SWDs received during the school year did not allow them to catch up to their general education peers.

Subgroup-specific perceptions, which were reinforced through social interactions such as the administrative and department meetings described above (Horn, 2007), meant that gaps identified in student performance data related to disability and language status garnered less urgency than those related to race and gender at GMS. At stake was the normalization and, thereby, the persistence of disability and language gaps.

Drawing on attribution theory, Bertrand and Marsh (2015) similarly argue that teachers' perceptions of SWDs and ELs influence how they make sense of data related to these two subgroups. They find that teachers' lowered academic expectations for ELs and SWDs make them more likely to attribute their performance (as evidenced by data) to student characteristics and less likely to instruction or to the nature of the test. Teachers' decreased self-efficacy with ELs and SWDs meant that it was less likely they would make instructional changes in response to these subgroups' data. I propose that subgroup-specific perceptions also condition how a school receives its citation under subgroup accountability, which is based on student achievement data.

In the context of subgroup-specific perceptions, a school's response to subgroup accountability would likely vary. A school cited for the lagging performance of racial or gender subgroups is more likely to respond to a citation with urgency than schools cited for the performance of ELs and SWDs. These subgroup-specific perceptions help explain why GMS did not make a particular effort to improve the performance of SWDs, one of the subgroups cited by the state.

Interventions for Black Boys

GMS's efforts to address its achievement gaps reflect school-based data practices rather than the state's determinations under subgroup accountability. The teachers and administrators at GMS drew on their analyses of student performance data to resolve that Black boys suffered from the most acute achievement gap at GMS. How educators make sense of data influences their subsequent instructional and organizational response (Bertrand & Marsh, 2015; Horn, 2007), and changes to the curriculum or to student grouping are more typical than instructional reforms that require critical self-reflection and result in more significant improvements to student learning (Bocala & Boudett, 2015; Marsh, Bertrand, & Huguet, 2015). In accordance with this research, at GMS, curricular reforms were instated that aimed to better engage Black boys (e.g., the inclusion of more male authors in ELA) and behavioral incentives that the staff reasoned would appeal to Black boys were introduced (e.g., sports video games during lunch). GMS's efforts to address subgroup inequalities were piecemeal, and they did not target the subgroups cited by the state, suggesting that the pressure exerted by subgroup accountability was minimal.

Conclusion

Prior research has found that the effects of subgroup accountability pressure are uneven; in some cases, identified subgroups saw progress the year following a citation, and in other cases, they did not. This variation can be traced, in part, to how practitioners understand and, thereby, respond to a citation. In this chapter, I draw on an ethnographic study of a middle school to argue that teachers' and administrators' data practices mediate the potential of subgroup accountability policy to promote equity. Technical discussions about data disaggregation and the most appropriate units of comparison, as well as debates about how to interpret data based on the subgroup at issue served as sites where staff co-constructed understandings about the gravity of GMS's achievement gaps. By invoking the intensive needs of the student body and subgroup-specific perceptions during these interactions, teachers and administrators decreased the urgency around GMS's achievement gaps and, thereby, created conditions that lessened the pressure exerted by subgroup accountability.

Although subgroup accountability is designed to exert uniform pressure across schools and subgroups, findings from GMS indicate that the effects of subgroup accountability vary based on (1) school demographics and (2) teachers' and administrators' perceptions of students.

Subgroup accountability is applied in a uniform manner across all schools and thereby constitutes one part of the effort to bring about educational equity without integration (Superfine, 2013). However, teachers and administrators understood the intensive needs of GMS's economically and racially segregated student body as relevant to their analysis and interpretation of student achievement data. GMS's demographics decreased the urgency and increased the ambiguity surrounding their achievement gaps, creating conditions that minimized subgroup accountability's influence. In contrast to staff at GMS, teachers and administrators at low-poverty, high-performing schools may respond to a citation with urgency since the lagging performance of a student subgroup would be difficult to attribute to the challenges students bring to school. Further research is needed to compare the effects of receiving a citation in high-poverty and low-poverty schools.

Past research has shown that racial and economic segregation between and within schools is the most important factor that predicts student achievement. In this chapter, I suggest that while segregation is ignored by accountability policies that attempt to promote equity, it may actively undermine their success. The primary federal policy lever for promoting equity in schools is misaligned with the segregated landscape of US schools.

Findings at GMS also suggest that teachers and administrators respond differently to a citation depending on the subgroup at issue. Staff believed that the lagging performance of ELs and SWDs were reasonable to a certain extent, in contrast to racial and gender achievement gaps. Unless practitioners hold similar expectations for all students, the pressure of subgroup accountability will vary by subgroup. Schools cited for gender and racial achievement gaps may be more likely to respond to subgroup accountability than schools cited for disability- and language-based gaps. Studies across school sites are needed to investigate the effects of subgroup accountability based on the subgroup(s) identified. In schools where staff have high expectations of low-income students and perceptions about students do not vary significantly by subgroup, the pressure of subgroup accountability is likely to have a more uniform and intense effect. The belief that SWDs and ELs can learn at a comparable rate as general education students is necessary for subgroup accountability to effectively pressure schools to focus their energies on these two subgroups. Teacher and administrator preparation programs, as well as ongoing training for practicing professionals that promotes high expectations for all students, provide a foundation for equity-oriented policy.

Subgroup accountability policy relies on the assumption that teachers and administrators will respond to a citation based on achievement data by providing targeted supports to the state-identified subgroups. However, the progression from data to practice is not linear. Subgroup accountability would be more effective at fulfilling its intentions if it accounted for the ways that school-based data practices mediate a school's response to its citation. Policymakers assume that teachers and administrators will rationally transform a citation into practice even when they are excluded from the data analysis process that triggers a citation. Bringing school-based actors closer to the data analysis process by, for example, creating more transparency around the state's calculations and holding training to walk staff through the state's process for citing a school, may lead teachers and administrators to construct understandings of student achievement data that more closely align with the state's conclusions. Moreover, these efforts would need to be informed by further research on the relationship between segregation and school-based data practices. The case of GMS suggests that this relationship is one more reason that subgroup accountability policy is unlikely to compensate for the inequalities produced by economic and racial segregation.

Acknowledgments

This article is based on research that was made possible in part by financial assistance from the Ruth Landes Memorial Research Fund, a program of the Reed Foundation.

Note

1. The names of the school and all individuals are pseudonyms to maintain confidentiality. I also report approximate student demographic and performance data to maintain confidentiality.

References

Ball, S. J., Maguire, M., Braun, A., & Hoskins, K. (2011). Policy actors: Doing policy work in schools. *Discourse: Studies in the Cultural Politics of Education*, 32(4), 625–639.

Berliner, D. C. (2009). *Poverty and potential: Out-of-school factors and school success*. Boulder and Tempe: Education and the Public Interest Center & Education Policy Research Unit.

Bertrand, M., & Marsh, J. A. (2015). Teachers' sensemaking of data and implications for equity. *American Educational Research Journal*, 52(5), 861–893.

Bocala, C., & Boudett, K. P. (2015). Teaching educators habits of mind for using data wisely. *Teachers College Record, 117*(4), 1–20.

Booher-Jennings, J. (2005). Below the bubble: "Educational triage" and the Texas accountability system. *American Educational Research Journal, 42*(2), 231–268.

Center on Education Policy. (2003). *From the capital to the classroom: State and federal efforts to implement the No Child Left Behind Act.* Washington, DC: Author.

Coburn, C. E. (2004). Beyond decoupling: Rethinking the relationship between the institutional environment and the classroom. *Sociology of Education, 77*(3), 211–244.

Coburn, C. E. (2005). Shaping teacher sensemaking: School leaders and the enactment of reading policy. *Educational Policy, 19*(3), 476–509.

Coburn, C. E., & Talbert, J. E. (2006). Conceptions of evidence use in school districts: Mapping the terrain. *American Journal of Education, 112*(4), 469–495.

Coburn, C. E., & Turner, E. O. (2011). Research on data use: A framework and analysis. *Measurement, 9*(4), 173–206.

Coburn, C. E., & Turner, E. O. (2012). The practice of data use: An introduction. *American Journal of Education, 118*(2), 99–111.

Daly, A. (2012). Data, dyads, and dynamics: Exploring data use and social networks in educational improvement. *Teachers College Record, 114*(11), 1–38.

Datnow, A., & Hubbard, L. (2015). Teachers' use of assessment data to inform instruction: Lessons from the past and prospects for the future. *Teachers College Record, 117*(4), 1–26.

Datnow, A., & Park, V. (2018). Opening or closing doors for students? Equity and data use in schools. *Journal of Educational Change, 19*(2), 131–152.

Datnow, A., Park, V., & Kennedy-Lewis, B. L. (2012). High school teachers' use of data to inform instruction. *Journal of Education for Students Placed at Risk, 17*(4), 247–265.

Datnow, A., Park, V., & Kennedy-Lewis, B. L. (2013). Affordances and constraints in the context of teacher collaboration for the purpose of data use. *Journal of Educational Administration, 51*(3), 341–362.

Downey, D. B., & Condron, D. J. (2016). Fifty years since the Coleman Report: Rethinking the relationship between schools and inequality. *Sociology of Education, 89*(3), 207–220.

DeSimone, J. R. (2009). Principals' perceptions of the No Child Left Behind's adequate yearly progress requirements as it relates to students with special needs. *Journal of Education and Human Development, 3*(1), 1–9.

Diamond, J. B., & Cooper, K. (2007). The uses of testing data in urban elementary schools: Some lessons from Chicago. *National Society for the Study of Education Yearbook, 106*(1), 241–263.

Farley-Ripple, E., & Buttram, J. (2015). The development of capacity for data use: The role of teacher networks in an elementary school. *Teachers College Record, 117*(4), 1–34.

Garver, R. (2017). Orienting schools toward equity: Subgroup accountability pressure and school-level responses. *The Educational Forum, 81*(2), 160–174.

Glaser, B. G., & Strauss, A. L. (1967). *The discovery of grounded theory: Strategies for qualitative research.* Chicago: Aldine.

Hallett, T., & Ventresca, M. J. (2006). Inhabited institutions: Social interactions and organizational forms in Gouldner's *Patterns of Industrial Bureaucracy. Theory and Society, 35*(2), 213–236.

Hemelt, S. W. (2011). Performance effects of failure to make Adequate Yearly Progress (AYP): Evidence from a regression discontinuity framework. *Economics of Education Review*, *30*(4), 702–723.

Henig, J. R. (2012). The politics of data use. *Teachers College Record*, *114*(11), 1–32.

Horn, I. S. (2007). Fast kids, slow kids, lazy kids: Framing the mismatch problem in mathematics teachers' conversations. *Journal of the Learning Sciences*, *16*(1), 37–79.

Horn, I. S., Kane, B. D., & Wilson, J. (2015). Making sense of student performance data: Data use logics and mathematics teachers' learning opportunities. *American Educational Research Journal*, *52*(2), 208–242.

Ingram, D., Louis, K. S., & Schroeder, R. G. (2004). Accountability policies and teacher decision making: Barrier to the use of data to improve practice. *Teachers College Record*, *106*(6), 1258–1287.

Jennings, J. L. (2012). The effects of accountability system design on teachers' use of test score data. *Teachers College Record*, *114*(11), 1–23.

Jimerson, J. B. (2014). Thinking about data: Exploring the development of mental models for "data use" among teachers and school leaders. *Studies in Educational Evaluation*, *42*, 5–14.

Krieg, J. M. (2011). Which students are left behind? The racial impacts of the No Child Left Behind Act. *Economics of Education Review*, *30*(4), 654–664.

Lachat, M. A., & Smith, S. (2005). Practices that support data use in urban high schools. *Journal of Education for Students Placed at Risk*, *10*(3), 333–349.

Ladson-Billings, G. (2006). From the achievement gap to the education debt: Understanding achievement in US schools. *Educational Researcher*, *35*(7), 3–12.

Lauen, D., & Gaddis, M. (2012). Shining a light or fumbling in the dark? The effects of NCLB's subgroup-specific accountability pressure on student performance. *Educational Evaluation and Policy Analysis*, *34*(2), 185–208.

Lipsky, M. (1980). *Street-level bureaucracy: Dilemmas of the individual in public services*. New York, NY: Russell Sage Foundation.

Marsh, J. A. (2012). Interventions promoting educators' use of data: Research insights and gaps. *Teachers College Record*, *114*(11), 1–48.

Marsh, J. A., Bertrand, M., & Huguet, A. (2015). Using data to alter instructional practice: The mediating role of coaches and professional learning communities. *Teachers College Record*, *117*(4), 1–41.

Miles, M. B., Huberman, A. M., & Saldaña, J. (2014). *Qualitative data analysis: A methods sourcebook* (3rd ed.). Thousand Oaks, CA: Sage Publications.

Owens, A., Reardon, S. F., & Jencks, C. (2016). Income segregation between schools and school districts. *American Educational Research Journal*, *53*(4), 1159–1197.

Roderick, M. (2012). Drowning in data but thirsty for analysis: Commentary on "interventions to promote data use." *Teachers College Record*, *114*(11), 1–9.

Simmons, W. (2012). Data as a lever for improving instruction and student achievement. *Teachers College Record*, *114*(11), 1–9.

Spillane, J. P. (2006). *Standards deviation: How schools misunderstand education policy*. Cambridge, MA: Harvard University Press.

Spillane, J. P. (2012). Data in practice: Conceptualizing the data-based decision-making phenomena. *American Journal of Education*, *118*(2), 1–29.

Superfine, B. M. (2013). *Equality in education law and policy: 1954–2010*. Cambridge: Cambridge University Press.

Vasquez Heilig, J., & Darling-Hammond, L. (2008). Accountability Texas-style: The progress and learning of urban minority students in a high-stakes testing context. *Educational Evaluation and Policy Analysis, 30*(2), 75–110.

Weick, K. E., Sutcliffe, K. M., & Obstfeld, D. (2005). Organizing and the process of sensemaking. *Organization Science, 16*(4), 409–421.

Weinbaum, E. H., Weiss, M. J., & Beaver, J. K. (2012). *Learning from NCLB: School responses to accountability pressure and student subgroup performance.* (CPRE Policy Briefs). Retrieved from http://repository.upenn.edu/cpre_policybriefs/42

Part III
The Legacy and Futures of Special Education

10 The Individuals With Disabilities Education Act

The Further Marginalization of Racially and Ethnically Diverse Students for More Than 40 Years

Jennifer M. McKenzie and Ambra L. Green

Public Law 94–142 (P.L. 94–142) in 1975 was the first law enacted by Congress on behalf of the education of students with special needs. P.L. 94–142, also termed the Education for All Handicapped Children Act (EAHCA), mandated that students with disabilities had the right to "(a) nondiscriminatory testing, evaluation, and placement procedures; (b) be educated in the least restrictive environment; (c) procedural due process, including parent involvement; and (d) a free appropriate public education" (Yell, Rogers, & Lodge Rogers, 1998, p. 226). This federal mandate also guaranteed funding to states to assist them with the education of students with special needs. In return for funding, states were obligated to guarantee a free appropriate public education (FAPE) to students with disabilities. This chapter focuses on the EAHCA, now referred to as the Individuals with Disabilities Education Act (IDEA), and the consequences of this law that, arguably, maintain the overrepresentation of racially and ethnically diverse (R/ED) students with disabilities. First, the chapter examines the spirit and stated intent of IDEA. Presented second is a discussion of the overrepresentation of R/ED students with disabilities in special education categories, placement, and exclusionary discipline practices and how teacher preparation programs perseverate such inequities. Last, the chapter discusses recommendations for policy, teacher licensure, and teacher preparation programs.

SPIRIT AND INTENT OF IDEA

The essence of the IDEA has changed very little since 1975: special education exists to provide educational services to students who have a disability covered by the law and need special education services to learn (Yell, Shriner, & Katsiyannis, 2006). The act's main purpose has always been to ensure "that all children with disabilities have available to them an free appropriate public education that emphasizes special education and related services designed to meet their unique needs and prepare them for further education, employment, and independent living" (IDEA, 20 USC §1400 (d)(l)(A)). IDEA contains several major principles on which to base discussion, including zero reject, nondiscriminatory assessment procedures, and provision of FAPE.

Prior to the enactment of EAHCA in 1975, Congress found the educational needs of millions of children with disabilities were not being met for several reasons. Many children were excluded completely from public schools and from being educated with nondisabled peers. Many others, although they attended public schools, did not receive appropriate educational services that met their unique needs either due to lack of adequate resources within the public school or undiagnosed disabilities (IDEA, 20 USC §1400 (c)(2)). From these issues arose the critical concept of zero reject. Zero reject asserts that no student may be excluded from public education on the basis of disability, regardless of the severity of the disability or the available resources of the public school (West & Schaefer Whitby, 2008). The act requires states to actively identify and evaluate students who are in need of special education and related services and to develop individualized education programs (IEP) for each student determined eligible (IDEA, 20 USC §1412 (3)(A)(4)). In order to determine student eligibility under the act, assessment procedures were developed.

According to IDEA, all children who are suspected of having a disability must be given a comprehensive assessment prior to determining their eligibility for special education. Furthermore, this assessment must be chosen and administered in such a way as to not discriminate against individuals from different cultures or who speak languages other than English (Smith, 2005), and consideration must be given to the impacts of socioeconomic status and other variables on evaluation outcomes (Boone & King-Berry, 2007). In addition, the evaluation process must be multidisciplinary, consisting of several types of assessments, to avoid an overreliance on any one measure that may be culturally biased (Boone & King-Berry, 2007). These provisions were incorporated to help ensure all students received an objective and unbiased assessment to inform decisions of eligibility and provision of appropriate services under the act.

The keystone principle of IDEA is the provision of FAPE to all students found eligible under the act. The original EAHCA defined FAPE as special education and related services that

(A) Are provided at public expense, under public supervision and direction, and without charge,
(B) Meet standards of the State educational agency,
(C) Include an appropriate preschool, elementary, or secondary school education in the state involved, and
(D) Are provided in conformity with the individualized education program. (IDEA, 20 U.S.C. § 1401(a)(18))

The pivotal component to providing FAPE is for school personnel to develop and implement an educational program that consists of specially designed instruction to meet the unique needs of each child with a disability (IDEA, 20 U.S.C. § 1401(a)(16)). From student to student, FAPE can look substantially different due to the individualized nature of the approach. The question of what actually constitutes FAPE has resulted in much controversy and debate and has frequently been the subject of due process hearings and court cases (Yell, Katsiyannis, & Hazelkorn, 2007). Mostly absent from the discussion, however, are the disparities in educational equity for R/ED students. Research has clearly documented that, when compared to the academic achievement of their White peers, students of color consistently perform at lower rates (Vanneman, Hamilton, Baldwin Anderson, & Rahman, 2009). Research into this discrepancy revealed an opportunity gap, in which students of color are more likely to be educated in underresourced educational settings, taught by underprepared or less experienced teachers, and have a lack of access to high-quality instruction and academic experiences (Barnett, Carolan, & Johns, 2013). Current legal guidance under IDEA says that school districts must provide sufficient instruction, support, and services to enable a child with a disability to benefit educationally and to provide equal educational opportunity (Yell et al., 2007). It can be argued that R/ED students with disabilities are not being provided with the instruction, support, and services to enable equal access and educational opportunities compared to that provided to their White peers, solely on the basis of overall lack of equity in educational opportunities.

Although it is well known in the educational community that schools serving primarily R/ED students are underresourced, very little discourse has occurred regarding solutions, and few concrete steps have been taken to remedy the issue of inequitable and homogenous education norms that privilege White students and further ostracize R/ED students. It should come as little surprise, considering those who determine the educational fate of R/ED students do not live in the communities these schools serve and are not part of these oppressed groups. The educational workforce, including lawmakers, school and district administrators, and classroom teachers, is primarily composed of the White middle class. This cultural mismatch leads to the ignoring of inequitable special education decisions and already-marginalized students becoming all but invisible.

It is clear that Congress intended the IDEA to be a guarantee of access to public education for all students with disabilities. Through a progression of reauthorizations, the spirit of the law has expanded far beyond access into a legal standard for educational appropriateness and equal educational opportunity for students with special needs. Despite this lofty effort, the *interpretation and implementation* of the federal law have resulted in negative consequences for students from R/ED backgrounds.

OVERREPRESENTATION OF R/ED STUDENTS RECEIVING SPECIAL EDUCATION SERVICES

About the same time as the passage of EAHCA, many researchers documented disproportionality, specifically overrepresentation, in special education services received by students from R/ED backgrounds (Dunn, 1968; Finn, 1982; Mercer, 1973). Disproportionality refers to a particular racial or ethnic group represented in a given category (i.e., special education disability categories or exclusionary discipline practices) at a higher or lower rate than other racial/ethnic groups (Skiba, Albrecht, & Losen, 2013). Overrepresentation is too many individuals of a specific group represented in a designated category than would be expected given the total population of that group. The overrepresentation of students from R/ED backgrounds has typically been found in special education categories where the identification of individuals is subjective, meaning the mostly White, middle-class stakeholders in educational decision-making positions have latitude in applying special education eligibility criteria. These categories include Learning Disabilities (LD), Intellectual Disability (ID), and Emotional and Behavioral Disorder (EBD; Skiba et al., 2013). Nationally, patterns reflecting disproportionality for students from R/ED backgrounds have been fairly consistent with minimal variability overtime (Chinn & Hughes, 1987; Losen & Orfield, 2002; Parrish, 2002; Skiba et al., 2013; Sullivan & Bal, 2013; US Department of Education, 2013). Students with disabilities from R/ED environments are overrepresented in IDEA disabilities categories, restrictive classroom environments, and exclusionary discipline practices.

IDEA Disability Categories

Concern about disproportionality in special education disability categories mainly centers on the subjective diagnoses of disabilities such as LD, ID, and EBD, rather than in objective disability categories, like hearing or visual impairments and orthopedic impairments (Skiba et al., 2013). As of 2008, African American students represented about 17% of the public school population and 20% of students in special education. Among students with disabilities, African American students were, and remain, overrepresented in all subjective categories: LD (21.51%), EBD (28.74%), and ID (31.48%; Aud, Fox, & Kewal Ramani, 2010). These data represent a steady increase in special education referrals. Federal law offers little guidance in the process of assessment and referral, leaving states to develop their own systems and criteria for eligibility. This results in vast differences between and within states with respect to assessment procedures, as well as which students get identified (MacMillan & Reschly, 1998).

Scholars agree that disproportionality in the subjective, high-incidence categories occur as a result of intricate interactions between student characteristics, teacher preparation, and attitudes resulting in bias and process and structural inequities (Sullivan & Bal, 2013). When members of the dominant majority are given the power to make nearly all educational decisions, including special education eligibility, it is to be expected that those decisions will be made using the lens of "deficit paradigm" that explains the lack of success in school as being due to problems with students, their families, their culture, or their communities (Weiner, 2003). Although these beliefs may remain unspoken, the racism or bias they contain corrupts the decision-making of those who hold them. This is especially true in judgments of acceptable social behaviors, as perceptions of behavior are so culturally biased and White teachers may not understand or may disregard the culturally appropriate behaviors of their R/ED students.

Additionally, assessment procedures for special education eligibility generally include standardized, norm-referenced cognitive and academic assessments to gather information regarding student functioning. Use of these assessments with students from R/ED backgrounds is problematic because cultural knowledge influences test performance. Assessments reflect the values and beliefs of the culture in which they were developed, creating an implicit cultural bias (Sattler, 1992). Often special education professionals put a significant amount of trust in standardized assessment scores with little regard to their appropriateness for R/ED students. These underresourced students may obtain lower scores on IQ tests simply because the assessment does not reflect their cultural and educational experiences, which results in an increased likelihood of being identified as having an intellectual disability.

Restrictive Classroom Environments

Educational placements and settings are less researched areas of disproportionality with most of the research conducted at the state and district levels (Fierros & Conroy, 2002; Serwatka, Deering, & Grant, 1995; Skiba, Poloni-Staudinger, Gallini, Simmons, & Feggins-Azziz, 2006), which is a major limitation in the field. Nonetheless, when compared to other disability categories, students with EBD are more likely to be educated in more restrictive environments (Smith, Katsiyannis, & Ryan, 2011; US DOE, 2013). National data from the Office of Special Education Programs' Annual Report to Congress (USDOE, 2013), demonstrates that about 45% of students with EBD are served inside the general education class 80% or more of the school day, about 18% are served inside general education classes between 40% and 79% of the day, and 20% are served inside the general education classroom 20% or less of the day.

There are further concerns that students with EBD who are also R/ED make up the percentage of students more frequently placed in more restrictive and segregated educational settings (Albrecht, Skiba, Losen,

Chung, & Middelberg, 2012). Using one year of a single state's data, Skiba and colleagues (2006) explored the extent to which African American students were placed in more and less restrictive settings within five disability categories, one being EBD. The statewide analysis indicated that while comprising 23.2% of the total EBD population, African American students represented only 14.2% of the students with EBD in general education classrooms (defined by the state statute as removal from general education for less than 21% of the school day) and 26.2% of students with EBD in separate classrooms (defined by the state statute as removal from general education settings for more than 60% of the school day). African American students with EBD were 1.2 times more likely than peers with the same disability to be placed in separate classrooms and, therefore, about 50% less likely to be placed in general education classrooms (Skiba et al., 2006).

Although the most overrepresented ethnic group in all subjective special education disability categories and therefore, most researched, African American students are not the only ethnic group receiving instruction in restrictive environments. Once identified, students from R/ED backgrounds are *all* more likely to be placed in more restrictive classrooms than their White peers (Fierros & Conroy, 2002). Obviously, this results in racial and ethnic segregation in public schools under the guise of special education. There is no scientifically based reason why R/ED students should be placed in more restrictive settings at rates higher than their White peers, other than inherent racism by the adults on IEP teams tasked with making these placements. The only ones who benefit from this segregated system are the general education teachers and administrators whose jobs are made easier by avoiding interactions with students whose behavior and learning differences make them uncomfortable. What needs to be understood is the ability to opt out of discomfort is part of White privilege, and it sustains systematic racism in schools.

Exclusionary Discipline Practices

Current disciplinary practices and policies in schools, such as zero tolerance, seem to have increased the vulnerability for R/ED students (Krezmien, Leone, & Achilles, 2006; Losen, Ee, Hodson, & Martinez, 2015). Out-of-school suspension of students with disabilities has increased over time (Krezmien et al., 2006; Zhang, Katsiyannis, & Herbst, 2004). Nationally, R/ED students with disabilities are at a greater risk of exclusionary discipline practices (Krezmien et al., 2006). In particular, African American students with disabilities represent about 19% of the total population but are 2.8 times more likely than other students to receive at least one of the categories of disciplinary exclusions monitored by IDEA (i.e., ISS, OSS, and expulsion; OCR, 2014; Skiba et al., 2013). Of R/ED student with disabilities, more than 25% of males and nearly 20% of girls, with the exception of Latino/Hispanic and Asian students, receive OSS (OCR, 2014).

In the 2004 IDEA reauthorization, racial and ethnic disproportionality in special education was designated one of the top three priorities by Congress (Albrecht et al., 2012). Under the new provisions, states are required to monitor disproportionality, or disproportionate representation as termed in IDEA, by race or ethnicity in disability categories, special education placements, and exclusionary discipline practices. The reauthorization included little to no guidance regarding steps to remedy identified problems and thus has maintained these disparities for nearly 50 years. For example, in OSEP's 35th Annual Report to Congress, African American students were 1.49 times more likely to be identified as EBD than their non–African American peers (USDOE, 2013), the same rate Oswald and colleagues reported in 1999 (Oswald, Coutinho, Best, & Singh, 1999). In addition to the disparities found among students from R/ED backgrounds in K–12 settings, the March 2014 OCR data collection survey found new evidence that although African American preschool students represent 18% of students enrolled in preschool settings, they are receiving suspensions at 42% (once) and 48% (multiple times; OCR, 2014). It would appear special education policy has identified disproportionality as a problem but have been slow to propose efficacious solutions.

The issue of disproportionality becomes even more problematic and questions the moral and ethical practices of education stakeholders when we consider that the nation's schools are becoming more racially, ethnically, culturally, and linguistically diverse (Oswald et al., 1999), yet the diversity of educational stakeholders is not. For example, according to the National Center for Education Statistics, in 1998 R/ED students consisted of approximately 32% of the total public school population while the population of White students was about 68%. Twenty years later, the percentage of R/ED students increased to 45% while the White population decreased to 55% (Aud et al., 2010), nearly eliminating the population gap between the "majority" and "minority" students in public schools. However, the racial and ethnic composition of teachers and school psychologists or diagnosticians in public schools is significantly less diverse than the student population (Brown-Jeffy & Cooper, 2011). In the annual report, *The Condition of Education (2011)*, the U.S. Department of Education provides three facts: (a) The American public education system is more diverse than ever before, (b) the diversity is expected to continue, and, conversely, (c) the racial and ethnic demographics of educators continue to remain stable; approximately 85% of teachers are White and 75% are female (Aud et al., 2011). While the predominately White workforce of teachers is likely more than capable of teaching students from various races and ethnicities, current research suggests there may be a cultural mismatch between the teachers and their multicultural students (Skiba et al., 2008). The cultural mismatch hypothesis holds that teachers are more likely to inappropriately refer, identify, make placements for, and discipline R/ED students because they do not understand or are dismissive of their cultures (Skiba et al., 2008). Therefore, reform regarding teacher licensure requirements and preparation programs are necessary to address cultural differences between the adult and the student.

TEACHER PREPARATION PROGRAMS: ISSUES PERPETUATING MARGINALIZATION

Teacher preparation programs are driven by state policy decisions, such as licensure requirements. Institutes of higher education's (IHEs') plan course requirements and sequences based on what their teacher candidates will be required to know and be able to do to obtain full licensure. While training in special education law and procedures is included in preparation for special educators, IDEA does not provide adequate guidance regarding decision-making or educational processes that could decrease disproportionality. Due to this and several other factors, educators carry forward their own biases into the referral process and into the classroom. Furthermore, if White teachers, who make up the majority of the teaching force, are not trained in culturally responsive practices and teachers from R/ED backgrounds are absent from the teaching environment, the concerns of R/ED students and their parents regarding their special education needs may continue to be silenced.

Composition of the Teaching Force

Recruitment and retention of teachers from R/ED backgrounds have been a critical issue in the field of education for decades (Valle-Riestra, Shealey, & Cramer, 2011). Although the 2004 reauthorization of IDEA included a significant focus on the preparation of "highly qualified" special educators, missing is the discussion of how to prepare educators who place a student's culture, values, and beliefs at the center of the teaching process (Valle-Riestra et al., 2011). Students from R/ED backgrounds, many of whom live in poverty, are most likely to be taught by inexperienced teachers in settings with limited resources (Berry, 2008). It is essential that preparation programs develop models of recruitment and retention that are sensitive to the unique cultural perspectives of R/ED teacher candidates, as well as address heightened accountability to produce highly qualified educators for high-need students (Valle-Riestra et al., 2011).

Since the 1980s, efforts to increase recruitment of R/ED teacher candidates have received considerable funding, which led to a growth in the minority teaching force of over two-and-a-half times the rate of the White teaching force, almost doubling in size (Ingersoll & May, 2011). Recruitment strategies alone do not directly address the shortage of R/ED teachers. Unfortunately, turnover among R/ED teachers is greater than their White counterparts, with more individuals citing career advancement or job dissatisfaction (Ingersoll & May 2011). A logical explanation for this dissatisfaction could be that if public schools are not responsive to the needs of R/ED students, they are equally inhospitable to R/ED teachers. R/ED teachers also cite a lack of teacher autonomy as a large factor in lessened job satisfaction (Ingersoll, 2007). Accountability reforms, which often remove from classroom teachers such decisions as text, topic, and content selection, may have led to increased teacher turnover among R/ED teachers (Ingersoll & May, 2011). The required text and content in most schools do not reflect any cultures other than that of White Europeans, which would be especially problematic for a teacher who wanted to include materials that are better suited to R/ED students. Additionally, when curricular standards become more important than creating student-centered philosophies, it is antithetical to the creation of transformative changes for R/ED students.

Field Experiences

Many preservice teachers have had few significant interactions with students from diverse backgrounds, which limits their knowledge and understanding of diversity issues (Terrill & Mark, 2000). Those same teachers often go on to work with students in communities in which they have limited experience (Sleeter, 2001). In a national survey conducted by Parsad, Lewis, & Farris in 2001, only 26% of teachers with three or fewer years of experience felt well prepared to address the needs of students from diverse cultural backgrounds. Furthermore, in a 2000 study, Terrill and Mark found preservice teachers expected higher levels of discipline, lower levels of parental support, higher levels of child abuse, fewer gifted and talented students, and lower levels of motivation in the schools with children of color (Terrill & Mark, 2000). These low expectations stem from the "deficit paradigm" (Weiner, 2003). Teachers often exhibit inappropriate techniques when working with culturally diverse students because they are not aware of their implicit pedagogical, curricular, assessment, and management decisions (Milner & Tenore, 2010). However, if structured correctly, studies have shown that field experiences can be an important means for achieving the goal of culturally responsive teaching (Lee, Eckrich, Lackey, & Showalter, 2010).

It is not sufficient, however, to simply take White teacher candidates to urban schools to "experience diversity". Research has shown that, even when provided with the research-based opportunities and effective practices for teaching in an urban school, preservice teachers did not demonstrate these skills in their classroom teaching (McKinney, Haberman,

Stafford-Johnson, & Robinson, 2008). Placing White preservice teachers in schools serving primarily R/ED students without the requisite knowledge and skills to be culturally competent can often reinforce negative stereotypes held by the new teachers. Teachers need an understanding of institutional racism within which to contextualize the schools where they are placed (Sleeter, 2001).

Culture and Classroom Management

As culture dictates how we approach situations and react in social interactions (Carledge, Lo, Vincent, & Robinson-Ervin, 2013), cultural biases or misconceptions can lead to teachers reacting to misbehaviors of students of color more harshly than their White peers. Being culturally competent is not simply an awareness of what teachers assume to be their students' cultures, but it is a thorough understanding of the teachers' own cultural identities, including how that culture is framed by students and affects perceptions of other cultures (Fasching-Varner & Dodo Seriki, 2012). In current teacher preparation programs, not only is there a scarcity of multicultural education; there is also virtually no recognition that European American students and teachers are cultural beings (Weinstein, Tomlinson-Clarke, & Curran, 2004). Difficult conversations regarding race and equity are carefully avoided in academic discourse, which helps perpetuate race-neutral course work and dialogue. More often than not, the issue of equity, its effect on students' academic achievement, and the important role teachers play in equity pedagogy is conspicuously absent from course objectives in teacher preparation courses (Ruiz & Cantú, 2013). This omission sends the message that studying racism in education is marginal, at best, and validates the behavior of White students who resist learning about racism.

Federal Regulations Issued in Response to Disproportionality

After several advocacy efforts from the field of special education since Congress identified disproportionality as one of the top three priorities of the 2004 IDEA reauthorization, the Department of Education Office of Special Education and Rehabilitative Services released regulations regarding IDEA and disproportionality. The regulations address key concerns of the field regarding how states and districts measure and report disproportionality and provide comprehensive coordinated early intervening services (Office of Special Education and Rehabilitative Services, 2016). Regulations were effective January 18, 2017, and although new, they have the potential to foster consistency in defining, measuring, and remediating disproportionality across states. These will be steps in the right direction only if states implement the regulations with fidelity and with the input from community stakeholders, instead of viewing the regulations only through the lens of the privileged majority.

Future Recommendations

Although many theoretical hypotheses have been provided to explain the inequitable treatment of students from R/ED backgrounds, there is a dearth of literature with results demonstrating how to reduce the problem. However, future research and policy development related to teacher preparation and licensure can be more targeted and focus explicitly on the development of cultural competencies and scientific evidence-based practices (Artiles, Kozleski, Trent, Osher, & Ortiz, 2010). The following recommendations for policy and licensure for teachers and school psychologists and teacher preparation programs are provided below.

1. **State policy and licensure should reflect the need to focus on cultural competency and evidence-based practices.** State policy and licensure requirements for teachers drive course sequences and course work at IHEs. Therefore, if these policies do not indicate the extent to which diversity, cultural competency, and classroom and behavior management is essential for teachers, administrators, and school psychologists, it is likely IHEs will not include, or explicitly focus on, these competencies in their preparation programs. Stakeholders at the state level must make an effort to engage R/ED communities in discussions regarding what makes good teachers for the students in their neighborhood schools. The voices of these systemically marginalized parents and community leaders can no longer be ignored.
2. **Teacher preparation programs must infuse culturally responsive instructional strategies and classroom management into all teacher education programs.** Single, stand-alone courses that attempt to "cover" all aspects of multiculturalism are not effective (Grant, 1994). Essential, research-based components of culturally responsive instruction should occur repeatedly throughout course work and practicum experiences. More important, programs must help prospective teachers recognize the ways that race and racism structure the experiences of all Americans, not only those from minority groups. Teacher candidates must examine their own cultures and recognize racism and implicit bias prior to beginning teaching; when IHEs avoid these uncomfortable conversations, oppression and racism are perpetuated in their classrooms. Additionally, the literature recommends that teachers use culturally responsive classroom management practices to create a common understanding of behavioral expectations and to create an environment where students feel valued and safe (Carledge et al., 2013). Classroom management is so much more than keeping order and control; teacher candidates must be challenged to investigate their worldview of appropriate behavior and how that view may inhibit their positive interactions with R/ED students. In order for educators to follow these recommendations,

they must be instructed in what it means to be culturally responsive and given ample opportunities to practice implementation of these strategies in classrooms in supportive field placements with experienced, culturally responsive practicing teachers.

3. **Whenever feasible, teacher candidates should be placed in urban schools for early field experiences and student teaching.** It is vitally important that preservice teachers are engaged in classrooms with diverse students as early in their preparation as possible so that their first interactions with R/ED students do not come during student teaching or during their first year of employment. Observation in classrooms should be paired with reflection and significant amounts of direct interaction with learners (Akiba, 2011; Hughes, 2009). Experiences can also be made more meaningful when there is a good working relationship between the school experience site and the IHE (Miller & Mikulec, 2014). IHEs need to cultivate rapport with schools in order to provide the very best learning experiences for teacher candidates. A large part of this relationship includes IHE outreach to schools that primarily serve R/ED students in order to identify excellent, culturally responsive, practicing teachers and provide them with resources, such as professional development. This is an investment in schools that are known to be underresourced and is an action step, rather than another admiration of the problem, toward closing the opportunity gap for R/ED students in these schools. Furthermore, R/ED students will have the opportunity to see preservice teachers using practices that create welcoming classrooms for diverse needs, which may, in turn, create interest within these students to choose education as a career goal.

4. **Efforts to recruit and retain R/ED teacher candidates must be strengthened.** Research has repeatedly shown the powerful role teachers play in making a great difference in positive student outcomes, especially for high-needs students (Darling-Hammond, 1999; Darling-Hammond & Berry, 1999). With the increasing racial and ethnic diversity in schools, there is a great need for the teaching force to resemble the makeup of the student population, creating more minority role models in schools (Banks, 1995). It should be no surprise that R/ED students do not grow up and choose a career working in a system that has oppressed them personally. The problem of systemic racism in education is cyclical: R/ED students are marginalized by their educational experiences and, in turn, few choose to become educators. Fewer educators from R/ED backgrounds leads to R/ED students being taught primarily by White teachers who are not fluent in cultural responsivity, thus sustaining the system of oppression. High-quality educators, committed to issues of equity and social justice, who have a direct, personal connection to the role of culture in student performance, are critical to ending disproportionality.

The disproportionality of R/ED students in special education has been a documented problem for more than 40 years. Policy makers, researchers, and practitioners emphasized the negative student outcomes that result from incorrect special education identification and more restrictive placements and exclusionary discipline practices for R/ED students. In order to remedy these negative consequences of the improper implementation of IDEA, policy makers, educator preparation programs, and R/ED communities must engage in difficult dialogues to better prepare future teachers to educate R/ED students by accentuating the importance of culture—both of students and teachers—on educational decisions and performance. The voices of marginalized and oppressed communities can no longer be rejected by educational stakeholders, as the voices of R/ED students, parents, and community members are vital to creating the necessary transformation in special education.

References

Akiba, M. (2011). Identifying program characteristics for preparing pre-service teachers for diversity. *Teachers College Record, 113*(3), 658–697.

Albrecht, S. F., Skiba, R. J., Losen, D. J., Chung, C., & Middelberg, L. (2012). Federal policy on disproportionality in special education: Is it moving us forward? *Journal of Disability Policy Studies, 23*(1), 14–25.

Artiles, A., Kozleski, E., Trent, S., Osher, D., & Ortiz, A. (2010). Justifying and explaining disproporitonality, 1968–2008: A critique of underlying views of culture. *Exceptional Children, 76*(3), 279–299.

Aud, S., Fox, M. A., & Kewal Ramani, A. (2010). *Status and trends in education of racial and ethnic groups.* Washington, DC: National Center for Education Statistics.

Aud, S., Hussaw, W., Kena, G., Bianco, K., Frohlich, L., Kemp, J., . . . Hannes, G. (2011). *The condition of education.* Washington, DC: National Center for Education Sciences.

Banks, J. A. (1995). Multicultural education: Its effects on students' racial and gender role attitudes. In J. A. Banks & C. M. Banks (Eds.), *Handbook of research on multicultural education* (pp. 617–627). New York, NY: MacMillan.

Barnett, S., Carolan, M., & Johns, D. (2013). *Equity and excellence: African-American children's access to quality preschool.* New Brunswick, NJ: National Institute for Early Education Research.

Berry, B. (2008). Staffing high-needs schools: Insights from the nation's best teachers. *Phi Delta Kappan, 89*(10), 766–771.

Boone, R. S., & King-Berry, A. (2007). African American students with disabilities: Beneficiaries of the legacy? *The Journal of Negro Education, 76*(3), 334–345.

Brown-Jeffy, S., & Cooper, J. E. (2011). Toward a culturally relevant pedagogy: An overview of the coneptual and theoretical literature. *Teacher Education Quarterly, 38*(1), 65–84.

Carledge, G., Lo, Y.-Y., Vincent, C. G., & Robinson-Ervin, P. (2013). Culturally responsive classroom management. In E. Emmer, E. Sabornie, C. M. Evertson, & C. S. Weinstein (Eds.), *Handbook of classroom management: Research, practice, and contemporary issues* (pp. 411–426): Abingdon, UK: Routledge.

Chinn, P. C., & Hughes, S. (1987). Representation of minority students in special education classes. *Remedial and Special Education, 8*(4), 41–46.

Darling-Hammond, L. (1999). America's future: Educating teachers. *The Education Digest, 64*(9), 18.

Darling-Hammond, L., & Berry, B. (1999). Recruiting teachers for the 21st century: The foundation for educational equity. *Journal of Negro Education,* 254–279.

Dunn, L. M. (1968). Special education for the mildly retarded: Is much of it justifiable? *Exceptional Children: Journal of the International Council for Exceptional Children, 35*(1), 5–22.

Fasching-Varner, K. J., & Dodo Seriki, V. (2012). Moving beyond seeing with our eyes wide shut: A response to "there is no culturally responsive teaching spoken here". *Democracy and Education, 20*(1), 5.

Fierros, E. G., & Conroy, J. W. (2002). Double jeopardy: An exploration of restrictiveness and race in special education. In D. J. Losen & G. Orfield (Eds.), *Racial inequity in special education* (pp. 39–70). Cambridge, MA: Harvard Education Press.

Finn, J. D. (1982). Patterns in special education placement as revealed by the OCR survey. In K. A. Heller, W. Holtzman, & S. Messick (Eds.), *Placing children in special education: A strategy for equity* (pp. 322–381). Washington, DC: National Academy Press.

Grant, C. A. (1994). Best practices in teacher preparation for urban schools: Lessons from the multicultural teacher education literature. *Action in Teacher Education, 16*(3), 1–18.

Hughes, J. (2009). An instructional model for preparing teachers for fieldwork. *International Journal of Teaching and Learning in Higher Education, 21*(2), 252–257.

Individuals with Disabilities Education Improvement Act of 2004, 20 USC §1400 et seq. (2004).

Ingersoll, R. (2007). Misdiagnosing the teacher quality problem. *CPRE Policy Briefs.* Retrieved from http://repository.upenn.edu/cpre_policybriefs/35

Ingersoll, R., & May, H. (2011). *Recruitment, retention and the minority teacher shortage.* Retrieved from http://repository.upenn.edu/gse_pubs/226

Krezmien, M. P., Leone, P. E., & Achilles, G. M. (2006). Suspension, race, and disability: Analysis of statewide practices and reporting. *Journal of Emotional and Behavioral Disorders, 14*(4), 217–226.

Lee, R. E., Eckrich, L. L., Lackey, C., & Showalter, B. D. (2010). Pre-service teacher pathways to urban teaching: A partnership model for nurturing community-based urban teacher preparation. *Teacher Education Quarterly, 37*(3), 101–122.

Losen, D. J., Ee, J., Hodson, C., & Martinez, T. E. (2015). Disturbing inequities: Exploring the relationship between racial disparities in special education identification and discipline. In D. Losen (Ed.), *Closing the school discipline gap: Equitable remedies for excessive exclusion* (pp. 89–106). New York, NY: Teachers College Press.

Losen, D. J., & Orfield, G. (2002). *Racial inequality in special education.* Cambridge, MA: Harvard Education Press.

MacMillan, D. L., & Reschly, D. J. (1998). Overrepresentation of minority students: The case for greater specificity or reconsideration of the variables examined. *Journal of Special Education, 32*(1), 10.

McKinney, S. E., Haberman, M., Stafford-Johnson, D., & Robinson, J. (2008). Developing teachers for high-poverty schools: The role of the internship experience. *Urban Education, 43*(1), 68–82. https://doi.org/10.1177/0042085907305200

Mercer, J. R. (1973). *Labeling the mentally retarded.* Berkeley, CA: University of California Press.

Miller, P. C., & Mikulec, E. A. (2014). Pre-service teachers confronting issues of diversity through a radical field experience. *Multicultural Education, 21*(2), 18.

Milner, H. R., & Tenore, F. B. (2010). Classroom management in diverse classrooms. *Urban Education, 45*(5), 560–603. doi:10.1177/0042085910377290

Office of Special Education and Rehabilitative Services, D. O. (2016, December 19). Assistance to states for the education of children with disabilities: Preschool grants for children with disabilities. *Federal Register, 81*(243), 92376–92464.

Oswald, D. P., Coutinho, M. J., Best, A. M., & Singh, N. N. (1999). Ethnic representation in special education: The influence of school-related economic and demographic variables. *The Journal of Special Education, 32*(4), 194–206.

Parrish, T. (2002). Racial disparities in the identification, funding, and provision of special education. In D. J. Losen & G. Orfield (Eds.), *Racial inequity in special education.* Cambridge: Harvard Education Press.

Parsad, B., Lewis, L., Farris, E., & National Center for Education Statistics, W. D. C. (2001). *Teacher preparation and professional development: 2000. E.D.tabs.* Retrieved from http://proxy.mul.missouri.edu/login?url=http://search.ebscohost.com/login.aspx?direct=true&db=eric&AN=ED458204&site=ehost-live

Ruiz, E. C., & Cantú, N. E. (2013). Teaching the teachers: Dismantling racism and teaching for social change. *The Urban Review, 45*(1), 74–88.

Sattler, J. M. (1992). *Assessment of children* (Rev. 3rd ed.). San Diego: Sattler Publisher.

Serwatka, T. S., Deering, S., & Grant, P. (1995). Disproportionate representation of African Americans in emotionally handicapped classes. *Journal of Black Studies, 25*(4), 492–506.

Skiba, R. J., Albrecht, S. F., & Losen, D. J. (2013). CCBD's position summary on federal policy on disproportionality in special education. *Behavioral Disorders, 38*(2), 108–120.

Skiba, R. J., Poloni-Staudinger, L., Gallini, S., Simmons, A., & Feggins-Azziz, R. (2006). Disparate access: The disproportionality of African American students with disabilities across educational environments. *Exceptional Children, 72*(4), 411–424.

Skiba, R. J., Simmons, A. B., Ritter, S., Gibb, A. C., Rausch, M. K., Cuadrado, J., & Chung, C. (2008). Achieving equity in special education: History, status, and current challenges. *Exceptional Children, 74*(3), 264–288.

Sleeter, C. E. (2001). Preparing teachers for culturally diverse schools research and the overwhelming presence of whiteness. *Journal of Teacher Education, 52*(2), 94–106.

Smith, C. R., Katsiyannis, A., & Ryan, J. B. (2011). Challenges of serving students with emotional ad behavioral disorders: Legal and policy considerations. *Behavioral Disorders, 36*(3), 185–194.

Smith, T. E. C. (2005). IDEA 2004: Another round in the reauthorization process. *Remedial and Special Education, 26*(6), 314–319. doi:10.1177_07419325050 260060101

Sullivan, A., & Bal, A. (2013). Disproportionality in special education: Effect of individual and school variables on disabiliity risk. *Exceptional Children, 79*(4), 475–494.

Terrill, M., & Mark, D. L. (2000). Preservice teachers' expectations for schools with children of color and second-language learners. *Journal of Teacher Education, 51*(2), 149–155.

U.S. Department of Education (USDOE). (2013). *Thirtififth annual report to congress on the implementation of the individuals with disabilities education act, Parts B and C*. Washington, DC: Author.

U.S. Department of Education Office for Civil Rights. (2014, March). *Civil rights data collection*. Retrieved from U.S. Department of Education ocrdata.ed.gov/

Valle-Riestra, D. M., Shealey, M. W., & Cramer, E. D. (2011). Recruiting and retaining culturally diverse special educators. *Interdisciplinary Journal of Teaching & Learning, 1*(2), 20.

Vanneman, A., Hamilton, L., Baldwin Anderson, J., & Rahman, T. (2009). *Achievement gaps: How black and white students in public schools perform in mathematics and reading on the national assessment of educational progress*. Washington, DC: National Center for Education Statistics, Institute of Education Sciences, U.S. Department of Education.

Weiner, L. (2003). Why is classroom management so vexing to urban teachers? *Theory into Practice, 42*(4), 305–312.

Weinstein, C. S., Tomlinson-Clarke, S., & Curran, M. (2004). Toward a conception of culturally responsive classroom management. *Journal of Teacher Education, 55*(1), 25–38.

West, J. E., & Schaefer Whitby, P. J. (2008). Federal policy and the education of students with disabilities: Progress and the path forward. *Focus on Exceptional Children, 41*(3), 1.

Yell, M. L., Katsiyannis, A., & Hazelkorn, M. (2007). Reflections on the 25th anniversary of the U.S. supreme court's decision in Board of Education v. Rowley. *Focus on Exceptional Children, 39*(9), 1–12.

Yell, M. L., Rogers, D., & Lodge Rogers, E. (1998). The legal history of special education. *Remedial & Special Education, 19*(4), 219.

Yell, M. L., Shriner, J. G., & Katsiyannis, A. (2006). Individuals with disabilities education improvement act of 2004 and IDEA regulations of 2006: Implications for educators, administrators, and teacher trainers. *Focus on Exceptional Children, 39*(1), 1–25.

Zhang, D., Katsiyannis, A., & Herbst, M. (2004). Disciplinary exclusions in special education: A 4-year analysis. *Behavioral Disorders, 29*(4), 337–347.

11 Civil Rights Remedies and Persistent Inequities

The Case of Racial Disproportionality in Special Education

Catherine Kramarczuk Voulgarides

Within the field of special education many researchers have been asking some version of the following question: *Are Native American, Black, and Latinx students over- or underrepresented in special education classification, placement, and/or in exclusionary disciplinary outcomes as compared to their White peers?* On one hand, decades of research evidence has shown that lower income students of color, particularly Native American, Black, and Latinx students labeled with a disability, are overrepresented in special education classification and placement outcomes and/or in disciplinary outcomes (e.g., Donovan & Cross 2002; Harry & Klingner, 2014; Losen, 2014). Research has also shown that these groups of students are underrepresented in gifted and talented programs (e.g., Ford, Grantham, & Whiting, 2008). On the other hand, in the past several years there has been a growing body of research that has questioned whether or not students of color are sufficiently classified and placed into special education (e.g., Morgan et al., 2017, 2018, 2015). The contradicting findings and the growing debate about racial disproportionality,[1] as it is formally defined in the single most influential piece of legislation affecting students with disabilities in schools—the Individuals with Disabilities Education Act (IDEA), has raised legitimate concerns about whether or not the civil rights and educational needs of nondominant students labeled with a disability are being met in schools across the United States.

For instance, in Morgan et al.'s (2015) study on the issue of over- and underrepresentation in special education the authors used nationally representative longitudinal data and found that "racial-, ethnic-, and language-minority schoolchildren in the United States are less likely than otherwise similar White, English-speaking schoolchildren to be identified as disabled and so are comparatively *underrepresented* in special education" (p. 285). The authors further argue that federal monitoring of racial disparities through IDEA "may be misdirected," due to the nature of their findings (p. 288). On the other hand, Skiba, Artiles, Kozleski, Losen, and Harry (2016) argue that Morgan et al.'s (2015) findings ignore the "deeply complex" factors that contribute to racial disparities in special education. They further assert that "the sweeping conclusion[s]" in the Morgan et al. (2015) study should not be used "to justify" their "startling policy recommendation that the entire federal policy apparatus in IDEA 2004[2] based upon an assumption of overrepresentation may be in error and should be reconsidered" (p. 223). The debate about the issue continues to date—with studies by Fish (2019) and Shifrer and Fish (2019) illustrating that the context of schooling provides some insights into the contradictory patterns of overrepresentation that have been outlined in previous research studies. It is also relevant to the recent delay and subsequent reinstatement of the refined federal IDEA policy remedies that were created to address the complex inequity.[3]

Given the central concern that is embedded in the ongoing academic debate about racial disparities in special education—that of whether or not the civil rights of students with disabilities are being met in schools across the United States, it is critical that researchers and policy makers assess how IDEA policy compliance relates to the inequity. Therefore, this chapter is focused on understanding why racial inequities in special education persist despite the presence of legal protections that were designed to address the issue. It engages with a paradox that exists between the guarantee of a free appropriate public education and the persistence of racial inequities in special education. Artiles (2011) outlines the contours of the paradox by stating "the civil rights response for one group of individuals (i.e., learners with disabilities) has become a potential source of inequities for another group (i.e., racial minority students) despite their shared histories of struggle for equity" (p. 431). In order to explore why this paradox exists, the chapter takes a historical perspective and outlines the legislative development of IDEA, and it critically assesses how some of the ideological and legal assumptions behind IDEA relate to broader academic and policy debates about racial inequities in special education.

Protecting Students With Disabilities in Schools: A Slow Progression of Earned Rights

Prior to the 1970s there were virtually no federal or state laws protecting students with disabilities in the United States. Rather, people with disabilities were segregated, marginalized, excluded, and denied basic social and educational services (Winzer, 1993). Compulsory education laws, enacted in the 1900s, intensified the segregation and exclusion of students with disabilities in schools, too. The principles of compulsory attendance laws were at odds with the eugenics movement and frustrated educators within schools (Spaulding & Pratt, 2015) as the idea of including all students in the educational process was a profoundly progressive idea. In addition, according to Yell, Rogers, and Rogers (1998), up to 1969, courts also "upheld legislation that excluded students whom school officials judged would not benefit from public education or who might be disruptive to other students" (p. 220). However, it was in the wake of the civil rights victories of people of color and women that disability rights eventually become a priority for the U.S. Congress (Minow, 2010; Skrentny, 2009).

Section 504, which passed in1973 and was part of the Rehabilitation Act of 1973, was the first federal law for people with disabilities in the United States. Section 504 took into account a nondiscrimination framework that was directly shaped by the civil rights laws passed in the 1960s, specifically Title VI (Skrentny, 2009), and it mobilized disability rights advocates (Ong-Dean, 2009). During this period, students with disabilities were "the other minority" (Miles, 2016) and advocacy efforts were framed around the arguments used in *Brown v. Board of Education of Topeka, Kansas* (347 U.S. 483); mainly that the segregation and exclusion of students with disabilities from educational services was a violation of Equal Protection and Due Process. This strategy helped shape the outcomes of influential court cases, *Pennsylvania Association for Retarded Children (PARC) v. Commonwealth of Pennsylvania* (334 F. Supp. 1257) and *Mills v. Board of Education, of the District of Columbia* (348 F. Supp. 866), which eventually led to the passage of the Education for All Handicapped Children Act (EAHCA; 1975), which later became IDEA.

PARC was focused on gaining rights for mentally retarded children who were excluded from the educational system. The case established that schools should remedy the historical discrimination of mentally retarded children by granting plaintiffs equal protection and equal rights to public education under the 14th Amendment. *Mills* was a class-action suit brought on behalf of seven children who had been identified as having behavioral problems and as being mentally retarded. The suit claimed that the students were excluded and denied their right to an education. The case set the precedent that schools must provide public education to all children regardless of their disability. The *PARC* and *Mills* courts "shared a fundamentally social orientation," establishing that students with disabilities were not solely defined by their disability but were also subject to "the consequences of cultural prejudices and institutional deficiencies" (Ong-Dean, 2009; pp 19–20) in the education system. In addition, *PARC* and *Mills* provided the procedural and substantive framework for the EAHCA in 1975 that was later renamed IDEA in 1990.

However, as school-based disability legislation evolved in the U.S. Congress and the courts, the substantive content of *Brown* was foregrounded (Kramarczuk Voulgarides, 2018; Zirkel, 2005). Zirkel (2005) states that "the IDEA itself, both currently and as originally passed in the form of the EAHCA, makes no mention of *Brown* in its findings or other provisions," further noting that Congress has focused on "procedural, rather than a substantive, standard of equal opportunity for students with disabilities, who had been denied access to education" (Zirkel, 2005, p 263).

For instance, in a prominent special education case *Board of Education of the Hendrick Hudson Central School District v. Amy Rowley* (1982), the *Rowley* court determined "the law's [IDEA] emphasis on procedural requirements reflected a 'legislative conviction' that the *substance* of an appropriate education would usually be realized by simply meeting the laws *procedural* requirements—in particular, the requirements for including parents in the formulation of the IEP" (Ong-Dean, 2009, p 32). Thus, the development of IDEA reflected a commitment to providing educational opportunity and access through due process and procedural protections, but it did not necessarily reflect *substantive* monitoring of civil rights concerns, which, in turn, affects how racialized inequities in special education are addressed through procedural compliance with IDEA.

Racial and Ethnic Inequities and the Development of IDEA

Issues of race, ethnicity, and language were always present in the legal cases that shaped the passage of the EAHCA and eventually IDEA. For instance, in *Hobson v. Hansen* (1967) unjust special education placement was examined in the District of Columbia where test scores were used to place students in educational tracks that adversely affected African American students and low-income students. The court determined the practice was unconstitutional and that it violated the 14th Amendment because African American students and low-income students were placed in educational tracks that provided little to no "educational benefit" (Miles, 2016). In *Diana v. State Board of Education* (1970), a student named Diana was given an IQ test in English even though she only spoke Spanish. Her low-test scores resulted in special education placement, which was then contested in court. A consent decree was created guaranteeing that students would be tested in their native language. In another case, *Larry P. v. Wilson Riles* (1979), plaintiffs challenged California school districts for violating IDEA Title VI and Section 504 by using IQ scores to identify African American students for special education placement. While the cases that are listed are nonexhaustive, they do illustrate how disability law intersects with race, ethnicity, and/or language differences. The cases also highlight a growing recognition that inequitable and culturally insensitive practices and procedures result in racialized outcomes in special education. However, despite these cases and a legacy of research that has highlighted the existence of racial disparities in special education (e.g., Dunn, 1968, Skiba et al., 2008), it was not until 1997 that disproportionality was formally recognized in IDEA legislation.

The 1997 amendments to IDEA (20 U.S.C. §1418(c), 1998) required that state and local education agencies (SEAs and LEAs, respectively) identify and monitor racial disproportionality in special education. Unfortunately though, the guidance proved ineffective in nationally reducing disproportionate outcomes (Albrecht, Skiba, Losen, Chung, &

Middelberg, 2012; Cavendish, Artiles, & Harry 2014; Hehir, 2002) and the policy approach for addressing disproportionality was later refined in the 2004 reauthorization of IDEA (20 U.S.C. §1412(a)(22, 24)). The 2004 reauthorization contains a twofold approach for addressing disproportionality (e.g., Skiba, 2013). It requires that states numerically monitor special education outcomes through State Performance Plan (SPP) indicators. States set a numerical threshold for identifying disproportionality in the classification, placement, and/or suspensions of students with disabilities by race and if LEAs are found to be numerically disproportionate, they must show compliance with the IDEA regulations that are associated with their citation for racial inequities. This twofold approach for addressing racial disparities in special education is highly problematic, however.

Education is not a guaranteed civil right in the U.S. Constitution. Rather, education is the responsibility of state governments. Due to this, states *can* and *do* interpret IDEA in ways that are responsive to the local political and legislative needs of SEAs and LEAs. This educational federalism (Robinson, 2013, as cited in Strassfeld, 2016), which favors state autonomy despite the fact that constitutional and federal rights are central to IDEA, leads to varying definitions of disproportionality that affect how SEAs and LEAs monitor and address disproportionality (Strassfeld, 2016). For instance, states have been allowed to independently define a threshold for identifying disproportionality that varies across the country (US GAO, 2013), and mounting evidence has shown that many school districts across the United States report compliance with IDEA mandates *despite* high numerical values of disproportionality (Albrecht et al., 2012; Cavendish et al., 2014; US GAO, 2013). Essentially, the highly proceduralized development of IDEA coupled with the unintended consequences of educational federalism generate consequential policy implementation gaps that affect how IDEA can be leveraged to address a systemic inequity like racial disproportionality within local contexts.

Compliance and Racial Inequity: A Tenuous Relationship

While the legislative history of IDEA birthed out of civil rights legal strategies, Court decisions, amendments, and reauthorizations of IDEA prioritized procedural protections in order to assure that all students have access to a free appropriate public education (FAPE). This has established an environment where evidence of compliance with IDEA's procedural protections serves as sufficient evidence that civil rights outcomes are achieved in practice; a form of legal endogeneity (Edelman, 2016; Edelman, Krieger, Eliason, Albiston, & Mellema, 2011). Legal endogeneity implies that courts, governing bodies, and other actors involved in the legal process take evidence of organizational structures, such as the presence of a discipline code or correctly completed individualized education program (IEP), as proof of compliance to the intent of a law. The theory illustrates how organizations, and in this case schools, respond to "ambiguous" civil rights and social reform laws by "creating a variety of policies and programs [that are] designed to symbolize attention to law" (Edelman, 2016, p 12) that may not actually lead to the realization of civil rights outcomes. Regardless of this fact, however, organizational actors, compliance monitors and auditors, and eventually the courts determine that the mere presence of these bureaucratic routines and the associated policies, procedures, and practices are evidence of compliance with the civil rights intent of a law like IDEA. Essentially, under this theoretical framework, it is easier for practitioners, or anyone within complex organizational systems, to symbolically comply (Meyer & Rowan, 1977) with policy and legal mandates rather than radically shift policies and practices to assure that all students are equitably educated—a form of loose coupling (Weick, 1976).

The social forces that are associated with legal endogeneity pose a serious equity concern from addressing disproportionality. If organizational structures, policies, rules, handbooks, and the like are relied on as evidence of compliance with a civil rights intent, a law's effectiveness is weakened (Edelman, 2016; Edelman et al., 2011). This is clearly evident in the way in which disproportionality is addressed through IDEA as SEAs and LEAs can exhibit persistent numerical racial disparities in the classification, placement, and/or suspension of students with disabilities by race while simultaneously showing legal compliance with IDEA mandates. It is also evident in the way in which something like a correctly filled out IEP can signal adherence to civil rights concerns without actually addressing the civil rights needs of a student with a disability. Because, while a correctly filled-out IEP illustrates proof of compliance with IDEA and it symbolically signals that educational opportunity and access was given to a student via the very existence of the document, it does not mean that high-quality interventions and services were provided to that child (e.g., Kramarczuk Voulgarides, 2018). In addition, when practitioners work in districts found to be disproportionate yet compliant with IDEA, paperwork compliance suggests to state auditors and monitors that educators are not explicitly or implicitly discriminating against students of color or erroneously placing and/or classifying them. Rather, they are faithfully applying the law and adhering to the principles of equal educational opportunity and access. It is here where the educational paradox that is associated with IDEA has the direst consequences because student failure and the need to be in special education are not associated with broader social forces or structural inequities but, rather, with students and their perceived failure to succeed in school or comply with school norms and expectations. And most problematically, this process *just happens to* result in racialized outcomes.

The difficulties that are associated with addressing racial inequities in special education through IDEA compliance are also compounded by prevailing legal theories about the sources of discrimination that have shaped civil rights jurisprudence since the 1960s: disparate impact theory and disparate treatment theory (Edelman, 2016). Disparate impact theory does not require that a plaintiff prove in their case that there is an explicit intent to discriminate. Rather, social systems and structures can be implicated in the production of discriminatory outcomes, and the approach is aligned with addressing institutionalized discrimination. In contrast, individual and systemic disparate treatment theory requires that a plaintiff show in their case that there was an explicit intent and motivation to discriminate against a particular group. According to Edelman (2016), the rise in claims about discriminatory intent over impact in the past 40 years has weakened civil rights legislation "as a tool for fighting discrimination and inequality" because judges are more likely to equate an organization's symbolic structures with the achievement of civil rights" (p. 55) so as not "to infer intent from statistical disparities alone" (p. 59). This has major implications for how disproportionality can be and has been addressed in U.S. courts.

Strassfeld (2019), in her analysis of the *Blunt v. Lower Merion District* (2007–2015) case, illustrates how disparate treatment theory has systematically limited plaintiff's capacity to assert their rights when racial disparities in special education are present. Strassfeld (2019) outlines how the plaintiffs in the *Blunt* case brought their challenges around racial disparities in special education by leveraging Title VI on Equal Protection Clause grounds, but they failed to achieve redress for any rights violations. The plaintiffs' concerns were dismissed despite the fact that there was statistical evidence of racial disproportionality. The *Blunt* court required proof of intentional discrimination even though there was some evidence of procedural violations related to IDEA implementation, too. Essentially, the *Blunt* court ruled in favor of the school district, illustrating how the social forces of legal endogeneity and the need to identify a singular explanation of explicit intent to discriminate cannot and does not account for the sociological complexity of how racial inequities in special education manifest and persist within schools.

Examining Colorblind Policy Approaches When Addressing Racial Inequities in Special Education

Given the evidence that current legislative efforts to address disproportionality have been ineffective, it is important to think critically about how race is operationalized in policy and law, which, in turn, affects how IDEA procedural compliance can be used to address racial disproportionality, too. Obasogie (2013), in his study on how people who are blind experience and understand race, finds that racial ideologies are deeply embedded in social interactions, policy, and law. He states that "social practices train individuals to look differently on certain bodies" (p. 62), regardless of a person's capacity to "see" skin color, finding that racial discrimination is not solely a reaction to visibly different skin colors but, rather, is embedded in the social fabric of everyday life. Obasogie asserts that notions of race, superiority, and inferiority are deeply ingrained in seemingly mundane social interactions and benign social practices that equally shape sighted and not sighted individuals' notions of race. These unspoken and unseen social understandings of race ultimately affect how policies and laws are conceptualized, created, and implemented across various social settings. However, sensitivity to this complex understanding of race and acknowledgment of often-unseen racial ideologies in the social world are not evident in the most well-intentioned policies—and especially not in the disproportionality monitoring mechanisms. This colorblind approach to law produces and sustains racialized outcomes.

Bonilla-Silva (1997, 2002) has described American society as a racialized social system, where seemingly race-neutral actions have racial consequences. This logic, commonly referred to as colorblindness (Bonilla-Silva, 2002, 2010), applies to policies that are not explicitly focused on addressing issues related to race yet produce racialized outcomes (e.g., Saito, 2009). IDEA is arguably a colorblind policy and law because even though race is recognized in the SPP indicators, the procedural protections and interventions that are embedded in IDEA and that are leveraged when an LEA is cited for disproportionality, do not explicitly attend to the impacts of racial, ethnic, and cultural differences on educational practice. Essentially, the SPP indicator solely detects a numerical threshold that is egregious, which then triggers procedural compliance with IDEA mandates. This policy approach does not interrogate the source(s) of the racial inequity. Rather, it identifies the existence of the inequity, but then it requires compliance with IDEA mandates that delete the sociological complexity of how "race" operates in society (also see Artiles, 2017). It also negates the impact of social context and human interactions on the production of educational inequities.

In addition, the promises of equal protection and due process, which are deeply embedded in the legislative framework of IDEA, also do not account for the sociological complexity of how race and racial inequities manifest and persist in the social world. According to Obasogie (2013), Equal Protection jurisprudence since the *Regents of the University of California v. Bakke* (1978) decision "has evolved in a manner that reduces race to a series of discrete categories that exist outside of any broader social or political process and whose significance and salience are thought to come from mere observation," causing "equal protection's moral sensibilities [to] shift from using law to remedy past injustices to using law to mandate no recognition of difference in the distribution of resources even when done to level a historically and sociologically uneven playing field" (Obasogie, 2013, p 157). Under this framework, social injustices that are associated with race and racial discrimination become decontextualized in both their conceptualization and remedies. And while both race and disability are protected classes under the U.S. Constitution, race is subject to strict scrutiny but disability status is not. Thus, remedying a problem like disproportionality, which exists at the intersection of disability and race, is incredibly difficult to achieve under the current legislative framework of IDEA. And when SEAs and LEAs are able to show procedural compliance with IDEA they are exhibiting an implied commitment to equal protection and due process, but this form of legal compliance does not account for the way in which structural and intersectional inequities and discriminatory social norms relate to racialized inequities.

What Now?

Legal attempts to address racial inequities in special education cannot be solely focused on assuring that the policies and procedures that are associated with IDEA implementation exist and are complied with in educational practice. They also cannot be focused on locating the micro-"racist" acts of individuals, organizations, or procedures. Rather, questions about the effectiveness of special education and the capacity of special education services and systems to provide *equitable* access and opportunity to *all* students should be focused on critically understanding how structural, interactional, and organizational social forces have an impact on students' lives and educational outcomes. And given the evidence presented in this chapter about the legislative development of IDEA, its civil rights intent, and the proceduralization of IDEA, it is imperative that the ongoing academic debate about racial disparities in special education includes a sustained conversation about the equity impacts of the policy implementation process on racial disproportionality. Essentially, the multidimensional contours of the educational paradox that exists between the guarantee of a free appropriate public education and the persistence of racial inequities in special education cannot be subject to one-dimensional solutions and remedies. Thus, when researchers, policy makers, and educators think about meaningfully addressing a complex inequity like disproportionality, it is necessary that they activate the sociological imagination (Mills, 2000) and creatively conceive of new ways to address the long-standing issue that has plagued the U.S. education system for decades.

Notes

1. Racial disparities in special education are formally known as disproportionality. The issue is defined by a group's over- or underrepresentation in an educational category, program, or service in comparison to the group's proportion in the overall population (Donovan & Cross, 2002). Also, see Cruz and Rodl

(2018) and Skiba et al. (2016 for examples of the academic debate that surrounds the issue.
2. The 2004 reauthorization of IDEA resulted in explicit monitoring of special education outcomes through 20 quantifiable and qualitative indicators (20 U.S.C. 1416(a)(3)), known as State Performance Plan (SPP) indicators. Three SPP indicators are specifically related to disproportionality: Indicators 4, 9, and 10. Indicator 9 refers to the disproportionate representation of racial and ethnic groups in *special education and related services* that is the result of *inappropriate identification*. Indicator 10 refers to disproportionate representation of racial and ethnic groups in *specific disability categories* that is the result of *inappropriate identification*. Indicator 4 has two components: 4A refers to significant discrepancies in the rates of long-term suspensions of students with disabilities compared to districts in a state, and 4B refers to significant discrepancies in the rates of long-term suspensions of students with disabilities, based on race and ethnicity, compared to districts in a state *due to inappropriate policies, procedures, or practices*. The SPP indicators have both a numerical and qualitative component. The numerical component alerts to *significant disproportionality*, which is a numerical threshold that is set by each state to determine whether or not there are racially disparate student outcomes within a particular locale. The qualitative component relates to *disproportionate representation*, which requires that SEAs and LEAs monitor IDEA statutory compliance through district self-directed and state monitored reviews of IDEA policies and procedures.
3. See recent news stories on the issue:

www.educationdive.com/news/department-of-education-delays-equity-in-idea-compliance-date-by-two-years/527035/
www.ncld.org/archives/action-center/what-we-ve-done/used-delays-the-equity-in-idea-regulation
www.washingtonpost.com/news/answer-sheet/wp/2018/03/20/why-devoss-plan-to-delay-obama-era-rule-on-minority-special-education-students-is-a-mistake/?utm_term=.6ace80249af2
http://blogs.edweek.org/edweek/speced/2019/05/special_education_disparity_rule_reimplemented.html

References

Albrecht, S. F., Skiba, R. J., Losen, D. J., Chung, C. G., & Middelberg, L. (2012). Federal policy on disproportionality in special education is it moving us forward? *Journal of Disability Policy Studies*, 23(1), 14–25.

Artiles, A. J. (2017, October). *Re-envisioning equity research: Disability identification disparities as a case in point*. 14th Annual Brown Lecture. Washington, DC: American Educational Research Association.

Artiles, A. J. (2011). Toward an interdisciplinary understanding of educational equity and difference: The case of the racialization of ability. *Educational Researcher*, 40(9), 431–445.

Board of Education of the Hendrick Hudson Central School District. v. Rowley, 458 U.S. 176 (1982).

Bonilla-Silva, E. (1997). Rethinking racism: Toward a structural interpretation. *American Sociological Review*, 465–480.

Bonilla-Silva, E. (2002). The linguistics of colorblind racism: How to talk nasty about blacks without sounding "racist". *Critical Sociology*, 28(1–2), 41–64.

Bonilla-Silva, E. (2010). *Racism without racists: Color-blind racism and the persistence of racial inequality in the United States*. Lantham, Maryland: Rowman & Littlefield.

Brown v. Board of Education, 347 U.S. 483 (1954).

Cavendish, W., Artiles, A. J., & Harry, B. (2014). Tracking inequality 60 years after Brown: Does policy legitimize the racialization of disability?. *Multiple Voices for Ethnically Diverse Exceptional Learners, 14*(2), 30-40.

Cruz, R. A., & Rodl, J. E. (2018). An integrative synthesis of literature on disproportionality in special education. *The Journal of Special Education, 52*(1), 50–63.

Diana vs. State Board of Education, CA 70 RFT (N.D. Cal. 1970).

Donovan, M. S., & Cross, C. T. (Eds.). (2002). *Minority students in special and gifted education/Committee on minority representation in special education*. Washington, DC: National Academy Press.

Dunn, L. M. (1968). Special education for the mildly mentally retarded: Is much of it justifiable? *Exceptional Children, 35*, 5–22.

Edelman, L. B. (2016). *Working law: Courts, corporations, and symbolic civil rights*. Chicago, IL: University of Chicago Press.

Edelman, L. B., Krieger, L. H., Eliason, S. R., Albiston, C. R., & Mellema, V. (2011). When organizations rule: Judicial deference to institutionalized employment structures 1. *American Journal of Sociology, 117*(3), 888–954.

Education for All Handicapped Children Act of 1975 (EAHCA). U.S. Public Law 94–142. U.S. Code. Vol. 20, secs. 1401 et seq.

Fish, R. E. (2019). Standing out and sorting in: Exploring the role of racial composition in racial disparities in special education. *American Educational Research Journal*. Advanced online publication. https://doi.org/10.3102/0002831219847966.

Ford, D. Y., Grantham, T. C., & Whiting, G. W. (2008). Culturally and linguistically diverse students in gifted education: Recruitment and retention issues. *Exceptional Children, 74*(3), 289–306.

Harry, B., & Klingner, J. (2014). *Why are so many minority students in special education?* New York, NY: Teachers College Press.

Hehir, T. (2002). IDEA and disproportionality: Federal enforcement, effective advocacy, and strategies for change. In D. J. Losen & G. Orfield (Eds.), *Racial inequity in special education* (pp. 219–238). Cambridge, MA: Harvard Education Press.

Individuals with Disabilities Education Act of 1997. U.S. Public Law 105–17. U.S. Code. Vol. 20, secs. 1400 et seq.

Individuals with Disabilities Education Act, 20 U.S.C. § 1400 (2004).

Kramarczuk Voulgarides, C. (2018). *Does Compliance Matter in Special Education?: IDEA and the Hidden Inequities of Practice*. New York, NY: Teachers College Press.

Larry P. v. Riles, 495 F. Supp. 926 (N.D. Cal. 1979).

Losen, D. J. (Ed.). (2014). *Closing the school discipline gap: Equitable remedies for excessive exclusion*. New York, NY: Teachers College Press.

Meyer, J. W., & Rowan, B. (1977). Institutionalized organizations: Formal structure as myth and ceremony. *American Journal of Sociology, 83*(2), 340–363.

Miles, A. (2016). Overrepresentation in special education: Does the IDEA violate the equal Protection clause. *Rutgers Race & Law Review, 17*, 245.

Mills, C. W. (2000). *The sociological imagination*. Oxford: Oxford University Press.
Mills v. Board of Education, DC. 348 F. Supp. 866 (D. DC 1972).
Minow, M. (2010). *In Brown's wake: Legacies of America's educational landmark*. Oxford: Oxford University Press.
Morgan, P. L., Farkas, G., Cook, M., Strassfeld, N. M., Hillemeier, M. M., Pun, W. H., & Schussler, D. L. (2017). Are Black children disproportionately overrepresented in special education? A best-evidence synthesis. *Exceptional Children*, 83(2), 181–198.
Morgan, P. L., Farkas, G., Cook, M., Strassfeld, N. M., Hillemeier, M. M., Pun, W. H., . . . & Schussler, D. L. (2018). Are Hispanic, Asian, Native American, or language-minority children overrepresented in special education? *Exceptional Children*, 84(3), 261–279.
Morgan, P. L., Farkas, G., Hillemeier, M. M., Mattison, R., Maczuga, S., Li, H., & Cook, M. (2015). Minorities are disproportionately underrepresented in special education: Longitudinal evidence across five disability conditions. *Educational Researcher*, 44(5), 278–292.
Obasogie, O. (2013). *Blinded by sight: Seeing race through the eyes of the blind*. Stanford, CA: Stanford University Press.
Ong-Dean, C. (2009). *Distinguishing disability: Parents, privilege, and special education*. Chicago, IL: University of Chicago Press.
PARC v. Commonwealth. 343 F. Supp. 279; 1972 U.S. Dist. LEXIS 13874.
Regents of University of California v. Bakke, 438 U.S. 265 (1978).
Robinson, K. J. (2013). The high cost of education federalism. *Wake Forest Law Review*, 48, 287.
Saito, L. T. (2009). *The politics of exclusion: The failure of race-neutral policies in urban America*. Stanford, CA: Stanford University Press.
Section 504 of the Rehabilitation Act of 1973, 34 C.F.R. Part 104.
Shifrer, D., & Fish, R. (2019). A multilevel investigation into contextual reliability in the designation of cognitive health conditions among U.S. children. *Society and Mental Health*. Advanced online publication. https://doi.org/10.1177/2156869319847243.
Skiba, R. (2013). CCBD'S position summary on federal policy on disproportionality in special education. *Behavioral Disorders*, 38(2).
Skiba, R. J., Artiles, A. J., Kozleski, E. B., Losen, D. J., & Harry, E. G. (2016). Risks and consequences of oversimplifying educational inequities: A response to Morgan et al. (2015). *Educational Researcher*, 45(3), 221–225.
Skiba, R. J., Simmons, A. B., Ritter, S., Gibb, A. C., Rausch, M. K., Cuadrado, J., & Chung, C. G. (2008). Achieving equity in special education: History, status, and current challenges. *Exceptional Children*, 74(3), 264–288.
Skrentny, J. D. (2009). *The minority rights revolution*. Cambridge, MA: Harvard University Press.
Spaulding, L. S., & Pratt, S. M. (2015). A review and analysis of the history of special education and disability advocacy in the United States. *American Educational History Journal*, 42(1/2), 91.
Strassfeld, N. M. (2016). The future of idea: Monitoring disproportionate representation of minority students in special education and intentional discrimination claims. *Case Western Reserve Law Review*, 67, 1121.
Strassfeld, N. M. (2019). Education federalism and minority disproportionate representation monitoring: Examining IDEA provisions, regulations, and judicial

trends. *Journal of Disability Policy Studies, 10*(20), 1–10. doi:10.1177/1044 207319835185

United States. Government Accountability Office. (2013). *Individuals with disabilities education act: Standards needed to improve identification of racial and ethnic overrepresentation in special education: Report to the chairman, committee on health, education, labor, and pensions, U.S. Senate*. Washington, DC: United States Government Accountability Office.

Weick, K. E. (1976). Educational organizations as loosely coupled systems. *Administrative Science Quarterly*, 1–19.

Winzer, M. A. (1993). *The history of special education: From isolation to integration*. Washington, DC: Gallaudet University Press.

Yell, M. L., Rogers, D., & Rogers, E. L. (1998). The legal history of special education: What a long, strange trip it's been! *Journal for Special Educators, 19*(4), 219–228.

Zirkel, P. A. (2005). Does Brown v. Board of Education play a prominent role in special education law. *Journal of Law & Education, 34*, 255.

12 "PAAP Season"

A New Rationale for Segregating Students With Significant Cognitive Disabilities

Maria Timberlake

"She's a nice young woman and she's doing a nice job with those kids." This is the complete and unedited transcript of my first teacher evaluation in rural Maine in the late 1980s. Students with intensive physical and intellectual disabilities were being welcomed into the district for the first time. My principal, a kind man at a loss to know exactly what to think about this new situation, completed my evaluation by simply appreciating that I was there. The expectations for students with significant cognitive (historically called severe or profound) disabilities were low, our portable classroom behind the school made us largely invisible, and our equipment and atypical bodies and behavior were a mystery to other teachers and administrators. Fast-forward to the present: Federal law now requires that students such as those in my first class have access to the general education curriculum and be assessed on the same academic standards as their nondisabled peers (Individuals with Disabilities Education Improvement Act [IDEA], 2004). Such a drastic shift in policy represents a complicated journey of social advocacy, litigation, and legislation. This chapter tells one part of this epic policy narrative, the implementation story of the Personalized Alternate Assessment Portfolio, hereafter, PAAP.

The story begins with an introduction to the education of students with significant cognitive disabilities and the federal assessment requirements that resulted in the PAAP. Next, we see how policy-implementors (teachers, administrators, state and university personnel) approached and then retreated from substantial change. Even as a new policy offered an opening for reform, a pervasive ideology of "otherness" of disabled individuals as fundamentally different than so-called normal students remained intact. "The seemingly benign category 'normal' is, in fact, a powerful notion that defines who is inscribed within and who is positioned outside of its circle" (Gallagher, Connor, & Ferri, 2014, p. 1125). Conflicting ideologies interacted during implementation—subtly at first and then more obviously until the power of existing norms around disability caused the transformative power of PAAP to subside. However, the story is not as straightforward as two distinct viewpoints vying to dominate implementation—ideological positions overlapped and contradicted each other between, and even within, individual actors. And although all parties were ostensibly motivated by the "best interests" of individuals with disabilities, PAAP Season also reveals how such students and family members were absent from a story that could have profoundly changed their schooling.

Conceptualizing PAAP in Social Context

The PAAP served as Maine's Alternate Assessment, the special type of test given to students who were previously exempt from statewide proficiency testing. The Alternate Assessment was federally mandated, first appearing in the 1997 reauthorization of the Individuals with Disabilities Education Act (IDEA) then clarified and expanded in No Child Left Behind (2002).[1] States were responsible for conducting the Alternate Assessments and reporting the results but could design the particular format of the test. These assessments were intended to increase academic achievement by bringing students previously considered "not ready" or unable to benefit from academic instruction into the same accountability system as the rest of the student population.

Historically, students considered to have "severe" or multiple disabilities were exempt from state tests and rarely taught academics because it was believed they were unable to learn complex content and that independent living skills such as grocery shopping, cooking, and brushing teeth were more important (Ryndak & Billingsley, 2004). The Alternate Assessment promoted "high expectations for academic learning and access to the general curriculum" (U.S. Department of Education, 2007, p. 3)[2] by not only measuring progress but also calculating scores into school accountability reporting. This previous policy of allowing exemptions, aligned with the experiences in my first teaching job, where students with disabilities were relegated to secluded classrooms and required only that teachers be "nice".

With the PAAP policy, students would be assessed on academic material and schools would be accountable to their scores. The implications of including students with significant cognitive disabilities in school accountability measures were potentially transformative—unsettling historical beliefs about ability and competency and enabling new educational practices as students were seen in this new light. But there was also the potential that these students could be pushed further to the margins and seen as responsible for low scores and districts' so-called failure. The PAAP gave students with significant cognitive disabilities recognition and validity. However, it also marginalized the same students because the social norms surrounding the students did not change. The belief in the "otherness" of disabled students was intractable and the tenacity of the belief surprised advocates who assumed that as schools complied with the assessment requirement, segregation would be impossible. Teachers were motivated by care and concern for students they perceived as vulnerable and were fiercely protective at the suggestion that students be taught academic content or, as some called it, "a waste of time" (Goldstein & Behuniak, 2012; Restorff, Sharpe, Abery, Rodriguez, & Kim, 2012; Roberts, Ruppar, & Olson, 2018; Timberlake, 2014). Many teachers, administrators, and state personnel articulated versions of the seemingly benevolent sentiment that students with disabilities be segregated "for their own good" in a place where "their needs can be met" whenever an opening for significant change appeared. Thus, the story of PAAP season is also a cautionary tale about the incredible power of social norms to maintain the distinctions between those providing and those receiving help, the benevolent, and the "needy". Deep-seated, unexamined beliefs about disability kept students confined to a status that allowed professionals to maintain their roles and the educational systems and structures to enact change but remain largely intact.

A Brief History of Legislative Intent of PAAP

One way to appreciate the significance of the PAAP is by understanding that prior to 1975, there were at least one million children with disabilities in the U.S. receiving no education at all (Hehir, 2005). The Education for All Handicapped Children Act in 1975 opened the doors of public schools to all students, but Congress explicitly based the act on access to opportunity and not on any particular level of quality or achievement (Blau, 2007; Eckrem & McArthur, 2001). In other words, students were provided physical access to schools but not necessarily academic access to content. Expectations changed incrementally as this first special education law was reauthorized over subsequent decades (and renamed IDEA in 1990).

Despite these legislative advances, students with significant cognitive disabilities remained highly segregated and were provided with special teachers, separate classrooms, and an individualized and functional curriculum (Jackson, Ryndak, & Wehmeyer, 2008). If academic skills were taught at all, they were to be practical, such as reading a fast food menu or choosing clothing appropriate for the weather (Browder et al., 2003). When IDEA was reauthorized in 2004, Congress saw access to an academic standards-based curriculum as a potential avenue for increasing expectations and making special education more effective (Yell, Katsiyannis, & Hazelkorn, 2007). Thus, 15 years after my first teaching job, students like mine were guaranteed *"access to the general education curriculum in the regular classroom to the maximum extent possible in order to meet developmental goals and, to the maximum extent possible, the challenging expectations that have been established for all children"* (20 U.S.C. § 1400(c)(5)(A) (2004).

The Promise and Excitement of the PAAP

The PAAP was a tool with the potential to uncover hidden academic capacity, revise perceptions of disability, and challenge the assumption that segregation was educationally necessary. The overall policy intent was accountability, but the Maine Department of Education (DOE) also hoped to use the PAAP to improve instruction provided to students with the most significant cognitive disabilities. The PAAP was piloted in four districts in 2000–2001 and then implemented statewide in 2002. The state DOE[3] disseminated policy guidance stating the PAAP will "inform teaching and learning", utilize multiple measures of learning, and provide understandable information to parents and educators". Meeting notes and work samples from these years show the stakeholder group (representatives from the state department of education, the state university, and special education administrators) working to create materials for teachers to guide implementation in a particular direction. In addition to compliance (meaning participation in the assessment), the aim was to simultaneously increase expectations for what students could accomplish. The diversity of opinions and agendas were not visible initially. The first DOE personnel involved in the rollout of the PAAP as well as the representatives from the university had experience teaching students with significant cognitive disabilities and sought to use the assessment requirement to enact larger change. The district administrators were focused on legal compliance and the potential philosophical changes seemed acceptable. Every participant had a vision of what the PAAP would accomplish, but the parties never explicitly described or debated their vision.

Document review from the roll-out period (2000–2002) also foreshadowed later problems. The state asked for outside assessment professionals to review the PAAP development and the written feedback contained the following phrases: "very impressed with overall philosophy and thoughtful dialog", "a lot of pieces are here but there could be more structure", "this is a good start but need more structure", and the word structure is repeated several more times. As will be described later, the first PAAPs required teachers to develop evidence of student performance such as photos, videos, and models. As the PAAP was "structured" and streamlined over the years, however, teacher creativity, inventiveness, and choice were removed. Over time, the rubrics became more general and teacher-created tasks were replaced by an online "bank" of items developed by a test company.

Materials were developed to support the implementation of the first PAAPs including rubrics that translated academic standards into student behaviors. These materials are quite important in the PAAP story because they illustrate attempts to alter the social status of students with disabilities through the PAAP. Essentially, to shape implementation in a way that changed long-standing assumptions that these students could attain only rudimentary daily living skills at best. The first rubrics were very comprehensive, spelling out activities that could be used to demonstrate mastery of content area standards. Every English language arts, math, science, and social studies standard had a rubric with "backed down" options and rubrics were bound into thick booklets by grade spans (K–2, 3–4, 5–8 and 9–12). Each page listed the academic standard; then columns moved across the page with simplified and less complex versions, ending with a basic foundational skill, or what was referred to in PAAP language as the "lowest level of complexity". For example, one of the first rubrics (dated 12/14/01) contained an elementary math performance indicator: *Students will demonstrate an understanding of what numbers mean and how they are used*. This was accompanied by a sequential list of progressively more concrete expressions of performance, culminating in *Using objects, words or symbols, student can copy a model set with up to 5 members with support*. The aim was to convince teachers that even their students who were considered intellectually disabled, used eye gaze or other nonverbal communication, and/or had limited voluntary movement could be working on academic standards.

Similarly, a social studies indicator stated *Students will understand that all nations have governments*, and the lowest level on the rubric for this standard is *Student can identify the person in charge of a particular group, with prompting*. Again, the aim of providing such detailed indicators was to increase the likelihood that the PAAP would push instruction in a new direction. By explicitly showing how to make standards meaningful, the PAAP could serve as more than an assessment; it could deliberately drive changes in perceptions of disability.

After a couple of years, the DOE staff who helped develop the rubrics were replaced by a full-time PAAP coordinator, a former superintendent whose sole responsibility was statewide PAAP implementation. The new coordinator had extensive assessment experience but no disability experience—which was the first clue that the state priority was efficiency—increasing compliance with the regulation rather than changing the educational status of students with disabilities.

As implementation began in full, small differences in orientation among the policy implementers at different levels (teachers, administrators, university, and state personnel) foreshadowed widening philosophical gaps. First, despite a strong background in assessment, the new leadership at the state level lacked experience and understanding about teaching students with complex physical, sensory and communicative disabilities. Therefore, the directions for how to administer the PAAP were oversimplified and ended up creating more frustration and resistance. Teachers were required to list the cues they gave while administering the PAAP to students. So, in addition to the rubrics, examples of potential prompts were now disseminated to support implementation. For example, teachers were advised to "use verbal cues such as '*what strategies do you use to figure out a word you don't know'?"* This example illustrates the implication of valuing assessment expertise without equally seeking knowledge of disability supports from those who could have provided it. More extensive supports were needed, such as tactile symbols, picture communication, and physical cues, for example, gently stroking a child's cheek to indicate you were going to give him or her a bite of food or a photo of the music teacher as a cue that a transition to music class was coming.

Second, the message of "high expectations" became ubiquitous and conflicting priorities emerged. If a teacher questioned the PAAP, the assessment specialists considered them to have a "deficit perspective" or as not believing that "all children can learn". For example, when a teacher protested administering a test item to count the number of toy trucks on a worksheet and circle the answer because the student had low vision and her cerebral palsy interfered with manipulating a pencil, they were met with "[Y]ou need to have high expectations!" Those who wanted to use the PAAP to enhance the status of students with disabilities recognized the absurdity of some of the test items but did not protest because there was, in fact, a history of low expectations. If some of the PAAP tasks were questionable (counting trucks), the trade-off was worthwhile because the students would have to go into a general education math class and count the trucks with nondisabled children. Once there, modifications such as counting the number of times a peer put a truck in her hand and indicating an answer using a voice output app would be easily accomplished. Thus, the social change agenda was more important to the university personnel who were willing to compromise on the validity of the test to move inclusion forward, while the state co-opted the arguments for inclusion (increasing expectations and believing in competency) to increase compliance.

The Emergence of PAAP Season

"PAAP season" was the way a teacher described the time spent putting the pieces of the PAAP together. The season began when the teacher started organizing tasks in the late fall and ended in early spring when "everything's packaged up". An elementary teacher summed up the concept of PAAP season by reporting, "There's certain pockets of time you say OK let's just get this done!"

After being implemented statewide in 2002, the years from 2004 to 2008 were a critical and somewhat chaotic time. Teachers struggled to accept and accommodate the PAAP, and the state struggled to refine expectations and settle on a version of the PAAP that satisfied the growing Alternate Assessment movement across the country (Quenemoen, Kearns, Quenemoen, Flowers, & Kleinert, 2010). The differences in what each defined as a valued outcome were becoming more pronounced. The advocacy position had been to persuade teachers that since they must now teach academics to students seen as "severely" disabled, why not teach those academics in inclusive classrooms alongside nondisabled peers? This position viewed the PAAP as a vehicle to increase inclusion and the status of students with very diverse abilities. The assessment position focused on bringing the PAAP into alignment with other standardized assessments. Although both agreed on the value of the assessment, the definition of successful implementation was quite different.

The significance of the term *PAAP season* was that it demonstrated compliance with the law but showed that educators were not necessarily seeing this assessment as representing anything more than a required activity to fit into already busy schedules. As the state focused on technical validity, the PAAP became further removed from classroom practice (teachers were no longer creating tasks) and was therefore even less able to influence philosophical shifts in those practices. The measures that were taken to standardize the PAAP in the name of increasing reliability, resulted in the test being less able to provide any kind of personalized feedback. The state personnel were diligent in carrying out their implementation tasks, but had they paused to learn about who the students were, what they needed from an assessment, and how the PAAP could serve to improve their overall participation in curriculum and instruction, this story would be very different.

Numerous variables contributed to producing "PAAP season" but one stands out as particularly significant: the evolving composition of the PAAP. Most notably, some element of the test changed every year. The continual changing and "tweaking" kept the PAAP process just slightly chaotic and unpredictable. The standards were revised, or the required number of assessment tasks was changed, or the forms that accompanied the tasks were altered, or the process for submitting a completed PAAP was updated, or the scoring language changed . . . and so on. The PAAP instruction manual was updated and reissued every year.

The constant changes kept special educators struggling to keep up; one could not learn the elements of the PAAP and then move ahead to become proficient and thoughtful in its use because the following year it would be a little different. Teachers were frustrated and increasingly cynical as "the state" (teachers' term for legislative requirements) kept changing what was expected. The "state" was continually responding to larger national conversations about standards and seeking more sophisticated technical validity (Kleinert & Kearns, 2010). Importantly, this is another unanticipated consequence of differing roles and perspectives among those navigating the implementation of a new policy. Teachers were sincere in their attempts to learn the PAAP and state personnel were sincere in their attempts to improve the PAAP. And yet, their very efforts served to inadvertently frustrate each other. While points of contradiction can act as important spaces for transformation, in this case, the perspectives of those in the assessment position dominated the conversation and process.

Another consequence of the continual changes was eventual resignation—a distancing from a personal investment in the assessment toward an attitude of "what is the state going to want from us next?" Interviews conducted in 2009 suggested that special educators viewed the PAAP requirement from slightly different perspectives: as a consequence for underperforming teachers ("there are a few bad apples so we're all being punished") to a bureaucratic necessity to an insult to their professionalism. However, none expressed a view that the PAAP was part of social justice or related to the status of the students they supported. While some teachers did report rethinking their academic expectations, many simply taught selected "PAAP" skills during PAAP season (Timberlake, 2011).

Three areas also contributed to the impression of continual flux and made the PAAP less attractive to teachers and less able to advance reform in special education: (a) format, (b) professional development, and (c) sameness as equity.

The decision to change the PAAP from teacher developed portfolios to a paper-and-pencil test occurred during this period. Teachers were directed to stop creating tasks and choose from a selection of assessment items created by a test company. Special educators gave this change (from teacher-created to standardized tasks) mixed reviews but agreed that it depersonalized the process as well as "made it easier". Later, the option to select from an array of tasks was discontinued. Teachers were instructed which test items to administer and did so by downloading them from a secure website using a confidential password. This final level of standardization served to discourage any critical analysis of the underlying rationale of the PAAP as the assessment was formalized into another regulation to be followed.

Second, professional development focused heavily on procedural compliance and the mechanics of assembling a PAAP. Attendance was required at state workshops at least annually to learn the most recent years' new process for preparation and submission. Early workshops brought together hundreds of teachers each time, and although there were negative reactions expressed toward the PAAP, the focus of professional development remained on the test itself. Teachers were there to learn procedural compliance rather than to contribute expertise on disability and help determine how the PAAP could best reflect student progress. Teacher knowledge was silenced in the face of the contradiction between those giving the information (state education) and those whose only role was to receive it (teachers). However, the situation is even more complex because there were also significant contradictions within the teacher population. Participants at the workshops expressed mixed reactions to the PAAP and much of the resistance came from a concern that the standards were inappropriate for the targeted students. For example, some teachers were genuinely perplexed by the requirement to assess students with the most significant cognitive disabilities. Participants would stand up at the workshops and passionately try to explain how disabled their students were in the belief that if the state just understood, they would see that the PAAP was unreasonable. Thus, the complexity of PAAP Season is not merely that the state did not ask teachers for their expertise but that many teachers were also operating under a traditional view of disability. They kept their students safe and comfortable but viewed them as incapable of learning the level of academic content the PAAP required. It is possible to see in hindsight, that discussing feelings and expectations (in addition to forms) may have made a difference. The focus on the mechanics of the PAAP left teachers to process a range of emotions and make meaning of this extraordinary change without discussing the bigger picture—the evolution of disability in society.

In addition, while the early annual professional development was provided at multiple locations and in-person, it was changed after 2010 to an on-demand video with procedural updates. This is another key moment. It shows how a policy with such monumental potential for social change did not sustain the vision or commitment. The direction of the PAAP moved away from trying to influence teacher beliefs, values, and instructional choices to simply ensuring the assessment was submitted correctly.

Third, "sameness as equity" refers to the original policy intent, that using the same standards for students with disabilities would remedy historical inequities. The academic standards, while increasing students' participation in state assessment, could not, in and of themselves, change the segregation of students with complex disabilities. The PAAP was being guided by assessment experts with a strong belief that compliance and participation equaled equity. The early emphasis on teaching via detailed rubrics in order to convince teachers that academic standards could be a good thing was replaced by a focus on assessment expertise. This allowed the PAAP to be redesigned for efficiency (the booklets of rubrics became thinner every year and were eventually discontinued) and honed to a more streamlined process. Every student taking the PAAP was given the same choice of items, the items were evaluated by statisticians for technical validity and this stage of implementation began to close with the perception that the work was "done"—compliance with the Alternate Assessment policy had been achieved, all students were working on standards, and progress was being measured and reported.

PAAP Season Winds Down

As the PAAP approached 10 years of age, the novelty wore off, and the social justice mission stalled as PAAP season became a routine part of the special education process. Looking back, delivering the PAAP to teachers rather than inviting their expertise was problematic. The most immediate way to enact such a large-scale policy change was to provide materials and instructions to those responsible for implementing it. However, research conducted after more than a decade found no evidence that participants recalled a social change agenda. The contradictory views and the challenging conversations about disability that could have added a richness to the development gave way to efficiency and uniformity thinking. Districts were complying, and students with disabilities were part of the accountability system as envisioned in the federal laws. Although research showed some lingering resistance to the PAAP, teachers' reasons were about autonomy and not about the social status and isolation of the students (Timberlake, 2016).

Today, in 2019, there is little remaining of PAAP Season. English language arts and math tasks are computer-based and part of a multistate assessment no longer unique to Maine. The PAAP consists solely of science items that teachers (with the required confidential password) download and administer. The story of the PAAP began with an enormous policy shock to the entrenched system of providing often caring, but mainly custodial and segregated, educational programming for the most disabled students. The story peaked with statewide implementation and the struggles, opportunities, and insights obtained by such an ambitious project and ends with the PAAP functioning as one of a multitude of special education provisions.

The Legacy of PAAP: Reform as Repackaging and Reification of Segregation

The story of PAAP season shows positive outcomes for students with disabilities but at great cost. The largest gain was in bringing an academic focus to the education of students historically considered unable to benefit, the greatest loss was in reifying segregation and providing a new rationale for separateness. The overall policy intent was achieved. All students participated in state assessment, assessment tasks were aligned with academic standards, and students who may not previously have had access to academics received at least some instruction in reading, math, and science. Students with significant cognitive disabilities were visible in policy and on spreadsheets, they were identified at the district level as eligible for the PAAP and their scores were reported. Such results were unimaginable when my first students and I entered the portable classroom behind our elementary school decades ago. This policy outcome is deeply valuable and should not be underestimated. However, participation was accompanied by missed opportunities and the inadvertent reification of segregation. Paradoxically, while academic access increased, academics often came to be treated as perfunctory and devoid of real expectation and context. Teachers complied and "fit" the PAAP into their existing routines and minimized disruption by putting the PAAP together efficiently but with little change in the context surrounding academic instruction. As one teacher explained, "If through the course of the year, say from Oct-March I have to give 12 ELA and 12 math, these tasks are short . . . seriously, I can give them in study hall, they don't impact anything at all." While the intended accountability outcomes were achieved, the legacy of marginalization remains. And a new complacency emerged as PAAP season receded into recollections told by veteran teachers about "that time the state got involved" with kids with the most significant cognitive disabilities.

Academic Exposure at a Cost: The Construction of a New Language for Segregation

The most encouraging outcome of PAAP season has been a lasting change in access to academics. During research interviews in 2009, a participant shared, "I have seen growth with kids where I didn't expect I would, particularly around coin identification. Two of the kids I had—I really didn't think they'd be able to i.d. coins, but I found when sort of being forced to identify coins, they could!" In a subsequent study, a special educator stated that "the days of not teaching academics are over" (Timberlake, 2014). The lasting impact of PAAP was reinforced when teacher participants were asked about their instructional planning and all described some form of standards-based academics. Although these results still showed a persistent level of self-contained instruction, academic access had remained more than 10 years after the introduction of the PAAP (2014).

Another legacy of PAAP season is the teaching of science. Science was a content area not widely taught to students with disabilities prior to 2002 and appears directly attributable to the PAAP. Maine special educators were asked if they had added anything to their instruction because of the PAAP requirements and science was offered by multiple respondents. For example, "Things like some of the science concepts. . . . I wouldn't have thought to teach. Now that the tasks have come along, I've had to add to my curriculum a little bit" (Timberlake, 2011).

These outcomes are important, and mandating academics for students previously considered too disabled to benefit from it certainly improved the situation. However, the PAAP inadvertently served to cement existing inequalities by enabling academic access to be implemented in isolation from general education.

The entire PAAP process—from choosing test items, conducting the assessments and scoring the tasks, was implemented separately from general education. Special educators began to use a new and more sophisticated vocabulary (i.e., Alternate Assessment Grade Level Expectations [AAGLEs], Levels of Complexity [LoCs]),[4] but this change only served to provide a separate "language" spoken only by a few, again unintentionally cementing isolation of students whose status in schools was already very separate because of the complexity of their disabilities. Teachers and administrators began to refer to those eligible for the assessment as "PAAP kids", the required professional development as "PAAP training", and the time spent on the test as "PAAP Season". Whereas earlier segregation could be challenged by arguing for students to be seen as competent learners, the PAAP inadvertently provided a sanctioned reason for segregation—the requirement to prepare for the PAAP.

Beyond Disability: The Broader Lessons of the PAAP

The lessons of PAAP season can be understood as illustrating both the incredible power of policy as well as the incredible strength of resistance. When policy pushed too hard against the status quo by seeking substantial change in the status of individuals from lower (receiving charity and compassion) to equitable (receiving respect and inclusion), there were gains and losses. Why did the PAAP accomplish so much and yet fail to change the marginalization of students with the most complex disabilities? There is compelling evidence for two reasons: (1) The policy intent was not interpreted and implemented the same way by all involved, and (2) contradictions between a call for competency and inclusion were less powerful than existing norms defining ways to educate children and youth with complex physical and intellectual disabilities.

Interpretations of Policy Intent

Participant observation at PAAP professional development sessions, as well as investigations of teacher perceptions showed unequivocally that the policy intent was unclear to the teachers responsible for implementation. (Timberlake, 2011, 2014, 2016). Some saw value in the increased expectations, but there was also resistance and confusion. A key lesson is how teachers made their own meaning. In the face of ambiguity and continual change (the evolving PAAP structure), teachers created meaning, and it was neither the advocacy nor the academic achievement that those in charge of the implementation envisioned. For example, one teacher created a story she could accept:

> You gotta get it done so the school can get money! . . . After the first few years getting fumed about it, I got it in my head that it's a fund raiser. By doing this [PAAP] my school is receiving money and that helps a little bit to support my job and the kids. And that's how I accept it, it's kind of a fundraiser . . . without doing it [PAAP] & passing something in we won't get as much money or we'll be fined and be a 'needs improvement' school or whatever.

This view showed how the teacher complied with a policy she didn't value. Her words also reflect previous theoretical work suggesting that regardless of policy intent, individuals make meaning of policy in the context of their daily work (Brodkin, 2003; Lipsky, 2010).

On the other hand, other teachers believed the early portfolios (before the task bank and standardized administration) were a chance for students to showcase their work. These teachers expressed disappointment when realizing "the state" seemed unimpressed with student work. An elementary teacher lamented,

> Really, in the beginning I had hope because—I thought "well, we're showing things kids were using . . . they [PAAPs] were mammoth size! I thought OK, people really want to take a look at what kids are doing—what they're really doing in classrooms and I made these big beautiful PAAPs that took an enormous amount of time to complete.

And another teacher shared,

> You know earlier on it really seemed like wow this is great, this portfolio really shows what my kids can do! It's a huge amount of work—but I really felt when it was all done, wow—it was a thing of beauty. I mean some of those earlier PAAPS were amazing and then . . . last year I just had to shake my head.

These responses reveal differences in understanding policy intent and a poignant view of teacher cooperation. While teachers were willing to showcase student work, they were understandably disappointed to realize that the state was less interested in viewing "beautiful work", and more interested in progress toward the standards. Maine DOE's written policy articulated the purpose of the PAAP as "achievement of standards and accountability for results". The word *personalized* (the first "P" in PAAP) was misleading because progress and achievement did not, in the end, require a personal look at student work.

The Strengths of Existing Norms

The history of severe disability is a complicated one including neglect, fear, and pity (Baynton, 2013). One of the most enduring norms is segregation for "one's own good". Special education for these students is rooted in caregiving, and policymakers and state personnel underestimated the attachment to specialization that was challenged by implementing the PAAP.

The PAAP requirement shook many teachers' core beliefs about their students and their role. Professional development focused mainly on the mechanics of putting the PAAP together, and without the opportunity and support to reflect on what it meant to expect academics in individuals where it was considered unlikely, the policy could not lead to progressive philosophical changes. The shift in values that was hoped for with the advent of the PAAP was actually threatening to traditional roles and identity. The field of special education is based on "otherness", and despite very real civil rights gains, special education has also resulted in a system of assessing, diagnosing, labeling, and segregating individuals deemed "different". While PAAP provided openings to challenge the way students are educated, the change took the place of reform within current systems rather than transformative, systems change.

Despite the strength of existing norms, there are points in the PAAP story where actions that seem small in the face of systemic change, may have redirected the path of the PAAP and increased social inclusion. Requiring that a general educator participate in a minimal way (i.e., complete one social or communication task) could have decreased student isolation. For example, the special education law, IDEA, requires a general educator attend every IEP (individualized education program) meeting. While attendance does not guarantee participation, the requirement makes participation more likely. This same recommendation—to merge the PAAP with general education initiatives—could alleviate some concerns about protection. The participation of their general education colleagues would be necessary if special educators were to be convinced that the mainstream could be a safe welcoming place for vulnerable students.

Conclusion

While the PAAP was responsible for significant change, something was missing from the entire policymaking and implementing process: individuals with disabilities. Despite the noble aim, the policy that was designed to decrease marginalization of students with significant cognitive disabilities did not invite such individuals or their families or caregivers to help design or provide feedback about the PAAP. Including parents, caregivers, and disability advocates in developing ways to implement education policy would be logistically challenging, but the challenge is also the very reason to do so. Speaking about disability as "other", even when trying to better the circumstances for the "other" presaged the outcome. The lesson of PAAP Season is not to diminish the importance of caring. Almost 30 years after my first teaching job, "nice" still matters. But policy is a powerful way to ensure that care for others comes from a position of equity and inclusion.

Notes

1. The regulatory language for students eligible for Alternate Assessment is "students with the most significant cognitive disabilities".
2. https://www2.ed.gov/parents/needs/speced/learning/learning-opportunities.pdf
3. Personal records of committee document March 2000.
4. Alternate Assessment Administration Manual 2007–08.

References

Baynton, D. C. (2013). Disability and the justification of inequality in American history. In L. Davis (Ed.), *The disability studies reader* (4th ed.). New York, NY: Routledge.

Blau, A. (2007). The IDEIA and the right to an "appropriate" education. *Brigham Young University Education & Law Journal, 1*, 1–22.

Brodkin, E. (2003). Street-level research: Policy at the front lines. In M. C. Lennon & T. L. Corbett. (Eds.), *Policy into action implementation research and welfare reform* (pp. 145–163). Washington, DC: The Urban Institute Press.

Browder, D. M., Spooner, F., Ahlgrim-Delzell, L., Flowers, C., Algozzine, B., & Karvonen, M. (2003). A content analysis of the curricular philosophies reflected in states' Alternate Assessment performance indicators. *Research & Practice for Persons with Severe Disabilities, 28*(4), 165–181.

Eckrem, J. O., & McArthur, E. J. (2001). Is the Rowley standard dead? From access to results. *UC Davis Journal of Juvenile Law & Policy, 5*, 199–217.

Gallagher, D. J., Connor, D. J., & Ferri, B. A. (2014). Beyond the far too incessant schism: Special education and the social model of disability. *International Journal of Inclusive Education, 18*, 1120–1142.

Goldstein, J., & Behuniak, P. (2012). Assessing students with significant cognitive disabilities on academic content. *The Journal of Special Education, 42*, 117–127. doi:10.1177/0022466910379156

Hehir, T. (2005). *New directions in special education: Eliminating ableism in policy and practice.* Cambridge, MA: Harvard University Press.

Individuals with Disabilities Education Improvement Act. (2004). *Public law 108-446.* Washington, DC: U. S. Government Printing Office.

Jackson, L. B., Ryndak, D. L., & Wehmeyer, M. L. (2008). The dynamic relationship between context, curriculum, and student learning: A case for inclusive education as a research-based practice. *Research & Practice for Persons with Severe Disabilities, 33/34*, 175–195.

Kleinert, H. L., & Kearns, J. (Eds.). (2010). *Alternate assessment for students with significant cognitive disabilities: An educator's guide.* Baltimore, MD: Paul H. Brookes Publishing.

Lipsky, M. (2010). *Street level bureaucracy, dilemmas of the individual in public service.* (30th anniversary expanded ed.). New York: Russell Sage Foundation.

No Child Left Behind (NCLB) Act of 2001, Pub. L. No. 107-110, § 115, Stat. 1425 (2002).

Quenemoen, R., Kearns, J., Quenemoen, M., Flowers, C., & Kleinert, H. (2010). *Common misperceptions and research-based recommendations for alternate assessment based on alternate achievement standards* (Synthesis Report 73). Minneapolis, MN: University of Minnesota, National Center on Educational Outcomes.

Restorff, D., Sharpe, M., Abery, B., Rodriguez, M., & Kim, N. K. (2012). Teacher perceptions of alternate assessment based on alternate achievemet standards: Results from a three state survey. *Research & Practice for Persons with Severe Disabilities.* doi:10.2511/027494812804153570

Roberts, C. A., Ruppar, A. L., & Olson, A. J. (2018). Perceptions matter: Administrators' vision of instruction for students with severe disabilities. *Research & Practice for Persons with Severe Disabilities, 43*, 3–19. doi:10.1177/1540796917743931

Ryndak, D., & Billingsley, F. (2004). Access to the general education curriculum. In E. M. Horn & C. H. Kennedy (Eds.), *Including students with severe disabilities* (pp. 33–50). Boston, MA: Pearson Education, Inc.

Timberlake, M. (2011). Policy fact and policy fiction: Assessment, accountability and students with disabilities. *Journal of Maine Education*, 27, 31–33.

Timberlake, M. (2014). Weighing costs and benefits: Teacher interpretation and implementation of access to the general education curriculum. *Research and Practice for Persons with Severe Disabilities*, 39(2), 83–99. doi:10.1177/1540796914544547

Timberlake, M. (2016). The path to academic access. *The Journal of Special Education*, 49(4), 199–208. doi:10.1177/0022466914554296

U.S. Department of Education. (2007). *Learning opportunities for your child through alternate assessments*. Washington, DC: Office of Special Education and Rehabilitative Services.

Yell, M., Katsiyannis, M., & Hazelkorn, M. (2007). Reflections on the 25th anniversary of the US supreme court's decision in Board of Education v. Rowley. *Focus on Exceptional Children*, 39(9), 1–12.

13 Theories From Below
Imagining Policy Making and Policy Analysis Beyond "Achievement" Paradigms

Socorro Cambero, Miguel N. Abad, Briana M. Hinga and Gilberto Q. Conchas

The Kick It Spot: Uplifting the Paramount Perspective

The gates to the Rio De Los Angeles State Park opened on a balmy Saturday morning when I (i.e., Socorro, the first author of this chapter) was just shy of 12 years old. The balloons were in sync with the afternoon winds of spring, and the sunrays caressed my tender face. Childhood laughter rang through my ears, and I was surrounded by *mi comunidad* (my community), my buddies and *mi familia* (my family). *Todo era perfecto* (everything was perfect). I sensed that Papá was also exhilarated with this new neighborhood project. For Papá, the park symbolized a freedom that was unfamiliar to him but would hopefully be normal for his children and other young people in the community. This park would be our special place. This space would be free of negative experiences at home or school. There would be no parents working 12-hour workdays, no empty stomachs, or teachers who thought our *familias* (families) posed a threat to our educational performance—only Spanish jokes and games of tag.

After hours of games, sunlight and sugary snacks, Papá signaled it was time to go home. I trudged toward the sidewalk to cross the street. Suddenly, I felt a sharp grip from Papá on my hand. He looked both ways carefully while having the corner of his eyes alert on his five other children. There were no stop signs or lights to alert drivers of pedestrians, only the sound of drifting cars. One by one, they pass us, with no signal or awareness of our desire to cross the street. I voice my frustration to Papá.

SOCORRO: *¿Papá, porque no cruzamos? Los* vehículos *no paran.* (Dad, why don't we cross? The vehicles do not stop.)
PAPÁ: *Tenemos que esperar hasta que los* vehículos *paren. Ten paciencia, mi reina.* (We must wait until the vehicles stop. Have patience, my queen.)
SOCORRO: *¿Pero cuándo van a parar?* (But when will they stop?)
PAPÁ: *Has contacto con un* conductor *antes de cruzar, y cuando lo haces, se detendrá. Después otros* vehículos *también se detendrán.* (We have

to make contact with a driver before crossing, and when you do that, the driver will stop. Then, the other vehicles will also stop.)

We managed to cross the street, but I overheard a conversation between Mamá and Papá later that night. Papá shared that the missing crosswalk leading to the park would engender accidents. *How are children expected to cross the street?*

Since Mamá and Papá were active in community meetings, one of the city board members hooked up Papá with a meeting with the city mayor. Papá assembled an extensive list of reasons outlining why the implementation of a stoplight would be integral to ensuring the safety of young people. Papá outlined the collective responsibility of the city and the community in ensuring the safety of young people around the park. Papá kept it real. Community members must trust that the city will provide a venue for their children to stay safe while guardians are working to feed their families. Papá articulated a vision of society, communities and the state where collaboration and communication are essential.

Papá returned home from the meeting with the mayor. His head was drooped down, and I discerned the distress in his voice. The mayor informed Papá that it would take more than a community member's request to build a stoplight, such as an injury or perhaps a death. *Are community members' concerns not enough?* Papá was not content nor was he deterred. In fact, Papá realized that change does not emerge from individuals but by movements, by communities.

Mamá and Papá took me along as they canvassed community members' homes to gather the signatures of support. The Southern California heat was an impediment to the process, but Papá and Mamá were relentless; it motivated me. I walked diligently through the neighborhood, refusing the assistance from my father when he noticed a letup in my strides. Stubborn girl. Once we arrived at a door, Papá rang the doorbell, reassuring Mamá that knocks will amass support. Meanwhile, I peeked through windows or listened attentively, gently pressing my ears as close to the doors in search of the sound of footsteps, anything that signaled the presence of community members. Papá knew most community members because many hailed from towns in Mexico, often close to where Mamá and Papá grew up. It was a community of immigrants, the boldest people I knew who put everything on the line to provide for their children.

A tap on the shoulder meant that it was my turn to drop the line. Papá was strategic and clever. He figured that my perspective as a young person in the community was pivotal to acquire the most support. Additionally, since Mamá and Papá are Spanish-dominant, my bilingualism would be helpful when speaking to members who only speak English. *Hi, my name is Socorro. My parents and I are collecting signatures so that the city can plan a stoplight at the main street before the park. This will ensure the safety of the children like myself while the adults are working.*

We need the support of as many community members. Community members agreed, stating that the city plans must be presented to the community before they are implemented. Many reassured us with their support. Several community members also began collecting signatures from their co-workers and *familias*. They were the backbones of our communities' safety.

Together, community members, Mamá and Papá hustled to collect more than 2,000 signatures from community members. They stood at churches, neighborhood meetings and visited the park regularly. There were also community members who participated in subtle but loaded ways through word of mouth. Members became aware signatures were being collected. It was a collective effort. Papá presented the signatures of support to the mayor. He came back from his meeting with the same report. Still, a death or an injury were prerequisites to building a stoplight. Community members were startled with the outcome, as many were certain that signatures of support would coax the city to implement the crosswalk. This was offensive.

Who Knows

A few months later, Papá and I were on our way to the park. As we walked toward the end of the street leading to the park, we spotted the outlines of freshly spread concrete, gravel and yellow traces of newly painted sidewalk lines. Adjacent to the lines were glossy poles with stoplights. It had been done. We approached the sidewalk, but this time, Papá's eyes were relaxed, followed by a smirk across his face. *To this day, we do not know what prompted the city to implement the stop lights. Who knows?* The cars drifted by and slowed down within seconds after the walk button was pushed. Community members filled tables, and children were running across the new artificial grass. The teenagers walked around the playground, with their *mangoniadas*, dripping with *chamoy* from the street vendor's bountiful hand. It was what I remembered—poise.

Testimonios and Theories From Below

This chapter purposefully begins with Socorro's *testimonio*, which illustrates how theory emerges from the lives of everyday people as they struggle to live and create a better world. *Testimonios* are forms of counter-storytelling that serve as a methodological tool to piece together various experiences, "open new windows into reality" (Delgado, 1989, p. 2414) and challenge the status quo (Solórzano & Yosso, 2001, 2002). Socorro's papá and mamá's material conditions as parents, immigrants and part of the working class equipped them with a unique lens that allowed them to understand the vulnerabilities of the young people living in their community. Evidently, community members were not afraid of confronting the tension between celebrating a new implementation in the community and the root of the problem—the city's decision to disregard the concerns of those affected by community changes.

Saavedra and Pérez (2012) posit that "Chicana and Black feminisms can inform research and teaching while helping those living on or in the margins make sense of and heal fragmented lives" (pg. 431). Chicana feminism and Black feminism are radical theories because they hold a commitment toward social justice by pinpointing the root of the problem. Such theory centers the experiences of those most subjugated in society, as their material realities provide a unique lens that illuminates how sexism, capitalism and racism operate not only as abstract concepts but also within the lived realities of the economically nondominant, racially othered people. More important, they uplift those rendered invisible and center their experiences to inform a multitude of activisms and justice projects.

Testing and Achievement Regimes in Education Policy as Educational Enclosures

Ultimately, this volume has focused on illustrating the limits of what can be accomplished and imagined by education policies that are guided by technocratic projects. More important, we see how conventional education policy continues to be animated by the narrowing logics of achievement and testing. These logics are fully embedded within liberal ideological racial projects that produce our hegemonic notions of meritocracy and social mobility. The dominant regimes of achievement and testing severely limit how researchers, educators and policy-makers come to think about education.

As anthropologist Damien M. Sojoyner (2017) has written, schools in the United States often function as *enclosed places*, where only the most tepid reformist ideas are legible to the state. As such, the policy projects, research agendas and interventions that are taken up ultimately must not threaten hegemonic notions of education, achievement and testing. It is in the wake of this enclosure that collective action and resistance become key vectors of action that students, educators and parents can use for their voices to be acknowledged by the state. For instance, last year, we have witnessed students in Chicago and New Haven organize walkouts and protests in opposition to dehumanizing "no excuses" disciplinary policies at Noble and Achievement First charter networks. In the face of policy, research and practice entranced by a commitment to achievement defined narrowly defined by test scores, youth activists across the country remind us that "achievement" cannot be the justification for the everyday indignities that "no excuses" and testing regimes bring to bear on students educational experiences and realities. Therein lies the power of each case study in this anthology.

Section I, "False Choices", demonstrated the ways in which education policy, informed and guided by neoliberal logics, furthers a narrowed vision of education that is dictated by the market. Within this paradigm, education is defined top-down as policy makers ignore the knowledge and wisdom of parents, educators and young people. Moreover, the same market logic shapes ideas of citizenship and success for young people where order and compliance are rewarded above all else.

Section II, "Technical and Market Solutions for Issues of Justice", reminds us how mainstream notions of achievement based on testing impoverishes our imaginations of what education ought and should be. This narrowed imagination tends to privilege the expertise of administrators and technocrats while marginalizing the knowledge of community members that are subject to "education reform". Additionally, even data practices at the school level, as described in Rachel Garver's chapter, can reinscribe "gaps" while technically making accountability efforts more "efficient". Mirroring the intersection of capitalism and education, we are more clearly beginning to see how market solutions are vulnerable to the rent-seeking desires of politicians, administrators, policy makers and "education entrepreneurs".

The chapters from Section III, "The Legacy and Futures of Special Education", illustrate how historiographic, humanistic and critical perspectives are sorely needed within an education subfield where much research is still largely operating within damage-centered paradigms (Tuck, 2009). Positioning students with disabilities or neurodivergent young people through deficit lenses is consistent with neoliberal logics of our era, in which all kinds of deficiencies and failures are located within the individual (e.g. "character", biology, psychology) and within the cultural tropes that shape our imaginations of (especially poor) Black, Indigenous, Brown, and other racialized peoples.

This chapter introduces a discussion for how feminisms of color and "theories from below" can offer more expansive imaginations for education policy. Such theories remind us how parents, youth and community members hold valuable standpoints, rooted in their material realities, which are shaped by intersecting systems of oppression. Moreover, we lift up Chicana feminisms as an example of a theoretical lens for education research and policy analysis; its origins spring from the material and political struggle of activists who have dared to imagine and demand that another world is possible. By grappling with Chicana feminist frameworks, we are impelled into a space of imagination; *un espacio especial* (a special place) where theory and the experiences of *nuestra gente* (our people) are integral for education policy.

Lastly, we end this chapter and this book by returning to Lopez and Baca's chapter on turnaround efforts in Native schools. We spend special time revisiting this case study as it encapsulates the multitude of dimensions that are elided when policy-makers, researchers or administrators are guided by technocratic projects narrowly focused on testing and conventional modes of achievement. Feminist, Indigenous and other critical perspectives allow us to bring to light the other elements of education and schooling that much conventional policy making and analysis overlooks—in this case, issues of tribal sovereignty and cultural life.

Chicana Feminism and Views From Below

Feminist theories provide us a way to recognize the material and ideological manifestations of gender in shaping racial domination and economic exploitation. One of the most prominent contributors to Chicana feminism is Gloria Anzaldúa—Chicana feminist writer, poet, activist. Gloria Anzaldúa is widely known for her work on Borderlands Theory, which presents the border as a metaphor and a third space of ambiguity (Anzaldúa, 1987). She draws on her experience as the daughter of farmworkers living in poverty near *la frontera*—the Texas–Mexico border not being fully Chicana nor fully of American—and illuminates how living in the borderlands creates a third space between social institutions and cultures where ambiguity and contradictions are embraced. The *frontera* becomes an integral geographical location that captures the subordination specific to Chicanas/mestizas.

Anzaldúa's work provides us with tools to theorize on how people grapple with and navigate through contradictory power structures such as languages, locations, sexualities, nation-states and cultures. Anzaldúa's Borderlands theory also presents the concept of the *mestiza consciousness, una consciencia de mujer*. The *mestiza* occupies a special place and garners knowledge while living in radically different worlds. Anzaldúa (1987) asserts that living in the borderlands—a space of ambiguity and contradictory power structures—garners special knowledge from being within a system while also cherishing the knowledge of an outsider who comes from outside the system. Evidently, the *mestiza* "outsider within" status creates a unique and complex layer to a Chicana's sense of self.

Anzaldúa's insight further provides us with tools to theorize about the lives of individuals who are exposed to radically different roles—cultures, social classes, languages, colonization—to develop the ability to challenge dominant notions of reality. Chicana feminisms and other theories from below are rooted within the material realities and experiences of subjugated women. Their perspectives allow us to understand how social forces such as homophobia, racism, sexism and capitalism are manifested in everyday life. Hence, Chicana feminism is appropriate to complicate contemporary educational policies and practices.

Chicana Feminism as Political Struggle

The history of Chicana feminism traces back to the 1960s during the Chicano movement. The Chicano movement presented a list demands advocating for issues including social justice and educational reforms to better Chicano communities. This revolutionary movement was the genesis for several smaller movements such as the Chicano student movement, land tenure, farmworker unionization and educational reform (Escobar, 1993). Chicanas were prominent participants in the movement and demanded that the movement recognize how gender and racial oppression simultaneously impacts their lives. Chicanas asserted that sexist behavior present in the movement mirrored the very patriarchal structure that was the root to their oppression, therefore, recognizing gender oppression was critical. However, men and cultural nationalists believed feminism to be an individualist search for identity that was a distraction from the Chicano movement's "real" issues such as racism. Chicana feminists were read as advocating for antimale ideology, as "feministas", and "vendidas" (sellouts) who were "anti-Chicano movement" (Nieto-Gomez, 1974).

Rowbotham (1972) avers that women develop feminist consciousness as a result of their experiences with sexism in political organizing or social movements. The feminist consciousness propels people to mobilize change, even though subtle acts, evident in Papá's and the community members' actions. We note the similarities and interconnectedness between movements and theory. Anzaldúa's work on Borderlands Theory also runs in parallel to others Black feminist interventions such as *intersectionality* (Crenshaw, 1991) and *identity politics* (Combahee River Collective, 2014 as structural oppressions and vulnerabilities are concretized through social locations. This lineage of activists and theorists are what that have informed the development and evolution of Chicana feminisms and other critical perspectives. *Vis-à-vis* education, critical perspectives provide researchers and policy-makers a way to understand how policy is lived out every day in the lives of nondominant youth, parents and educators.

Unsettling Contemporary Achievement Paradigms

Jameson D. Lopez's and Evelyn C. Baca's chapter on American Indian School turnaround elucidates how decolonizing frameworks illuminate the deeper moral and ethical problems that are not legible to most conventional education research and policy analysis. At the heart of this chapter are the ways in which mainstream education policy analyses overlook the host of consequences of policy when the fixation on academic achievement becomes a myopic animating force for policy makers and researchers. This impasse is emblematic of the conflicts between what Leigh Patel (2019) has described as the "achievement-measured desires of a settler state" and the desires of Indigenous peoples to sustain Native life in the face of settler colonialism.

In this contemporary era of "education reform", success and failure are often guided by narrow metrics such as achievement scores and tests. A policy-maker might glance at the increases in math and reading scores in this case study and declare a major victory for the school, the teachers, the students and the tribal communities. Baca and Lopez problematize this conventional narrative not only as incomplete but also as unequipped to attend to the historical and contemporary realities of Native American schools.

By centering the voices and perspectives of tribal educators and school leaders, they illuminate how this "success" must be understood in relation to the enduring structures of settler colonialism, and the desires of tribal sovereignty and self-determination among tribal educators and officials. Baca and Lopez illustrate how tribal leaders were often left out of decision-making processes of school turnaround policies. "Data-driven instruction" ultimately left teachers feeling there was an overemphasis on testing, thus neglecting culturally sustaining pedagogies that revitalize American Indian/Alaskan Native cultures into the classroom. Moreover, student absences due to coming-of-age ceremonies—an important ceremony for the tribal life for White Mountain Apaches—were deemed as counterproductive to the state achievement logic that guided turnaround policies as determined by nontribal administrators and policy makers. Through policy imposition, these nontribal administrators reinscribed deficit perspectives of tribal life in the name of education reform and achievement.

As we look beyond the singular indicators of test scores, it becomes clear how such school turnaround policy reproduced settler colonial logics and undermined the tribal sovereignty of the school community. Baca and Lopez's case study provides an example of how critical frameworks can make clear the antagonisms and the host of dynamics that are often overlooked and undervalued by technocratic policy-making frameworks. The use of critical frameworks unsettles the privileged positioning of technical experts by centering the knowledge and expertise of tribal members. Most important, this approach allows us to question technocratic projects and reexamine the purpose of education and schooling, as well as redefine "success" outside of testing paradigms.

It is a refusal of both the ends and the means. A radical imagination looks not only at refusal and abolition but also at redefining the terms—even if we have yet to envision what those terms might be.

The Only Thing I Know—by Socorro Cambero

It was the only thing I knew
Mamá, Papá, and Abuela spoke it
My five siblings did, too
It was beautiful until I met you

I was sent to you at the ripe age of 5
You are a place I can trust, Mamá says
I did not question what you said
Or notice the damage inside

I begin to speak your language
Mamá urges I speak *my* language
No Mamá, *this is the right language*
I don't care! En mi casa, you speak our lenguage!

Mamá and Papá don't know shit
Can't even fucking understand what the teacher says
I call them uneducated
Basta with the bullshit, Mamá says

My teachers tell me to pick between the two
Mamá conseja, *pick what is best for you*
I ask, *the best for who?*
Another Brown girl who destroys her blood for you.

References

Anzaldúa, G. (1987). *Borderlands: la frontera* (Vol. 3). San Francisco: Aunt Lute.

Combahee River Collective. (2014). A Black feminist statement. *Women's Studies Quarterly, 42*(3/4), 271–280. Retrieved from www.jstor.org/stable/24365010

Crenshaw, K. (1991). Mapping the margins: Intersectionality, identity politics, and violence against women of color. *Stanford Law Review, 43*(6), 1241–1299.

Delgado, R. (1989). Storytelling for oppositionists and others: A plea for narrative. *Michigan Law Review, 87*(8), 2411–2441.

Escobar, E. J. (1993). The dialectics of repression: The Los Angeles police department and the Chicano movement, 1968–1971. *The Journal of American History, 79*(4), 1483–1514.

Nieto-Gomez, A. (1974). La Femenista. [The feminist]. *Encuentro Femenil*, 34–47.

Patel, L. (2019). Fugitive practices: Learning in a settler colony. *Educational Studies*, 1–9.

Rowbotham, S. (1972). *Women, resistance and revolution*. London: Allen Lane.

Saavedra, C. M., & Pérez, M. S. (2012). Chicana and Black feminisms: Testimonios of theory, identity, and multiculturalism. *Equity & Excellence in Education, 45*(3), 430–443.

Sojoyner, D. M. (2017). Another life is possible: Black fugitivity and enclosed places. *Cultural Anthropology, 32*(4), 514–536.

Solórzano, D. G., & Yosso, T. J. (2001). Critical race and LatCrit theory and method: Counter-storytelling. *International Journal of Qualitative Studies in Education, 14*(4), 471–495.

Solórzano, D. G., & Yosso, T. J. (2002). Critical race methodology: Counter-storytelling as an analytical framework for education research. *Qualitative Inquiry, 8*(1), 23–44.

Tuck, E. (2009). Suspending damage: A letter to communities. *Harvard Educational Review, 79*(3), 409–428.

Index

Note: Page numbers in italics indicate figures and in bold indicate tables on the corresponding pages.

1:1 program *see* educational technology
21st-century learning opportunities 124

accountability policies, subgroup 154–155; conclusion on 165–167; contextualizing data with school demographics and 160–162; data practices, handed-down and homegrown for 158–160; findings on 158–165; interventions for black boys and 165; research methodology on 157–158; school-based data practices and 155–157; theoretical framework on 157
achievement gaps 159–160; contextualizing data with school demographics and 160–162; interpreting data through subgroup-specific perceptions and 162–165; interventions for black boys and 165
adultism 104
adult teacher culture promoting integration 113–114
aggressive White peer cultures 107–111
Althusser, L. 4
American Federation of Teachers 139
American Indian/Alaska Natives (AI/AN) education: conclusion on 92–93; discussion of participants and stakeholders in 90–92; introduction to 76–78; leadership in 84–85; lessons from school turnaround process in 83–90, 87, 89; methodology in researching 81–83; outcomes with 85–88, 87; relevant literature on 78–79; sustainability and 88–90, 89; tribal critical race theory (TribalCrit) an 79–81
Antonio, A. L. 26–27
Anzaldúa, G. 223, 224
Artiles, A. 125, 134, 189, 190

Baca, E. C. 224
Beamon, R., Sr. 69–70
Beaver, J. K. 155
Bertrand, M. 164
bifocality, critical 3–4
Black feminism 221, 224
Black Resilience Neoliberalism 56–58
Bland, S. 53
Blunt v. Lower Merion District 195
Board of Education of the Hendrick Hudson Central School District v. Amy Rowley 192
Boggs, G. L. 15
Bonilla-Silva, E. 27, 196
Borderlands Theory 223, 224
Brayboy, B. M. 80, 92
Brooke, J. 62
Brown, E. 66, 68–72
Brown, W. 8
Brown v. Board of Education 24, 25–26, 42n6, 71, 100, 191; failure of 28
Brownview Community School District (BCSD) 23, 41n2, 42–43n8, 42n3–4; context and methodology in studying 29–31; context of

24–25; discussion and implications of 40–41; findings on 32–40
Budde, R. 139, 141
Bush, G. W. 99
Bush, J. 141–142
Butler, O. 1

Cambero, S. 218–220, 225–226
Capitalism and Freedom 139
Carter, P. L. 124
Chai, C. S. 123
Chang, M. J. 26–27
Character Counts! Coalition 54
Charter School Commission (CSC) 147
charter schools: advocates of 142–144; complications with management companies and 149–150; evidence in closures of 144–147, **145, 146**; evidence in litigation related to *147*, 147–149; Florida 141–142; promise of 139–141, *140*; what went wrong with 150–151; *see also* school choice
Chicana feminism 221; as political struggle 223–224; views from below and 223
Chiles, L. 141
Chin-Chung, T. 123
Christensen, C. 125
civil rights 189–190, 198n2; compliance and racial inequity and 193–195; examining colorblind policy approaches when addressing racial inequities in special education and 195–197; protecting students with disabilities in schools and 190–192; racial and ethnic inequities and development of IDEA and 192–193
Clinton, B. 6
Coburn, C. E. 157
colonization and tribal critical race theory (TribalCrit) 79–81
colorblind ideology 27–28; special education services and 195–197
Common Core–based PARCC (Partnership for Assessment of Readiness for College and Careers) 130
Condition of Education, The 179
Connecticut State Law Tribune 64
Cooper, K. 157

Corsaro, W. A. 103
creative appropriation of racism 104
critical bifocality 3–4
critical race theory (CRT) 7–8, 47
cultural enrichment 58–59
culturally sustaining pedagogy (CSP) 79
culturally sustaining/revitalizing pedagogy (CSRP) 79
culture and classroom management 182

data-driven decision making (DDDM) 155–156
Davis, M. R. 66
Davis, T. M. 102–103
de-democratizing of the state 8
DeVos, B. 99
Diamond, J. B. 157
Diana v. State Board of Education 192
Diaz, R. 69
digital divide 122–123; *see also* educational technology
diversity 27, 28, 30, 31; culture and classrom management and 182; 'experiencing,' in teacher preparation programs 181–182; as policy 37–40, 43n9–10; systemic inequality and 34–37; willingness to accept 32–34
Dorn, S. 125
Dubois, W. E. B. 41
Dumas, M. 10

earned rights, slow progression of 190–192
Economic Opportunity Act of 1964 (EOA) 49
Edelman, L. B. 195
educational policy: critical bifocality in 3–4; framing the culture of 63; implications of school choice for 40–41; need for ambitious imaginations in 15–16; political dimensions of so-called technical problems and 2–3; testing and achievement regimes in, as educational enclosures 221–223; theories from below in 218–226; unsettling contemporary achievement paradigms and 224–226
educational technology: conclusion on 135–136; engagement for all

with 132–134; literature review on equity and 122–123; model program for 126–127; need for more 123–125; policy details and socioeconomic and cultural implications of 1:1 program in 128–132, *131*; from redistribution to recognition and representation with 134–135; study methods on 125–126; toward an equity-oriented analysis of 121–122
Education for All Handicapped Children Act (EAHCA) 173, 174, 176, 191, 204; *see also* Personalized Alternate Assessment Portfolio (PAAP)
Elementary and Secondary Education Act (ESEA) 154
enclosures 1; in the neoliberal era 5–8; testing and achievement regimes in educational policy as 221–223
equity-oriented analysis of educational technology 121–122
Every Student Succeeds Act 77, 154
exclusionary discipline practice 178–180

Fair, W. 141
field experiences in teacher preparation programs 181–182
Fine, M. 3
Fish, R. E. 190
Florida Department of Education (FLDOE) 142–144, 145
Foundation for Excellence in Education (FEE) 142
Fraser, N. 126, 134
free appropriate public education (FAPE) 173, 174–175
Friedman, M. 139, 141
Fukuyama, F. 1

Germaine Middle School (GMS) *see* accountability policies, subgroup
Giordano, P. 64
Goodson, I. 63
Gray, F. 53
Great Society 48–50
Guinier, L. 28
Gutiérrez, K. D. 3

Harry, E. G. 189
Harvey, K. 69, 70

Henig, J. R. 66
Hess, F. M. 66–67
Higher Education Act of 1965 (HEA) 47–50
Hobson v. Hansen 192
Holme, J. J. 41
Hunger Games 53–54
hyper-individualism 6

identity politics 224
implicit cultural bias 177
Indian Education Act of 1972 76
Indian Reorganization Act 76
individualized education programs (IEPs) 193–194
Individuals with Disabilities Education Act (IDEA) 203; civil rights and 189–197, 198n2; colorblind policy approaches and 195–197; compliance and racial inequity and 193–195; disabilities categories within 176–177; exclusionary discipline practice and 179; federal regulations issued in response to disproportionality and 182; future recommendations and 183–185; racial and ethnic inequities and development of 192–193; spirit and intent of 173–175; *see also* Personalized Alternate Assessment Portfolio (PAAP); special education services
institutes of higher education (IHEs) 180
intersectionality 224

Jefferson, T. 41
Jim Crow 54
Johnson, L. B. 48–50, 52, 56
Johnson, P. 3
justice-oriented citizenship 47, 52, 53

Kahne, J. 47
Kirst, M. 66–67
Kozleski, E. B. 125, 189

Ladd, H. F. 123
Ladson-Billings, G. 160
Larry P. v. Wilson Riles 192
Lee, T. 79–80
Leonardo, Z. 4, 27, 40
Lessard, L. 70
life history methodology 65

Index

Lim, C. P. 123
Lipman, P. 67
Lopez, J. D. 224
Losen, D. J. 189

magnet schools 99, 102; integrative peer cultures in 113–115; *see also* school choice
Marsh, J. A. 164
Martinez, E. 123
Mass Insight 77
McCarthy, P. 67
McCarty, T. 79–80
Melamed, J. 10
Meriam Report 76, 92
micro-aggressions 102, 103; hidden racial/ethnic 115; racial/ethnic, in the suburbs 106–113
Milem, J. F. 26–27
Milliken vs. Bradley 100
Mills v. Board of Education, of the District of Columbia 191
Morgan, P. L. 189–190

National Alliance for Public Charter Schools (NAPCS) 142, 144, 146
National Center for Education Statistics 179
Native American Education Improvement Act 76–77
neighborhood effect 139
neoliberal governmentality 55
neoliberalism: educational reform driven by 15; enclosures in 5–8; school choice and (*see* school choice); technocratic realism and 8–9; Upward Bound (UB) program and 47–50
'new' sociology of childhood 104
New York Times 62
Nixon, R. 6
No Child Left Behind (NCLB) 76–77, 154, 203

Obama, B. 6, 99, 100, 116, 154
Obasogie, O. 195–196
Ohio University 48
O'Leary, N. 67–68
"otherness" of disabled persons 202
Oullette, K. 68

Parents Involved in Community Schools v. Seattle School District 100
Paris, D. 79

participatory citizenship 47, 52, 55
Partnership for Leaders in Education Program 78
Patel, L. 224
Pennsylvania Association for Retarded Children (PARC) v. Commonwealth of Pennsylvania 191
Pérez, M. S. 221
Personalized Alternate Assessment Portfolio (PAAP) 202–203, 215; brief history of legislative intent of 204; broader lessons of 213–215; conceptualized in social context 203–211; construction of new language for segregation and 212–213; emergence of PAAP season and 207–210; legacy of 211–212; promise and excitement of 205–207; winding down of PAAP season and 210–211
personally responsible citizenship 47, 52, 55
Povinelli, E. 6
Pratt, R. J. 76
Pryor, S. 71

Race to the Top program 77
racial capitalism 6
racial/ethnic integration and school choice *see* school choice; youth peer culture
racialized peer cultures 103–104
racism and school-based peer cultures 103–104
Reed, A. 7
Regents of the University of California v. Bakke 196
restrictive classroom environments 177–178
"river of struggle" 3
Robinson, C. 6
Rogers, D. 190
Rogers, E. L. 190
Rowbotham, S. 224
Rowland, J. J. 64

Saavedra, C. M. 221
Santopietro, J. 64
school choice 99; conceptual orientation in studying 26–28; context and methodology in studying 29–31; context of Brownview Community School District and 24–25; discussion

and implications of, for policymaking 40–41; diversity as policy and 37–40; findings on 32–40; introduction to 23–24; original intentions of 42n5; racial/ethnic integration during era of 100–103, **101**; racism and school-based peer cultures and 103–104; review of literature related to 25–26; transportation issues with 35–36; *see also* charter schools; magnet schools; youth peer culture
School Improvement Grants (SIG) 77
school turnaround leadership *see* American Indian/Alaska Natives (AI/AN) education
Scott, J. 41
Scott, R. 150
Scott, W. 53
segregation of students with significant cognitive disabilities *see* Personalized Alternate Assessment Portfolio (PAAP)
selective enrollment schools *see* school choice
Shanker, A. 139–140
Shen, F. X. 66
Shifrer, D. 190
Sikes, P. 63
Skiba, R. J. 189
Smith, L. T. 4–5
Sojoyner, D. M. 221
Southwest School District (SSD) *see* educational technology
special education services: examining colorblind policy approaches when addressing racial inequities in 195–197; exclusionary discipline practice and 178–180; future recommendations for 183–185; Individuals with Disabilities Education Act (IDEA) and 173–175; overrepresentation of racially and ethnically diverse students receiving 176–180, 189–197; protecting students with disabilities in schools and 190–192; restrictive classroom environments and 177–178; for students with significant cognitive disabilities 202–215; teacher preparation programs and issues perpetuating marginalization in 180–182
Spence, L. K. 6, 7

St. Petersburg Times 141
Strassfeld, N. M. 195
Stronger Together 99, 100, 116
structural euphemisms 5, 7, 8
student resistance 58
systemic inequality 34–37

Talbert, J. E. 157
Tampa Bay Times 150
teacher preparation programs 180–182; future recommendations for 183–185
technical problems, political dimensions of 2–3
technocratic realism 8–9
technology *see* educational technology
testimonios 218–220; theories from below and 220–221
Thatcher, M. 1
TINA (There Is No Alternative) 1
Tondeur, J. 123
tribal critical race theory (TribalCrit) 79–81
Trump, D. 99

Upward Bound (UB) program: Black Resilience Neoliberalism and 56–58; data analysis on 52–58; discussion and conclusion on 58–59; funding for 49–50; introduction to 46–47; neoliberal roots of 47–50; perspectives on inequality and action among youth in 52–56; research questions on 50–52, **51**

Vigdor, J. L. 123
Violent Crime Control and Law Enforcement Act 6

Wagner, A. 69
Waitoller, F. R. 134
Walsh Elementary School *see* Waterbury Connecticut school district
Waterbury Connecticut school district: conclusion and implications of 71–72; dirty water in neighborhoods of 63–65; framing the culture of education policy and 63; insight from people of 64–65; introduction to 62–63; life history methodology in studying 65; turnaround in dirty water in 66–67; what mayoral control means for 67–71

Weinbaum, E. H. 155
Weis, L. 3
Weiss, M. J. 155
Welner, K. G. 124
WestEd West Comprehensive Center 78, 81–83
Western science 4–5
Westheimer, J. 47
White adult culture 106–107
'White flight' 102
White Mountain Apache Indian Reservation *see* American Indian/Alaska Natives (AI/AN) education
Wirt, F. 66–67
Wong, K. K. 66
Wright, J. S. 68, 69, 70

Yell, M. L. 190
Yin, R. 30
youth participatory action research (YPAR) 50–52, **51**; perspectives on inequality and action in 52–56
youth peer culture 99–100, 116; critical methodology in study of 104–106; integrative, in magnet schools 113–115; racial/ethnic micro-aggressions in the suburbs and 106–113; racism and school-based 103–104; results of study of 106–115; theoretical framework on 104

Zhao, Y. 123
Zirkel, P. A. 191